O Canada

Chicken Soup for the Soul: O Canada
101 Heartwarming and Inspiring Stories by and for Canadians
Jack Canfield, Mark Victor Hansen, Amy Newmark. Foreword by Amy Sky
With bonus stories by Amy Sky, Marc Jordan, Matt Duchene, George Kourounis, Laura
Robinson and lyrics by Liona Boyd

Published by Chicken Soup for the Soul Publishing, LLC   www.chickensoup.com

The publisher gratefully acknowledges the many publishers and individuals who
granted Chicken Soup for the Soul permission to reprint the cited material.

Front cover photo courtesy of iStockphoto.com/mpruitt (© mpruitt) and
iStockphoto.com/visual7 (© visual7). Back cover photo of Amy Sky
courtesy of David Wile. Interior photo courtesy of iStockphoto.com/walik (© walik).

Cover and Interior Design & Layout by Pneuma Books, LLC
For more info on Pneuma Books, visit www.pneumabooks.com

Distributed to the booktrade by Simon & Schuster. SAN: 200-2442

Publisher's Cataloging-in-Publication Data
(Prepared by The Donohue Group)

Chicken soup for the soul : O Canada : 101 heartwarming and inspiring stories by
  and for Canadians / [compiled by] Jack Canfield, Mark Victor Hansen [and] Amy
  Newmark ; foreword by Amy Sky.

  p. ; cm.

  Summary: A collection of 101 personal stories by Canadian celebrities and other
Canadians about their lives, Canadian traditions, being Canadian, and other aspects
of the Canadian experience. Also includes a few stories by Americans about Canadian
hospitality.
  ISBN: 978-1-935096-75-7

  1. Canadians--Literary collections. 2. Canadians--Anecdotes. 3. National
characteristics, Canadian--Literary collections. 4. National characteristics, Canadian--
Anecdotes. 5. Canada--Social life and customs--Literary collections. 6. Canada--Social
life and customs--Anecdotes. I. Canfield, Jack, 1944- II. Hansen, Mark Victor. III.
Newmark, Amy. IV. Sky, Amy. V. Title: O Canada

PN6071.C26 C455 2011
810.8/02/0811   2011936063

20 19 18 17 16 15 14 13 12 11   01 02 03 04 05 06 07 08 09 10

Chicken Soup for the Soul®

O Canada

101 Heartwarming and Inspiring Stories by and for Canadians

Jack Canfield, Mark Victor Hansen, Amy Newmark
Foreword by Amy Sky

With bonus stories by Amy Sky, Marc Jordan, Matt Duchene, George Kourounis, Laura Robinson and lyrics by Liona Boyd

Chicken Soup for the Soul Publishing, LLC
Cos Cob, CT

Chicken Soup for the Soul

www.chickensoup.com

Contents

❸
~Slice of Life~

❹
~The Cultural Mosaic~

❺
~Wilderness and Wildlife~

❻

~Absence Makes the Heart Grow Fonder~

❼

~Holidays and Traditions~

❽

~Summer Memories~

❾

~Life Lessons~

❿

~Winter Wonderland~

⓫
~Inspiring Canadians~

⓬
~That Famous Canadian Hospitality~

Foreword

This land is your land, this land is my land,
From Bonavista, to Vancouver Island,
From the Arctic Circle to the Great Lakes waters,
This land was made for you and me.

What Canadian school kid doesn't know the words to "This Land Is Your Land," made famous by the Travellers and adapted from the original American folk song written by Woody Guthrie? In Canada, some argue that much of Canadian culture is an adaptation of American culture.

But having lived and worked in both countries, I can tell you that we have two very distinct cultures. We may have some common roots, but the blossoms on our tree are uniquely ours. Steeped in our British and French traditions, seasoned by our Native culture and simmered in the broth of multiculturalism, we are a country that loves words, ideas and nature. We are a gentle people, who at our best, take care of ourselves and of each other.

I grew up in Toronto, with my five brothers and sisters, swimming in the summer at Lake Simcoe and Algonquin Park, skiing in the winter in Collingwood and Quebec. My parents took us on a trip through the Rockies from Banff to Vancouver and up to Victoria when I was a teen.

But I really got to know this country by being a travelling musician. When I was asked to write the foreword to this book, I started to think about all the places I had performed in Canada, and I realized that music has taken me to every province and territory (except technically Nunavik, which was established after I had performed in the Northwest Territories).

I have had some ordinary visits, and some extraordinary visits. Let me take you on a musical guided tour of the country from "Vancouver Island to Bonavista."

In 1986, the summer I moved to Los Angeles, I also visited the World Expo in Vancouver. There, I saw the future in two ways: automotive and musical. The theme of the fair was transportation and communication, and on display were some wildly futuristic cars—all the square corners were rounded and aerodynamic—a shape that foreshadowed the vehicles of today. I also saw the band Parachute Club perform there—and wanted so badly for that to be me up on that outdoor main stage. That vision came to be a reality years later when I was a featured performer at the PNE in 1998. I also have a soft spot in my heart for Vancouver because it is where one of my favourite collaborators, David Pickell, lives. We have written three of my favourite songs together—"I Will Take Care of You," "Ordinary Miracles" and "Phenomenal Woman." I always take a long walk through Stanley Park, along the ocean's edge, when I am there—hoping to catch a glimpse of sea lions or whales.

My first experience performing in Alberta was in February of 1983, when I was a backup singer in Ronnie Hawkins' band, and we played at a Snowmobile Festival in Wetaskiwin! I will never forget every inch of my face freezing, so I covered all of it except for my eyelashes—and then my eyelashes froze. It was then that my grade school geography book made sense—Edmonton was on the same latitude as Moscow—and that was some kind of crazy Dr. Zhivago cold there!

Alberta also brings to mind playing at the Calgary Stampede, and Edmonton Klondike Days. Whenever I tour there and play both cities, I like to spur their notorious rivalry by telling whichever city I play in that I played in their sister city the night before—and that the audience was FANTASTIC! And that they better not let their rival outdo them in the enthusiasm department… and they naturally rise to the challenge.

It was in a hotel room in Calgary in early 1997 that I turned on the TV to find out that my video for my song "Til You Love Somebody" had gone to number one.

It was also in a hotel room in Calgary in September 2001, the morning after the Country Music Awards Show, that I turned on the TV to see a plane crashing into the World Trade Center. Hundreds of us from the music industry from all over North America were trapped there for four days, until the planes were able to fly again. We gathered dumbstruck and horrified, in hotel lobbies and bars, trying to make sense of the senselessness. And we did what Canadians do, and what Canadian musicians do—try to help in any way we can. A benefit concert for the victims was hastily put together, with all the performers who were in town for the Awards. It was affirming and healing to know that in the face of insanity, humanity could still prevail.

Using music to come together for the greater good is the idea behind the heartwarming Telemiracle telethon in Saskatchewan. I have done the twenty-hour weekend show twice—once in Saskatoon and once in Regina. I was told it is twenty instead of twenty-four hours because the volunteers who run the show have to get up early Monday morning to work on the farms! On my way out the first time, my friend, the singer Michael Burgess told me, "Oh I looove Saskatchewan." "Really?" I said. "What do you love about it?" "The people!" he said. And I came to understand what he meant.

Since 1977 this province of just over a million people has raised over eighty-one million dollars, more per capita than any other telethon. The funds are to help Saskatchewan residents to access special needs equipment and medical assistance that is beyond what is funded by the government and wouldn't otherwise be affordable. On my second appearance in 2008, blue-eyed soul singer Johnny Reid and I laughed ourselves silly at all of the crazy and inventive schemes the locals came up with to raise money during the year, with the incentive of a moment of TV glory when they get to present their donation on camera. Jalopy Drop? Drive an old car onto a frozen pond in late spring and take bets on when it will fall through the ice. Gopher Painting? Literally. Buy a piece of gaffer tape until enough is sold to tape the principal to the portable? Sounds fun to me! Wheel a bathtub from Saskatoon to Regina? A no-brainer. Never mind the traditional pancake breakfasts—these people have raised the fund-raising bar to the sky!

Another memorable benefit concert I performed at was in Winnipeg to help the victims of The Red River Flood of 1997. That natural disaster resulted in more than $500 million in damages in Manitoba. I flew out with my daughter Zoe, then six, and together we sung my song "I Will Take Care of You" to a crowd of over 40,000 people outside at Grand Forks. I was thrilled that many of them were singing along, which was new for me, since my first CD had only come out the year before. I also performed my song "Love, Pain and the Whole Damn Thing" with one of Manitoba's favourite sons, the literate and passionate rocker Tom Cochrane. The crowds were shaken by the devastation, but grateful and appreciative of the dozens of performers who came to help out.

Ontario—my home—I have played cities and towns big and small across this province. In the north: Thunder Bay, Elliot Lake, Kirkland Lake, Timmins, Cobalt, North Bay, Sudbury. In the south: Windsor, Sarnia, London, Hamilton, Wingham, Kitchener Waterloo, Barrie, Orillia, St. Catherines, Gananoque, Belleville, Ottawa and more… and of course Toronto many times.

Too many shows and too many stories to mention… But I do remember my very first show of my very first tour—flying out to Thunder Bay with a guitar player and a keyboard player. After we checked in, I got distracted in the book shop and I got to the gate just as the plane with my bandmates on it was pulling away. They knew that I am a little bit psychic—and thought I had had a vision that the plane was going to crash and so I decided not to get on. They wrote goodbye love letters to their wives on the plane… for real! When I finally got to Thunder Bay we laughed so hard at our mutual goofiness.

Quebec brings back memories of another natural disaster—the Ice Storm of 1998. I was in Montreal recording a string quartet for my CD *Burnt by the Sun*. As I drove to the airport in the evening, I could see ice eerily coating all the hydro wires. I was lucky to be on the last flight out before the storm closed down the airport and cut off power and essential services to millions for a frightening few days. On a sunnier note, the summer before I had performed on Canada Day in an outdoor square in downtown Montreal in front of 50,000 happy partiers! Nobody celebrates like the French, with their joie de vivre and carpe diem mentality. And nobody eats like the French... Can you say Croissant? Canadians can! Americans—not so much.

One of French Canada's treasures is the lavishly gifted Roch Voisine. We had written a hit song together for him called "Deliver Me" for his CD *Kissing Rain*, and in 1997 I toured with him, opening his shows in twenty-three cities across the country. While in his native New Brunswick, one night after the show his family treated the whole band to a beachside barbeque. Buckets of smoked arctic char, and lobster for everyone.... it was a magical midnight feast!

Nova Scotia again brings to mind triumph and tragedy. I had played many fun outdoor festivals there—always enjoying being near the ocean and participating in impromptu ceilidhs with Celtic musicians at all hours in the hotel. I enjoyed working with some of Cape Breton's finest—the amazing fiddler Natalie MacMaster, the engaging singer-songwriter Bruce Guthro. But my husband Marc Jordan and I were also guests on The Rankin Sisters Christmas Special, filmed in October 1998, just a few weeks after the Swissair crash at Peggy's Cove. We learned that the residents of Peggy's Cove and surrounding communities did what they have learned do in times of crisis: they pitched in to help. Many took their own boats out onto the turbulent waters to help search, hoping to find survivors, but instead finding their remains. The community was shaken, but everyone still pulled together to do what they could.

My first part in a high school musical was as Mrs. Barry in *Anne of Green Gables*, so I was delighted to take my children to visit Green Gables and the rest of beautiful PEI. Marc and I had moved back to

Canada in 1993 from Los Angeles, to raise our kids in a safe, clean place. We had fun that summer driving them through that island's red countryside in a convertible with the top down—even though it rained every day. In my other public role, as a spokesperson for mental health issues, I returned to Summerside in 2009 to speak at a conference, and ambled along the charming ocean side boardwalk for hours.

I have only done one tour of Newfoundland, and was moved by the rugged beauty of the coastline, and delighted by the brightly painted houses in St. John's. It turned out not to be a very well organized tour, however, but the promoter gamely said that in Newfoundland if there are more people in the audience than there are on stage—they consider the show a success!

The shows I did back in 1983 with Ronnie Hawkins in the Yukon and the Northwest Territories were memorable to me for a reason different from climate and geography. We were playing small clubs—to be exact, they were what we would call a "dive" in any other city. The flights had been long and bumpy, the band house—well, one star accommodation was a generous description. I remember looking for lettuce in the grocery store and it was $5 a head! That is like $20 in today's money.

But I also remember hitting the stage late at night—and the moment I grabbed the mike, and the band kicked in to some high voltage rockabilly and I started to sing—I thought—I love this! I love performing! I love music!

I don't care where I am—in a dive in the Arctic or a swanky theatre in Toronto—wherever I get to open my mouth and sing—it feels like home to me.

Lucky me to have had music give me wings to fly over this magnificent land and see the sights, and best of all, meet the people in this great country of ours.

This wonderful Chicken Soup for the Soul book will give you wings too, to visit our country from west to east, and from north to south. You'll read stories from other proud Canadians about what being Canadian means to them, you'll read stories from other performers who tried out the States but couldn't stay away from Canada, including my husband Marc Jordan, and my friends Liona Boyd and Laura Robinson. Liona tells her story through the song lyrics that will appear on her new album, *The Return*.

You'll read stories that will make you proud of our cultural mosaic, from immigrants who have been welcomed to our great land but encouraged to maintain their own traditions. I'm sure you'll enjoy the many amusing stories about our famously bad weather—after all, we are a hardy bunch and we like people to know that. Our own international storm chaser George Kourounis describes how he developed his love for bad weather as a child in Hull, Quebec. And you'll see plenty of stories about our short, but light-filled summers, and our love for our cottages. There are stories about Canadian traditions and holidays, including Canada Day, the Calgary Stampede, Maritime events, and of course, Hockey Night. And yes, there are plentiful hockey stories, including one from our young NHL star Matt Duchene, which is about his hometown roots and the joy of fishing.

This book will make you proud to be Canadian and remind you why you love Canada so much, and if you are reading it on foreign shores... or just across the border in the States... I won't be surprised to see you soon, whether it's in Bonavista or on Vancouver Island, in the far north or just across the river from Michigan. This "great land is made for all of us," and I am happy to present you with this book about that great land, made *by* us and *for* us.

~Amy Sky

Chapter 1

O Canada

Proud to Be Canadian

This is my country.
What I want to express is "here" and I love it.
Amen!

~Emily Carr

"Canada, My Canada"

From the CD *The Return* by Liona Boyd

Lyrics courtesy of Liona Boyd ©2011

Mid-Continental Music SOCAN

The spirits of our lakes and rivers gently sing to me
The mighty forests add their voice with mystic majesty
I hear the rhythm in the wings of wild geese as they fly
And music in the Rocky Mountains reaching for the sky

Canada, my Canada
My country proud and free
We'll give the world
A song to sing of
Peace and harmony
Canada, my Canada
Land I call my own
Canada, my Canada
You'll always be my home

Our people are a symphony, a multi-cultured voice
From far and wide we fought, we cried, we came
        and made the choice
Let's sing as one and harmonize our many different themes
And build the greatest nation for our children and our dreams

Canada, my Canada
My country proud and free
We'll give the world
A song to sing of
Peace and harmony
Canada, my Canada
Land I call my own
Canada, my Canada
You'll always be my home

From the rocky Western Shore
To the coast of Labrador

From the Gaspe's rustic charms
To the prairies and the farms

From the coves of Come-By-Chance
To Quebec, la belle province

From the cities and the mines
To the misty Maritimes

United we shall always be
From North to South, from sea to sea

Canada, my Canada
Mon grand et beau pays
Where native peoples bless this land
Of peace and harmony
I'm proud to be Canadian
Just look at how we've grown
Canada, my Canada
You'll always be my home
Canada, my Canada
You'll always be my home

(This Is Not) A Hockey Story

It's never felt more Canadian to be Canadian than it does now.
~Douglas Coupland

I've always been Canadian, but never felt as Canadian as I did one fateful February day in New York City. My story probably happened all over the world that day.

My husband and I gathered our infant son, clad in his "Canada" T-shirt (a special occasion deserved a change from the sleepers he'd been sporting) and headed out to a bar. Our miniature Canadian had been born in New York City two and a half months earlier, thus American by birth. By that point, however, he'd already acquired a Canadian passport and made his first trip north of the border to visit his homeland. For us, he was Canadian by heritage, Canadian for the future, and definitely Canadian today.

We arrived at the bar and made our way to the back to meet with Canadian friends as well as some American ones who had agreed to be honourary Canucks for the day. Our baby, who had fallen asleep on the walk to the bar, woke up punctually to see the puck drop at his first hockey game and the most personal one we'd ever watched. Canada was battling the United States in the gold medal game at the Vancouver 2010 Olympics. It was the culmination of the Olympics, and, for every Canadian I knew living in the U.S. at the time, the potential affirming climax of the struggle we've had holding on to our Canadian-ism, quietly patriotic and proud of the country where our hearts remained while we spent a few years in the U.S.

Canada scored during the first period and we were cautiously ecstatic. We were Canadian. This was our game. These were our Olympics. We wanted to win this game. We needed to win this game.

By the end of the first period, with Canada leading 1-0, our baby had had enough of his first rowdy hockey spectator experience. We bid farewell and slowly made our way with our stroller through the now very crowded bar. We were met with both approval and friendly heckling as we inched towards the door through a rather jolly bunch, noticing first the baby, and then his T-shirt.

We settled back at home in time for the beginning of the second period. My husband and I had both grown up in Toronto, with our fair share of Leafs ups and downs, and we followed our homeland hockey team through various other Olympic medal chases. But we had never been as invested in a game as we were that day. You didn't have to be a hockey fan that day. In fact, you didn't need to like hockey at all that day. You didn't need to understand offsides and icing and hooking. You just needed to be Canadian. You needed to be Canadian to appreciate the gravity of that game, of that event, with its potential to cause as much pain as it could eternal pride and bliss.

We sat in our living room in front of the television, passing the baby back and forth between us in an effort to keep him calm so that we could watch history in the making. Our blood pressure, I'm sure, rose, and tears most certainly welled in our eyes. It was the end of the third period, with less than a minute to play, and Canada was leading 2-1. We had this. We had the game. We had the win. We just had to get through the next few moments, holding our breath.

With twenty-four seconds left in play, a U.S. goal tied the game and rocked our world. We were shocked. We yelled. We stared in disbelief. Could this happen to our country? Could this happen to us? Had we just lost this? I tried to balance fear with hope, but I worried deeply for my country. With the U.S.'s momentum, I was so worried. We hoped with all our might that the break in play before overtime would thwart the U.S.'s drive and bring our boys back to their game.

It was, after all, a beautiful game; if it weren't for the emotional and even physical investment we had in it, we would have certainly been able to enjoy watching it. But the mechanics didn't matter and the skill level didn't matter. Only one thing mattered. And that one thing was finally realized at seven minutes and forty seconds into overtime play. The epitome of Canadian hockey, Sidney Crosby, scored an unbelievable goal and won the game. The Olympic gold. Words could not express the triumph, the jubilation, the honour that enveloped Canadian hearts at that moment.

Our game. Our Olympics. Our soil. Our land. Our CANADA. And we won. It truly was bliss.

Thinking back to that moment fills my eyes with the same tears that welled in me that day, the tears that my husband and I both shed that day. Our little family, alone in our apartment in New York, miles away from our Canadian home, could not have felt any more Canadian.

I had never been so in love with Canada as I was at that moment. I had never been so happy for Canada as I was at that moment. At that moment, Canada was a living being, one that you wanted to hug, and to high-five, and to lift up on your shoulders and to introduce to everyone as "my Canada." Canada was my child that day, the child who deserved love and a congratulations card and a voice to brag on his behalf. Canada was my mother that day, the mother who nurtures, who makes everything safe, who makes everything right and good in the world.

Every few years, I'm sure, for every citizen of the world, there is a moment that defines us as our country. A moment that takes a person out of his body, out of himself, and moulds his being into his country. For me, that was it. That achievement by our hockey team, Canada's hockey team, continues to rattle my being, to bring tears to my eyes. That moment continues to flow through me, having forever changed me, as Canadian pride runs through my veins.

~Inbal Ondhia
Canadian living in Mountain View, CA, USA

You Might Be Canadian If...

Canadians can easily "pass for American"
as long as we don't accidentally use metric measurements
or apologize when hit by a car.
~Douglas Coupland

Y ou might be Canadian if:

- You have ever apologized when someone bumped into you.

- You're fiercely proud of the fact that Canada is known as a humble nation.

- You have eaten poutine, beaver tails, moose meat, and Nanaimo bars—possibly all in the same meal.

- You have a Canadian flag sewn onto at least one backpack or item of clothing.

- You can read all the French on the back of any cereal box.

- You can locate Head-Smashed-In Buffalo Jump on a map.

- You have been known to tear up while recounting where you were when you saw Sidney Crosby's "Golden Goal" during the Vancouver 2010 Olympic and Paralympic Winter Games.

- You have a stash of Canadian Tire money somewhere in your house.

- You recognize only two seasons: hockey season and the rest of the year.

- You know what a toque is and how to wear it.

- You know that the last letter of the alphabet rhymes with HEAD, not BEE.

- You're unfazed by several feet of snow appearing overnight—unless you live in Vancouver or Victoria, in which case you're unfazed by three months of non-stop rain.

- You have at least two boxes of Kraft Dinner in your pantry.

- You're not bilingual, but you do know all the cool swear words in French.

- You can proudly rattle off a list of Canadian celebrities who made it big in Hollywood: Ryan Reynolds, Pamela Anderson, Jim Carrey, Mike Myers, Kim Cattrall, William Shatner.

- You know what a Double Double is, and you also know how to Roll Up the Rim to Win.

- You're delighted when American pop culture mentions Canada in any way. You're especially thrilled when American pop culture makes fun of Canada. Favourite examples: when the song "Blame Canada" was nominated for an Academy Award, and the classic line from *The Simpsons*: "I moved here from Canada and they think I'm slow, eh."

- You know Molson's "I Am Canadian" rant off by heart.

- You know that maple syrup truly is the nectar of the gods.

- You can find Saskatchewan on a map—and pronounce it correctly.

- You know the "correct" way to spell COLOUR, HONOUR, and LABOUR.

- You're proud of the fact that Canadians invented insulin, the zipper, the telephone, the pacemaker, the electric wheelchair, the hockey goalie mask—and, most significantly, the retractable beer carton handle.

- You know all the words to "The Hockey Song" by Stompin' Tom Connors.

- You love Canadian actors but rarely watch Canadian movies.

- You have vacationed in Cuba.

- You've never seen a gun in real life, only on American TV.

- You love to see Canadian musicians honoured at the Grammy Awards but have never watched the Juno Awards.

- You know exactly how much the Canadian dollar is worth in relation to the U.S. dollar—and the location of the nearest cross-border outlet mall.

- You define our national identity by what we're not: American or British.

- You love donuts more than Homer Simpson does.

~Sheri Radford
Vancouver, BC

Made in Canada

*We're very patriotic. It's hard to pinpoint, the Canadian thing.
It's almost like a small-town mentality.*
~Mike Weir

I buy Canadian. This sounds old-fashioned nowadays. I just had a baby and the sleepers I received as gifts were made everywhere from China to Tunisia. I am grateful and I dress my baby in them every day and night.

But if I have a choice, I buy goods made in Canada. I check the labels. I buy honey from the farmer down the road. Our neighbour keeps cows (Belted Galloway steers, to be exact) on our land, and if we eat beef, I try to buy it from him.

One day, I was working in the emergency room and the nurses started talking about cross-border shopping. We work in Cornwall, Ontario, an economically-depressed town with a handy bridge to upstate New York. The nurses raved about how much more cheaply they could buy groceries and clothes across the border.

"It's so worth it," said one.

"I love it," said another. "The border guards don't give you too hard a time if you've got groceries and baby clothes. What about you, Melissa?"

I shook my head. "I don't do it."

"But it's so much cheaper. Don't you want to buy clothes for Max?"

I tried to explain without hurting anyone's feelings. "I have a lot of hand-me-down clothes for Max. I've hardly bought anything for him between that and some gifts."

"What about for yourself, then? They have lots of nice stuff."

"I don't really need another shirt. So if I'm going to buy something, I prefer to buy it from someone local. There are a lot of cool designers in Montreal." Montreal used to be a clothing manufacturer's hub and you can still find Canadian-made baby goods, well-cut boots, and women's clothing with a certain je ne sais quoi. I've also driven in the other direction, to Ottawa, for their designers. I've searched online to support artisans. I'd rather buy a few well-made items than many cheap ones that fray and stain and end up in a rag pile or, worse yet, a landfill site.

One other nurse said she shopped locally, too, but the three cross-border shoppers stared at us in incomprehension. I thought about pointing out that all of us had relatively well-paying jobs. Heck, just the fact that we had jobs put us ahead of many people in Cornwall, especially since the paper mill closed down. If the locally-employed people didn't support the stores in town, those shops would close down too and we'd lose even more jobs.

But I could tell I wasn't going to change anyone's mind that day, so I quietly went back to work, armed with my conviction.

When I can, when it's available, I shop Canadian.

~Melissa Yuan-Innes
North Lancaster, ON

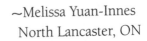

Hockey Life in Canada

*[Hockey] is the passion that brings us all together. On frozen ponds.
At the community rink. And in our living rooms. It's the feeling you got the
first time you stepped on the ice. The feeling you had when you scored your
first goal. Hockey is in our driveway. It's in our dreams. In every post game
celebration. It's in the streets, every time your friend yells "car." In every rink
across the country. It's in our hearts...*

~Tim Hortons commercial (2010), Sidney Crosby

My mom grew extremely frustrated with me as I cried my eyes out in the back of our old silver Ford Windstar. "Mommy, I don't want the white skates! I want the black ones! The sticks!"

My mom had made an understandable, but nevertheless completely wrong, decision signing me up for figure skating. I didn't want figure skating. I wanted hockey. My six-year-old brain was already wired to love the sport. Some of my first words were a tribute to the Leafs. At the tender age of two, clad in full Toronto Maple Leafs pyjamas, I would sit on the carpet, shrieking, "Go Leafs go!" Of course, I had no idea what the words meant; I just watched in awe as the figures on the grainy television screen dashed down the length of the ice, evoking cheering from both the rink and my family.

On that cold December day in 1999, with the minivan stopped in the parking lot of the local rink, my mom didn't have the slightest hope of winning against my determined six-year-old self. And she knew it.

I was the stereotypical Canadian kid: my world revolved around hockey. At the tender age of seven, I played in the local house league, realizing that I was made to be a goaltender. I've played rep hockey since I was eleven, dedicating countless hours to long practices, far away games, and "sleepover" tournaments.

Winter afternoons were spent on the pond, attempting to master the latest move we saw the pros do in a recent game. My parents showered me with hockey related presents at Christmas time.

I have stacks of hockey books, twice the size of encyclopaedias resting on my bookshelf. These books are stained with my eager fingerprints, as I was constantly sifting through them find information on everything hockey related. My hockey card collection is enormous, a result of begging for a new pack in the line-up at the supermarket on every shopping outing.

My summers were spent playing road hockey with the neighbourhood kids until our sleepy parents ushered us in around midnight. Saturdays were spent at a family friend's house. Our parents would stay upstairs in the living room, lounging on the couches, watching the game. Meanwhile, we were downstairs in the unfinished basement with the Leafs game blaring from the tiny television in the corner, engaged in an intense and heartfelt game of ministicks (a form of indoor hockey played with foam balls and tiny sticks). By the end of the evening, the bottoms of our socks were ripped from the concrete. We barely made it to our beds before falling asleep from the exertion, but we all fell asleep with hockey in our dreams.

This fascination with hockey is not just a childhood pastime for Canadians. It encompasses our nation. Hockey is our pride and joy. The Saturday morning hockey routine is simple. Early in the morning, countless Canadian families cram an oversized hockey bag into the family car, sliding the stick anywhere it will fit, go through one of the many local Tim Hortons drive-throughs to grab a cup of coffee, and head to the local rink. They watch their kids play, socialize with other hockey parents, and nurse that cup of Timmies for the entire game.

This hockey loving spirit is not only for the minors, but extends to our professional and international teams, too. When our team is in the Olympics, World Juniors, or any major international competition, Canadians are anxiously biting their nails in their living rooms with their fireplaces roaring beside them. From the five-year-olds learning to skate with hockey sticks limply in their hands, to the passion that ignites every Canadian when we see our country win gold, Canada truly lives and breathes hockey.

An inexplicable thrill surges through the hearts of hockey players. No words can truly explain the giddy feeling in our guts when the ice is freshly zambonied. Words are futile when trying to express the feeling of blades cutting through ice, and the gloriously sharp sound it creates. The English language has no words capable of expressing the feeling of being cheered for, winning a seemingly impossible game as a team, or accomplishing something new as a player.

That's why when that specific Tim Hortons commercial appears on television, and I listen to Sidney Crosby speaking, I get goose bumps. It is the most precise description of Canadian hockey I've ever heard.

True Canadian hockey is the moment your friend yells, "Car!" in the midst of a street hockey game. True Canadian hockey is your family gathered in the living room, shielded from the harsh elements of the Canadian winter, watching a game together. True Canadian hockey is the small town arenas, where fans and players alike gather to witness the most glorious sport ever created. As the images of my childhood splash across the screen, I can feel my heart expand with pride. Again, I realize my love for hockey and the beautiful country it belongs to. By the end of the commercial, I am breathless, nearly in tears. I realize that wherever the chaotic journey of life takes me in the future, I will always come back to my humble, hockey playing, Canadian roots. That's probably why the familiar sound of the Hockey Night in Canada theme song is still my favourite sound in the entire world.

On a global scale, Canada is known for its beautiful landscape, its peaceful nature, and its freezing cold winters—but to us Canadians, hockey is a synonym for Canada.

~Daniella Porano
Aurora, ON

The Hockey Jersey

Make no mistake, Canada's people were the stars of these Games. They jammed the streets of Vancouver, cheered the most obscure sports as long as a Canadian was competing and all but drowned themselves in a sea of red...
~quoted from the Chicago Sun-Times

My husband Paul and I live in downtown Vancouver, which means we were right in the middle of all the excitement during the Vancouver 2010 Olympic and Paralympic Winter Games. All we had to do was lean out our windows to see red-and-white-clad Canucks thronging the streets, belting out "O Canada" with a fervour hitherto unheard of. I embraced Olympic fever wholeheartedly, volunteering for the Games at Canada Hockey Place and scooping up Olympic paraphernalia as fast as my Visa card would let me. I proudly sported my Canada jacket over my red and white "True North Strong and Free" T-shirt, topping it all off with a Canada toque and red Olympic mittens. I also became something of a pin nerd, wearing dozens of Olympic pins and trading them with other nerds from all over the world.

My husband's Olympic fever was slower to catch on fire, but once it did it burned brightly. Paul decided that he, too, needed some patriotic gear. He hemmed and hawed over a Team Canada hockey jersey with Sidney Crosby's name and number on the back, then considered a classic Canada Cup jersey with Bob Gainey's name and number. Eventually, he decided on a jersey that he felt epitomized Canadian hockey: a Montreal Canadiens jersey. I protested that this wasn't an Olympic jersey, but he felt strongly that it represented Canada. It is, after all, the jersey referenced in Roch Carrier's classic story "The Hockey Sweater," which is quoted on the back of Canada's five-dollar bill. So he bought a Habs jersey and wore it constantly for the duration of the Games.

Everywhere Paul went, shouts of "Go, Habs, go!" followed him, yelled by happy Canadians often leaning out bus windows. Random strangers wearing huge Canadian flags as capes high-fived him enough times that he risked getting carpal tunnel syndrome. Cars honked at him. People kept stopping him to chat, especially people from Montreal who spoke in halting but friendly English about their beloved hockey team.

RCMP officers from all over Canada were everywhere in Vancouver during the Games—on horses, on bikes, walking, driving. Mostly they were chatting with folks, giving directions, and snapping photos for happy visitors. One day, an RCMP officer noticed my husband's jersey, grabbed him roughly by the shoulder and said, mock sternly, "I think we have to take you in for wearing a jersey like that." Another officer pulled the two apart and said, with a heavy French accent, "Whoa, let him go." Both officers laughed and clapped Paul on the back.

Even police officers couldn't resist commenting on a Montreal Canadiens jersey. And even though red clothing was everywhere during the Winter Games, the Habs jersey stood out as being truly Canadian.

~Sheri Radford
Vancouver, BC

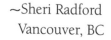

Lost and Found

Whether we say it in French with a Saguenay accent or in English
with an accent from Newfoundland, and wherever we come from or
wherever we live, we all share the most precious heritage that can be given to
humankind — our Canadian citizenship.
~Kim Campbell

From early childhood, my brother Bud was idolized by my two sisters and me. In spite of this, he was very much down to earth, fun to be with, an avid Boy Scout and later, a beloved teacher. During his studies, Bud met Cathie, a particularly attractive classmate, who our family came to adore. Soon they were a couple. Unfortunately, the war intervened.

In July of 1941, Bud joined the Royal Canadian Air Force where he trained to become a pilot. In March of 1942 Bud received his "wings" and was assigned as Squadron Leader of 427 Bomber Command. In August of 1943, the crew received orders to depart for overseas and was posted to England. During this time he and Cathie had parted ways, but it was obvious to all of us that they were made for each other.

My mother never interfered in our private lives, but this was different. A major situation simply had to be rectified! Would Bud go overseas without contacting Cathie? Could our mother possibly do something to prevent this tragedy?

Finally a solution was hatched. Mother asked Cathie to meet her at the train station in Montreal. Bud was then contacted and asked to meet Mother at the same time and place. Imagine their surprise when they found each other and not our mother! Needless to say, the ruse worked. The happy couple reunited and became engaged shortly before Bud left for England. What a relief! Cathie joined the Air Force too and was based in Halifax, working in a control tower nearby.

Slowly the months passed. After two years, we received word that Bud and his entire crew had been shot down over Denmark. This was to have been their final tour, a dangerous mission while laying mines over the Baltic. After scrambling for his flight jacket, to which was pinned a good luck charm, Bud parachuted to the ground, breaking a leg in the fall. After hiding for a time, Bud was discovered by a farmer and shipped off to a hospital where he was taken prisoner of war on Valentine's Day, 1945. The surgery on the broken leg resulted in excruciating pain and other complications that lasted for the remainder of his life. During this time my mother's positive attitude never wavered. She had no doubt that her son would return safely and if she shed tears, they were well hidden.

After an eternity, or so it seemed, in April of 1945 with the war nearly over, the Germans were scrambling to retreat. Under no apparent supervision, Bud was wandering down the road outside the prison, when, out of nowhere, American troops stormed in and scooped him up. On Easter Sunday, we received a telephone call informing us that Bud had been freed. We literally danced with joy. I jumped on my bicycle and raced up and down the streets screaming out the news, "He's free. He's free."

Now for the highlight of the story! Just how did Cathie find out that all was well and Bud was free? There she was, sitting in an Air Force hostel in Halifax, utterly despondent and unaware of the good news. Turning her head, Cathie happened to notice a copy of *Life* magazine on a table close to where she sat. On the cover was a picture of American soldiers freeing prisoners. In the centre, on crutches and easily noticed because of his famous brush cut and sweet smile, was Bud! She hurriedly ripped the cover from the magazine, leaving a jagged edge and excitedly ran to call home. Framed copies of the picture, complete with jagged edge, hang in our family homes today.

After weeks of recuperation in England, Bud was flown to a hospital near Montreal, only a few miles from our home, for continued therapy. What a joyous reunion we had! Upon release from hospital, Bud was honoured with notable awards which included the Distinguished Flying Cross and the Operational Wing. Happily reunited again, Bud and Cathie made plans for their wedding day.

At war's end, Bud returned to his studies and in the fall of 1949, we graduated together from Macdonald College, McGill University. Our father, vice principal of the college, proudly presented the two of us with our diplomas. In later years, Bud would become Federal Deputy Minister of Veterans Affairs.

My life's plan has been to recount Bud's story of love and heroism. The year of the Veteran seemed the appropriate time to gather details. Sadly, Bud was hospitalized before being able to read the final draft and died soon after. A memorial service and burial was held in the Military Cemetery in Ottawa, with Cathie and family members attending from near and far. On that warm, sunny, fall afternoon as we sat quietly listening to the memorable words of the padre, one solitary airplane flew overhead. At that moment, I wished only to give thanks for Bud's heroism in war and the peace and love he provided throughout his life.

I truly believed my wonderful brother was content with his life and now at peace. I love you Bud, and hope I "did you proud."

~Bonney Bohan
London, ON

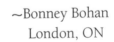

When Do You Stop Being Canadian?

I wouldn't let someone take my Canadian citizenship from me for anything.
~Jim Kale

When do you stop being a Canadian? This question has haunted me since I moved to the United States almost thirty-two years ago. My family had decided that enough was enough after watching one too many Tournament of Roses Parades in Pasadena on television, seeing the locals in shirt-sleeves in January. Despite our "tough" Canadian exterior, the caché of bundling under yet another blanket to stave off the biting chill of a harsh Edmonton winter had long ago worn off.

The talk of possibly moving to California seemed to warm my face, even as I breathed ice crystals into my woollen scarf as I waited for the school bus. I'll never forget how long it took to thaw my clenched hands, painful pins and needles coursing through my flesh as I wriggled my blanched digits. I dared not tell my friends about this exciting prospect in fear of being ostracized. During the time my father travelled to San Diego for his job interviews, I kept this secret close to my heart, vowing only to reveal the truth once it became an actuality.

Once my dad confirmed our move to San Diego, I finally told my friends, who despite my fears, were more intrigued than jealous. I promised to "send some sunshine" in my letters and invited them to visit once we got settled. I knew I'd miss them, but the anticipation of this new life helped soften the scariness of change.

Less than two years later, following a trip downtown for the required INS photographs and a seemingly endless plane ride, we touched down on the tarmac at LAX.

The first thing I noticed was, of course, the palm trees. So many of them! They seemed almost artificial, as if Hollywood had set out its best props to make a stunning first impression. It worked. Everyone looked so happy and the sun seemed brighter here. Did they have their own special effects or was it just my excitement?

We ended up first in La Jolla, a gorgeous coastal town just outside San Diego. Dad's new office was close to base camp, a motel complete with kitchenette and within walking distance to the beach. The beach! I kept pinching myself.

As we settled in, everything seemed magical. Traversing the winding streets, the fragrant sea air mixed with the pungent aroma of the bougainvillea and filled us with wonder. These new experiences remain imprinted in my mind. So many differences to take in! Seaside cliffs, towering palms, Bird of Paradise plants, all added to the mystique of this new landscape.

Early on I realized we were foreigners when we gathered in a local diner and my father ordered fish and chips. What was brought to the table only remotely resembled the newspaper-wrapped, vinegar-sprinkled treat we had enjoyed at home. While this dish looked familiar, it came "naked," with only ketchup as an accompaniment. Weird, I thought, where's the newspaper?

Meanwhile our house hunting efforts, while entertaining to me and my brother Jason, were proving taxing for our parents. We toured prospective neighbourhoods and Jason and I were sold on each home that came with a built-in pool. This luxury was rare in Canada. In Edmonton, or my home town of Toronto, a pool was truly a short-term treat that was soon covered over for yet another winter. In contrast, it seemed that every other house had a pool, and Jason and I drove our parents batty as we pleaded for such an oasis. Even the one with the water so dank that I swear there were creatures living within the murk didn't put us off. We swore we'd clean it every day!

We did not get that house.

We settled on a house in a suburb called Mira Mesa. (I loved all the Spanish names—so different than at home.) Jason and I staked claim to our prospective rooms and the moving-in process began in earnest.

A month later another transition occurred as I passed through the doors of Wangenheim Junior High, facing seemingly millions of new peers. Soon enough, I realized how I stood out. Ending many sentences with "eh" was met with blank stares. Evidently Americans spoke a different dialect than I. The quirky sayings of my home country would only serve to isolate me further at precisely a time when assimilation was so important.

The "eh" was dropped immediately.

Soon after this incident, the questions followed. Many times I found myself confirming that yes, Canadians did have indoor plumbing; no, we did not all live in igloos; and no, not all of us loved to play hockey! Frequently I felt more an oddity than a normal teen, trying desperately to be cool and "all-American;" acutely aware of my differences and alternately fretting and relishing in my uniqueness. One thing I did not adopt was spelling "American." I'd debate my teachers about the importance of using "her Majesty's English," even opting to get a few markdowns out of deference to the Oxford English Dictionary. I'd insert the letter "u" into words such as "color" and "favor" and I'd reverse letters in words—thus "metre" and "centre" would appear on my reports. Some teachers eventually chose to overlook my "misspellings," winking even as they got out their correction pens.

Eventually I became more comfortable with my adopted country and noted fewer differences between myself and my American compatriots. I felt more "normal," and spent less time obsessing about my "Canadianness."

Except for one thing. I never gave up my citizenship.

While I was proud to carry a green card and appreciated my

parents' efforts to immigrate to the United States, something kept me from losing that last vestige of my affiliation with Canada.

Despite becoming involved in politics and current affairs, enjoying the freedoms shared by my American friends, and relishing the culture, something kept me tied to Canada. I could not get my mind around relinquishing that final attachment to my country of birth. It seemed so harsh, so final, so rejecting. I chose, therefore, despite my being a political "junkie" and giving up my right to vote, to remain Canadian. It was often hard to explain to my American friends why I would live so long in the States without "making the commitment" to become a citizen. I'd counter this argument by asking them, "Could you give up your American citizenship?" Most would say no.

See, despite my growing to love fish and chips sans newspaper and vinegar, proudly flying the Stars and Stripes on the porch of my country farmhouse, actively participating in the political process, carting my son to Boy Scout meetings, and being an avid San Diego Chargers (sorry Toronto Argonauts!) fan, even after almost thirty-two years, I still consider myself Canadian. I proudly fly my flag on Canada Day, adorn my luggage with maple leaf tags, and persist in spelling "English-English" in all but my business correspondence.

If you aren't from Canada, you might not get it.

But as I have always said, you can take the girl out of Canada, but you can't take Canada out of the girl.

Eh?

~Dawn Edwards
Canadian living in Sandwich, IL, USA

Having a Ball

*I am sure that no man can derive more pleasure from money or power than I
do from seeing a pair of basketball goals in some out of the way place.*
~James Naismith

"Honey, it would be great if you learned something about basketball; you'd probably enjoy the game more." My handsome, curly-haired six-foot-four husband, Dick, was so passionate about this sport he secretly bought tickets and orchestrated our honeymoon to include evenings in sports arenas. He wanted me to learn the names of the Canadian basketball players, so that the exhilaration of the game might capture my heart as much as it did his.

As a child, as soon as Dick was big enough to dribble and shoot a ball, he had his eyes on a hoop, a net and a shiny gym floor. As a gangly teenager he had loved his position as number 15 on the Penticton Senior Secondary School's basketball team. There was not an ounce of awkwardness in him; he was confident when he had a ball in his hands. A natural.

Marriage to Dick meant I had to make a choice: I could either become a basketball widow, or follow him around to games across the interior of British Columbia, where he coached and refereed. It wasn't long before I was on buses with groups of loud, jovial boys who loved to re-enact each game play by play. The fanatical excitement was infectious. Soon, even for me, the smell of a school gym evoked the anticipation of spending an evening cheering until I was hoarse and listening to the rhythmic squeak of running shoes.

Our son Donovan emerged from the womb into a world of basketball logos, team colours, and numbered jerseys. Dick couldn't wait to set up a basketball hoop on the balcony over the driveway. The combination of our home, our driveway and a batch of chocolate chip cookies became a favourite source of entertainment for our whole neighbourhood. As soon as the boys heard the dribble of the basketball on the cement, and the vibrating *ka-thunk* of the ball hitting the rim, the friendly competition would begin and well-earned sweat would appear on foreheads. I happily became the basketball mom, sitting on the grass for hours cheering them on, laughing and keeping score. I never picked a team; they were all my favourites.

While we were living in Lethbridge, Alberta, the Canadian National Basketball Team chose the Lethbridge Community College as their home training base. The college was only three gloriously short minutes from our home. Excitement stirred in our household when, in the summer of 1990, Dick became heavily involved in assisting the organization of the training camp. There was a new sparkle in his dark brown eyes and an energetic bounce in his step. He believed in these boys; he also admired and liked them so much that he would have them over to our home from time to time.

That year, on one warm summer evening, Dick and I stood at our front door, waiting for the team to arrive for a barbecue. We watched as these tall, handsome, athletic boys marched down our cul-de-sac in their red and white training outfits. As they came closer, they started singing "O Canada." I could feel the tears prickling my eyes. These were the colours and sounds of a country that I loved. They evoked feelings of humility and also pride, that I was a part of this Canadian culture and history, as unusual and beautiful as the sight of these boys walking down my street.

I stood back to let the boys in, chuckling as they ducked their heads to get in through the front door. These were big lads and they had appetites to match their size. In amazement, I watched them pile mounds of dinner onto their plates and then build sky-high banana splits for dessert. It was a delight for a seasoned basketball mom to see these boys devour the food and enjoy our hospitality.

Amidst the fun, jokes and camaraderie in our backyard, someone pointed out that there were bricks missing in our patio. Dick and I explained that this was a very busy time in our lives and our patio was yet another unfinished project. "We'll get around to it someday," we said, "in a different season when life slows down." That was the end of the conversation, but it felt oddly unfinished.

The following day Dick and I arrived home after work to find a crowd of long arms and legs on our back patio. I had to blink twice to absorb the image. There was the Canadian basketball team, laying the last of the interlocking bricks in our patio. These were true Canadian boys: eager and grateful enough for a home-cooked meal to expend their time and energy to lend a helping hand. There were no photographers, TV cameramen or journalists around to capture this unusual, unselfish event. It was just a brilliant, living example of Canadian grit, respect and kindness. I shivered with pride and gratitude.

One day in 1991, Dick excitedly said to me, "Honey, life doesn't get any better than this! I've been asked to be a Team Official at the World Junior Men's Basketball Championship games in Edmonton." The event took place from July 27th to August 1st, 1991, and when Dick came home he was bursting with exhilaration. He had met dignitaries from all over the world and had had opportunities to interact with basketball players from every country. He was a proud Canadian representative and I truly believe he felt he was born for this.

When we moved to Kelowna, British Columbia, in May of 1993, one of the first things Dick did was sign up for a basketball league. Even though he was getting older, he still played basketball at every opportunity and he loved it as much as ever.

On December 8th, 1994, Dick and I arranged to meet at one of our last choir rehearsals for a Christmas production at our church. Before going to the choir practice, I stopped at a friend's house, and while I was there Dick telephoned me. "Listen honey," he said. "Just so you know, I'll be slipping out of choir practice early tonight so that

I can play basketball. When you see me get up and leave, don't worry about it—I'll be heading out to play at Immaculata High School. I'll see you after the game."

Toward the end of the choir practice I looked back to see him give me a big smile and a little wave. That was the last time I saw him alive. He died that night on the basketball floor, playing the game that had been so dear to him for his entire life.

I know he died having a ball.

~Heidi McLaughlin
West Kelowna, BC

The Ring

Our maple leaf flag is a symbol that unites Canadians.
Associated with the values of freedom, peace, justice, and tolerance,
Canada's flag honours Canadians of all origins
who have helped build one of the best countries in the world.
~Jean Chrétien

I approached through the graveyard slowly. I was twelve kilometres outside the small town in which I was staying, with only my day pack and a rusty, rented bicycle. I was weighed down partly by the shock of so easily finding it within rural Italy and partly by the unobtrusive manner in which it stood. Everywhere I looked, I was scanning simply elegant white maple leaves carved into the perfectly symmetrical rows of stark tombstones. I glanced back at the crumpled note I had copied off the Veteran Affairs online records: grave reference: I. F. 13. Here was row F. Which way did the numbers go? It didn't matter, I saw his grave almost immediately. Robert Anderson. I fell to my knees in front of him. Tears were already streaming down my cheeks as I reached out to trace the letters. He was my age when he died, only twenty-four.

"In loving memory.
What we would give,
His happy smiles to see,
Wife, Mother, and Son."

It might seem foolish bend over the grave of a man who died in 1944, thirty-nine years before I was born, to whom I do not even have blood ties. This man, though, is my greatest symbol of love.

Before he was dispatched to this Italian ground, his platoon was stationed in England. There he met the love of his life. He married her, he gave her a son, and he died fighting for their rights. This woman was determined to continue on with life. She rode the bride ships to Canada with an infant son, despite having no husband waiting on the other side. Here, she faced the cold shoulder of in-laws. They refused to acknowledge that their son's love and affection could have been diverted away from them, or that his medal of honour should dare go to the boy that would never meet his father.

This woman faced life in a foreign country, as a single parent, and as a widow, alone. I would have hightailed it back to the safety of home. She stuck it out. She lived an amazing life. She remarried, and then had the pride and courage to kick out an alcoholic husband and continue raising the kids alone. She gave birth to ten children, had the pleasure of raising nine. When they all grew up and moved out, she continued working actively in the community, constantly volunteering and creating bonds everywhere she went. People told me she was extraordinary. They didn't need to. The youngest girl she had was my mother. She was not just my grandmother but the woman I aspire to be.

When she passed away, the wake was a public celebration of life, and later, when the family spread the ashes in the Georgia Strait, the mood was one of favourite memories and stories of strength. Repeatedly, I heard that her first husband was the man she would now share eternity with. He was the pinnacle of love in her life. The ring I inherited was fingered by aunts, suggesting it might have been her first engagement ring. I stared at the ring and imagined loving one person so much that a single year of life together could sustain you through the next sixty.

I stared at it again now as I sat collapsed in the grass. The sparkle of gold and tiny diamonds were only accented by my watery vision. I traced the words on the cold stone again and cried for her. For I knew, without a doubt, that this was her true resting place. The ashy remains may have been given to the sea, but her spirit would have come straight here. I missed her love and strength and insistence that I eat more. In this place, I could feel her in the air. I breathed in her very being.

I spent the afternoon there. I wandered by every grave, reading the names, silently thanking the young men who had died in the fight against hate. I slowed over the eighteen other men in Robert Anderson's platoon who had died the same day. Eighteen in one day! I struggled not to see it as tragic, pointless death — and instead the reason that I was freely standing there that day decades later. I paid respect on behalf of the hundreds of families that would never make the journey to Italy to see the grave. The grave that had been built within the boundaries of the war itself.

Returning again to his resting spot, I fondled the ring, twirling it around my finger. I considered returning it to him, to them and their love, but I couldn't bear the thought of losing my last piece of her. It had become a part of me in the years I had worn it. It connected us to a higher level than our blood could. Instead, I dug out a Canadian penny to represent the land he had come from and a British coin to honour her. I placed both on the grave, whispering to him: "Life might have made her wait decades, but she's with you now. Keep her safe, she's with you now."

I walked away, my feet like lead, knowing I would probably never be back, but grateful for the opportunity they had given me and the life they allowed.

~Kelly Marie Pohorelic
Vernon, BC

Chapter 2

O Canada

Ice Time

Sports is human life in microcosm.

~Howard Cosell

Music and Hockey

What this power is I cannot say; all I know is that it exists and it becomes available only when a man is in that state of mind in which he knows exactly what he wants and is fully determined not to quit until he finds it.
~Alexander Graham Bell

My two passions in life are hockey and music. I play music for a living, and hockey for fun. When I moved to L.A. to work in the music business, it was hard to find anywhere to go skating, let along play the pick-up shinny that I was used to playing on the outdoor rinks in Toronto. In a way, though, both passions led me back to my home in Canada.

There is no place on earth that I would rather live than Canada. In 1988, I had just married my beautiful wife Amy Sky, and we were living in Hollywood, California. We were both writing songs and making records, and although we had a great life in L.A., the pull of Toronto was very strong for me. In fact, the whole time I was writing in L.A., I drew on my life lessons from the streets of Toronto for inspiration.

One day I was working in a recording studio at the home of Kevin Cronin, lead singer of the band REO Speedwagon. He was from Chicago and was a Blackhawks fan. Kevin had turned his tennis court into a ball hockey rink. I saw the rink, walked over and picked up a hockey stick for the first time in twelve years. I took a shot, and knew as I looked at the stick (which seemed to be glowing in my hands) that I had to move home. It was a moment that has shaped the rest of my life.

I did move shortly after that, and called Toronto home once more. In 2009, I got a call to work on a film which was a musical about hockey. The movie was called *Score*. They wanted me to help with some music. I thought I had died and gone to heaven, until they asked me to audition for the part of the dad. I had never acted in my life, but I did the audition, and remarkably, I got the part.

Panic set in immediately. When I asked who my movie wife was going to be, they said they hadn't cast her yet. Amy suggested I call our friend Olivia Newton-John, who we met while living in California. She graciously said she would do the picture. Olivia was amazing to have in the cast. She ran lines with me, gave me pointers, and was an incredibly gracious presence on set. It was a wonderfully Canadian story about a hockey prodigy (my screen son) who loves to play but doesn't like to fight. It was also a love letter to the game of hockey itself.

The final scene of the movie was one that I did with Wayne Gretzky's father Walter. I played a new hockey dad who was looking for advice, and got it from Walter, the dad of the Great One himself. It was a wonderful film, and it was selected to open the Toronto International Film Festival.

While touring as a musician in Canada, I have crisscrossed this country at least ten times, and the phenomenon of the hockey families has always touched my heart. I see them in hotels on the prairies, driving hundreds of miles to a game so their kids can participate in what really is our national sport. The dedication and love is evident in these road-weary families. It is quintessentially Canadian, I believe, and something that I love about this country. The sound of pucks hitting the wooden boards in the outdoor rink at Ramsden Park in Toronto is inextricably connected to my childhood: the freedom, the fantasy, the feeling of the cold air rushing past your ears as you fly down the ice. I am Bobby Orr, I am Wayne Gretzky, and the great Rocket Richard. I am Marc Jordan, and I am Canadian.

~Marc Jordan
Toronto, ON

Growing Up with a Canadian Obsession

Ice hockey players can walk on water.
~Author Unknown

Hockey in Canada is more than a favourite pastime. It is an obsession. There is something stemming from the genes that pulls parents out of bed at 4:30 on dark weekday mornings to go sit in a cold arena, hunkering around travel mugs of coffee, to watch their children pass puck after puck around the slippery surface. Even the Canadian five-dollar bill pays tribute to the game with pictures of pond hockey and a quote from Roch Carrier's short story "The Hockey Sweater": "The winters of my childhood were long, long seasons. We lived in three places—the school, the church and the skating rink—but our real life was on the skating rink."

Being a creative, artistic sort, I had never understood the fixation on this game—it moves too fast and has an undercurrent of violence with all that body checking and clashing of sticks. Then, one cold January day, I gave birth to a baby boy. Maybe it was being born into the cold of winter that gave rise to his obsession with hockey. But I should have recognized something was up, when at one year of age, he turned a long shoehorn into a hockey stick to bat a small ball around the floor. I have the picture to prove it. Twelve years later, the hockey stick of choice costs over $200 and is made of lightweight composite wood with a flex 100 Sakic curve.

I chuckle at the memory of my five-year-old hockey player being forced to sit through a demonstration of his younger sister's dance class. "I don't like ballet," he said to me, with all seriousness, in the car on the way home. "There's no action."

As the years go by, the hockey skates get bigger and the hockey schedule gets fuller, with more trips to the arenas in surrounding towns. Hockey has given us reason to see more of our province than would have been our natural inclination. I may not have shopped the main streets in all the downtown cores but I have been to all of the hockey arenas.

I have finally figured out what "offside" means. And even though I don't always catch the penalty calls, I understand a bit of the strategy that goes into putting the puck into the net.

Every year, the play goes a little faster as the kids' skill increases. The shots get harder as do the body checks. I no longer wince when my son gets checked into the corner but we all still hold our breath and mentally will a downed player to get back up because we know that the next big hit could be against our own child.

I can finally hold my own in a hockey discussion with the other parents and understand why everyone gets so upset at a bad call. I roll my eyes and throw my hands in the air over missed scoring opportunities. The bird's-eye view from the stands get us every time, as the spectators criticize the plays not so obviously visible from the level of the ice. "Yes, I see the sign that reminds us that every referee is someone's child… but, come on, he should have called that."

With every passing year that my son gets older, it is like I am growing up with hockey just like the rest of Canada.

In our area, there is a small window of opportunity that is anticipated as soon as the last leaf falls from the trees. It is the moment when the little lake near our home freezes solid enough to hold the weight of a person. This window only lasts a few short weeks before the water moves again. But as soon as the ice starts to creep towards the lake centre, the kids daily ask, "Is it time yet?"

Last year, we watched as our small lake began to freeze. The kids enjoyed throwing stones onto the thin sheet of ice to hear the wobbling sound it made as the rocks skidded across the surface. Every day we checked the thickness of the ice on the way to school. Then, ice fishermen started to appear, dotted here and there across the white expanse. And sure enough, the shovels came out and small clearings for rinks appeared in the snow on the ice.

One sunny day after school, I brought the kids' skates so they could spend an hour on the small frozen inlet. Before we had arrived, another boy whom we had never met had spent some time clearing the snow off a small area of ice.

Once he saw that we had come to join him, his face glowed with excitement. He was proud of the small rink he had worked so hard to create and couldn't wait to try out his hockey skills. He had brought some extra pucks and animatedly talked about putting up boards around the edges so that the puck wouldn't escape.

The kids placed backpacks on either side of the rink to stand in as goal posts and started to play. I realized the cleared space wasn't quite large enough and decided to do some more shovelling for them.

I stepped onto the lake and looked through the clear ice at the fish swimming below. Surrounded by snow-covered mountains, the air was crisp and fresh. It was neat to see the world from this perspective, not available to us most months of the year, as we don't own a boat. Standing on the middle of the frozen water in my boots, I actually cursed myself for not bringing my skates even though they pinched my feet.

Other kids appeared out of the woodwork with skates and hockey sticks in hand. Previous players, where another impromptu game had broken out, had left a hockey net on another cleared rink across the lake. Our little lake was soon bustling with action.

But all too soon it was time for us to leave. The kids made plans with strangers to continue the game the following day.

I wouldn't say that I have caught the full all-consuming passion of hockey yet. But I do appreciate the appeal of the suspenseful adrenaline rush and camaraderie that bind Canadians to this game. I am not at a place yet where I will sit glassy-eyed and glued to the television to watch Hockey Night in Canada. We'll see when my son makes the NHL. But I will say this, "I get it." Shh... don't tell my husband.

~Rebekah Wilkinson
West Kelowna, BC

The Rookie Card

No matter how carefully you plan your goals they will never be more than pipe dreams unless you pursue them with gusto.
~W. Clement Stone

The older man perusing the leather loafers in the far corner of the shoe store seemed oblivious to the fact that Zdeno Chára was "in the house." I, on the other hand (a true Ottawa Senators' fan), was elated, especially at being introduced to such an imposing figure. Standing six feet nine inches tall, this premier player was hard to ignore. I couldn't wait to tell my kids.

I had travelled to Montreal by train that weekend with a couple of friends in order to watch our much-loved Sens face off against the Montreal Canadiens. Because one of my friends was closely related to an Ottawa team member, my son Michael knew the chances were good that I would have access to the visiting team after the game. Upon hearing about our plans a few days earlier, he charged up the stairs and began rustling about in his bedroom.

"You could get me some autographs," he excitedly proclaimed, bursting into the kitchen five minutes later, a big smile etched on his face, a small stack of hockey cards clutched in his hand.

"I can't take the cards," I said, trying my best to gently break the news.

Michael's countenance crinkled.

"I'm just glad to go to the game. Maybe see the players off on their bus. I really don't want to be bugging them."

My son did not understand my point of view and continued to pester.

"Okay, okay," I finally relented. "Tell you what. You choose one card that you want signed. Just one card. Pick any player from the Sens or the Habs and if I happen to run into that player in downtown Montreal this weekend, I promise I'll ask him for his autograph."

Undaunted, Michael had shuffled through the pile. "Here it is," he finally announced, grinning once again. "Dominik Hašek's rookie card." He carefully passed over the chosen piece of colourful card stock, along with a few instructions for its safekeeping. (Hašek was the Senators' goalie at the time, while Chára was one of their top defencemen.)

So there I was, lingering in the shoe store with the personable Chára, as my friends left, laughing together. Apparently, the sight of my measly five-foot stature was quite comical in light of Chára's towering frame. I glanced at his feet. Was he actually this tall, I wondered, or was he wearing heeled shoes? He was — about three inches worth. On the other hand, I was wearing my flat, ultra-comfortable shopping shoes, definitely not the ideal footwear to be sporting when meeting Zdeno Chára face to face. (Face to waist was more like it.)

Moments later I raced down the street, catching up to the others as they entered a sophisticated women's wear boutique. "Too... bad... I... I... didn't have... Chára's hockey card," I stammered, breathless from my run. Quickly, I explained about the deal I had made with my son.

While I was jabbering away, they began to laugh once again, this time uproariously. "Hašek was in the shoe store," one finally blurted.

My eyes widened. "You mean the older man in the corner, the one with his hat pulled low?"

I spun around and dashed back up the street, newfound appreciation for my low-heeled shoes. Hopefully, he would still be there. I was this close to getting what my son so badly wanted. I could not fail him now!

Hašek and Chára were standing together in the centre of the store.

"You're... Dominik... Hašek," I exclaimed, breathless once again. I hadn't done this much sprinting since high school track and field.

"Yes," he said.

"I can't believe it!" I cried. Then I told him about Michael and the rookie card, adding a bit more information about how our local hockey team (the one my son played on, the one my husband coached and I managed), had hosted a pee wee team from the Czech Republic in Peterborough, Ontario, billeting the players in our homes for a few days. And how we had held a garage sale as a fundraiser for that same team when the Vltava River overflowed its banks, flooding the arena in eský Krumlov. The team had lost all its equipment, which we helped replace. Our experience with the Czech hockey team was, in fact, the highlight of our son's minor hockey career.

Dominik Hašek was meticulous about finding the right pen. Of course, I didn't have one with me. Even though I'd prayed about it, I really didn't expect to run into him in downtown Montreal. The Senators could lose (they did) and my joy would not be shattered. I was ecstatic that I could grant my son's request.

~Judi Peers
Peterborough, ON

He Shoots — He Scores

Ice hockey is a form of disorderly conduct in which the score is kept.
~Doug Larson

I had been cooped up way too long because of a knee that had to be pinned and stapled back together after a cross-country skiing accident three weeks earlier. I felt any excuse to get out of the house was a good one... but ice fishing? Who in their right mind had thought up that particular form of barbaric torture?

"The whole day," my husband Paul whispered, like it was a secret just between us, "has been planned by the guys in the office." I was acquainted with a few of them and their wives but knew them more by sight than by name. There would be a dozen or more on this sojourn.

The sun was glorious but you only felt its warmth if you moved quickly. We gathered at a rest area along the highway, then drove in convoy since only a few of us knew the exact location and the rest had only vague directions. Despite going around in circles a few times we found the spot. We parked our car along the banks of a small lake just outside the village of Ste. Agathe in Quebec's Laurentian Mountains, a couple of hours from our downtown apartment.

Several small wooden shacks had been placed on the ice. Within minutes of our arrival someone came along with an auger and drilled a half dozen holes in the ten-inch-thick ice. Paul took our picnic basket into one of the huts and went back to the trunk to retrieve a couple of deck chairs. Everyone carried something out of their cars like they were on an assembly line. Each couple had brought a picnic hamper with sandwiches, a thermos of soup, and bags of good, old-fashioned junk food. Everyone had a bottle of wine and a six-pack of beer. Folding chairs, side tables, blankets, extra mitts and gloves, sweatshirts and jackets followed the food just in case the temperature dipped or someone got wet. We would not go hungry or thirsty or suffer in any way on this outing if it could be avoided.

Fishing poles, line, reels and bait were produced from the trunks and the men immediately went into action untangling, assembling and baiting the hooks. Within minutes almost everyone had a line in the water, including me. I made myself as comfortable as I could on the deck chair and went to work. I was handed a paper cup of wine. The distribution of the beverages started the festivities.

Thankfully the wine dulled my senses and I had no idea how long we were out there doing almost nothing. A few fish were caught but not enough to get excited about. Their size was nothing to brag about either. I think that if all the fish were going to one household they would have fit comfortably in a sardine tin with a little compart-ment for the crackers and room to spare for the dipping sauce.

We fished. We ate. We nibbled. We drank. When boredom set in the men decided to play hockey. Since we didn't have the necessary equipment the game had to be improvised. There were two teams, three on each side. Picnic baskets served as goal posts and I, sitting on the deck chair, was the puck.

My right leg, encased in a plaster cast from my toe to my hip, was stuck out in front like the lead dog at the Iditarod. With a team member hanging onto the back of the chair I was propelled willy-nilly down the ice towards the goal line. If a block was set up I was set free and pushed in the general direction to go sliding down the ice on my own and hopefully through the goal posts.

To this day, "He shoots. He scores," means far more to me than to most people who don't watch or play or have any interest in hockey. The game ended when the chair folded on its own and I went sliding through the goal posts on my side, my right arm stretched out in front of my body, the deck chair attached to my butt end, taking out the picnic basket along the way. I am living proof that God takes care of fools. I felt no pain... that day.

We cleaned up when the sun started to go down and it got cold. With the alcohol in my system there was no way I could actually freeze but I did need the warmth of the car heater. With the heat blasting out at us, it didn't take long before I was removing the top five or six layers of clothing.

We were again playing follow the leader. I thought we were heading back to the city, stopping for dinner along the way, but that was not to be. We stopped at a hotel in Ste. Agathe. A deep-fried chicken feast, with French fries, mashed potatoes, and two or three different kinds of salads had already been prepared and set on the table while we were still being seated. We toasted a fantastic day with lots of black coffee since we still had over an hour's drive back into the city.

No one talked about the fish that were caught since there wasn't much there to talk about. No one really knew exactly how many or what size they were, but I do know that most, or possibly all, mysteriously ended up, unwrapped, in the trunk of a car whose owner parked his vehicle in a heated garage!

~Joei Carlton Hossack
Surrey, BC

A Stone, a Broom, and a Daughter

We'll explain the appeal of curling to you if you explain the appeal of the National Rifle Association to us.
~Andy Barrie

It was ten o'clock on a Sunday morning and instead of sitting on the couch reading the paper, my father was putting on his coat. "Where are you going?" I asked. "It's Sunday."

He did up the last button before answering. "I'm going curling."

I stared at him for a moment. "Curling? Just because it's winter in Canada doesn't mean you have to go curling. You don't even like the cold and suddenly you're going to spend time slipping and sliding on a rink. I bet they're going to make you wear a silly sweater with big maple leaves all over it." I paused, thinking about my father's previous lack of interest in any winter sport. "Besides, since when did you get interested in curling?"

"Since this week. I joined a curling club."

My father joining any club seemed odd to me. He worked six and a half days a week. Sunday was his only day off and he usually spent it in the house, reading, watching TV or taking a nap on the living room sofa. Suddenly he was going out.

"Why? Curling's such a dumb sport. You throw rocks at each other. Oh, and you sweep," I continued, with all the disdain a sixteen-year-old could muster. "You've never swept a floor in your life. Why start now?"

My father shrugged. "It's stones, not rocks. And why not?"

I couldn't think of an answer. I just knew I didn't like the idea of him going out.

When he came back a couple of hours later, I was there to greet him. "So, hit any rocks?" I asked.

He just smiled.

For the next few months, I continued to kid him every Sunday morning about going out to throw rocks and sweep. Each time he'd shrug and head out.

Then one Sunday, his car was in for repairs so my older sister drove him to the club. A little after noon, she asked me if I wanted to go with her to pick him up. "Sure," I said, wanting to see the sport that got my father out of the house once a week. "Let's go a little early and watch him in action."

Twenty minutes later we arrived at the curling club. We parked the car and headed in. Just as we opened the door from the foyer into the main reception area, a man came running up to us. "You can't come in."

"What do you mean we can't come in?" I asked. "We're meeting our father. He's a member. We want to watch him curl."

The man stood in front of us, barring our way in. He shook his head. "You can't come in. It's men's morning only. You have to wait for him outside."

I shook my head in disbelief. "Outside? It's the middle of winter. You've got to be kidding."

The man glared at me. "Women aren't allowed in the club until 1:00." He made a big show of looking at his watch. "And it's only 12:30."

I started to open my mouth to complain but my sister yanked my arm. "Let's go. We'll wait in the car."

"But…"

She didn't give me a chance to continue, just pulled me out the door.

Fifteen minutes later, my father came outside. He'd barely opened the car door when I started in on him. "Some idiot at the club wouldn't even let us in. Said it was men's morning. That women couldn't come in. Why would you join a place like that?" I barely paused for breath before continuing. "I always thought curling was stupid but now I'm sure. If you go back to that club after what that man did, it means you care more about some stupid rocks than about your own daughters."

My father didn't say anything for a moment. Then he sighed quietly. "You know I love you both very much."

The next Sunday and every Sunday after that, my father stayed home. I felt smug knowing he had chosen his daughters over a sport.

Many years passed before I realized the Sunday morning curling had little to do with curling. It was really about my father having some time for himself.

It's true that the man at the club had been officious. He could have let us wait in the foyer. But I had also been unfair. Rather than punish that man, I had punished my father by making him choose between curling and us. In doing so, I had taken away a couple of hours of his freedom, hours in which he could put aside his work and his family and simply focus on a stone and a broom.

And because he was the man he was, he let me do that. Even after my sister and I moved out, he never went back to curling. I had taken the pleasure out of it for him.

To be honest, even though I now know curling is considered a sport of strategy and precision, I still think it's somewhat less than thrilling to watch, especially compared to other winter sports like hockey and skiing. Not even the fact that Canada boasts some of the world's best teams will ever change my mind about that, though I do feel reflected glory when we win gold at the Olympics and I've been known to grin, just a little, when I see the Scotties TV commercials for their annual women's national curling championships.

But mostly what curling means to me is a lingering sense of guilt. The guilt of a sixteen-year-old girl who gave her father an unreasonable choice. If I could give my father back those hours with a stone and broom, I would. And I wouldn't even care if he did wear a sweater with big maple leaves.

~Harriet Cooper
Toronto, ON

Finding Hockey

You miss 100 percent of the shots you never take.
~Wayne Gretzky

Canadians are well known for our passion for the game, whether as a player or spectator. We fit our youngsters into hockey gear and push them onto the ice when they can barely walk, we freeze in tiny arenas as our local teams play, we religiously gather and cheer on our Canadian teams in national pride, and scowl in disbelief if they meet defeat.

But not everyone in Canada loves hockey. We are one of those families who doesn't share Canada's love of hockey, and yet, it has changed our lives.

Having recently moved to a new town, we were looking for ways to make friends. Our kids—Noah, Avery, and Simon—were seven, nine, and eleven, and the move had been difficult.

This was a small one-grocery-store town, sporting a one-rink hockey arena that had seen some great players like Darryl Sittler growing up, and where the majority of school kids could be found after school hitting that black puck with their stick across the ice.

Hockey and arenas were foreign places to us, and our three kids were having trouble making new friends. People had known each other for years and didn't seem to need any new friends, especially ones who didn't know anything about hockey!

The previous town we'd moved from hadn't had much of an

emphasis on hockey. Play hockey or don't play hockey. Dance, golf, or swim, do what you like. Here, it was just PLAY HOCKEY.

Our new town was in full swing to win the coveted Kraft Hockeyville Award. Every business and home was plastered in hockey sweaters and paraphernalia. Banners hung everywhere screaming, "WE ARE HOCKEYVILLE!" The town was in a hockey frenzy, with hockey emblems suffocating every available advertising space.

My kids did not share in this enthusiasm. "They are forgetting all about Valentine's Day!" declared my daughter, Avery, as February 14th approached and the only signs around town were about hockey. She defiantly plastered our trees and the front of our house with giant plastic hearts, and a sign: "No Hockeyville — Happy Valentine's Day!" This did not win us any new friends either.

The kids were coming home from school each day, shrugging off their wet snow coats and mittens, and heading to their rooms to read or play on their computers. "Don't you want to invite anyone over?" I would ask. "Isn't there someone out there who would like to play?"

"I don't know anybody. They don't want to know me. Everyone just goes to the arena after school," were the answers I got.

This went on and on, until I decided it had to stop. I wanted my kids to get outside and enjoy the weather, to have some friends, to play! Walking downtown one day, I saw some big red hockey nets advertised in the local sports store.

Not sure what I was doing, I brought the nets home, set them up on the street beside our house, and handed my kids hockey sticks.

"What are we supposed to do with these?" they complained.

"Road hockey!"

They were hesitant at first, but soon learned how to handle the sticks, and a neighbour boy came out and joined them. Simon, who was seven, brought a friend home from school who wanted to try road hockey. We noticed a couple of kids who lived around the corner watching, and invited them to play too.

My husband began coming home early from work, and sometimes the other dads would join in too.

My older son, Noah, an introvert, surprised us all, as he

played—loudly yelling and smashing the ball through the street. More and more kids joined in, and soon it was an everyday occurrence, with the large group of neighbourhood kids coming over, dragging the nets out onto the road, selecting teams from all the kids who showed up. Sometimes other kids came to cheer the teams on, and someone would bring granola bars or hot chocolate.

I guess hockey wasn't so bad after all.

Now Simon plays real ice hockey, but road hockey is still his first love, and he'd gladly give up an ice game to race around the street hitting that bouncy green hockey ball.

I sit in the cold bleachers and cheer his team on, trying to understand the game, clutching my Tim Hortons just like all the other hockey moms. I never dreamed I would be sitting here watching hockey, but it is actually kind of fun now, and how could I miss seeing my son's first goal?

No, our town didn't win the Hockeyville title that year, but our family did. We went from resenting and avoiding hockey, to joining in outdoor road hockey, meeting a lot of new friends and having a real live hockey player in our own family.

And that is something to celebrate!

~Lori Zenker
Elmira, ON

Pink Curlers and Pucks

Forget about style; worry about results.
~Bobby Orr

The long-awaited hockey season returned to our household every September, along with the crisp autumn air. The familiar overture of the Hockey Night in Canada theme song was like our call to duty. Being die-hard Canadian hockey fans, we planned our social calendars around game times.

My love of hockey was shaped by my father. It wasn't because of any interest I had initially in the game. As a nine-year-old girl, I was quite convinced I wanted to be a hairdresser when I grew up. I had put together a collection of my mother's cast-off rubber hair curlers in a paper bag. They were bright pink and had stretchy elastic fasteners that would often get tangled up in your hair. There was a sacrifice involved with having curls. A prized possession in my hairdressing kit was a half-used jar of Dippity-do styling gel. Every time I'd approach my mom or sister clutching my paper bag, they'd make themselves scarce. Even the cat hid. How would I become a hairstylist without anyone to practice on?

My father watched hockey every Saturday night, his eyes riveted on the television screen. Mom kept the household quiet for him during game time. My young sister and brother spent time at the kitchen table over coloring books and a Tupperware full of crayons. Dad admired Foster Hewitt's ease in calling the play-by-play action but felt he had an obligation to tell the referees when he didn't agree with their penalty calls. All logic told me that he was anything but a good choice to practice on. He wasn't female. And he was from farming stock, a strapping son of immigrant pioneers who worked long days in the fields and prayed for abundant harvests. Would he be willing to sit in pink curlers? He'd have to do.

As he leaned forward on the sofa to get a better look at a pass, I made my move and slipped in behind him. Without taking a breath, I rattled off my sales pitch. To my surprise, he just nodded his assent but asked me to stay quiet and talk only during the commercial breaks. You can get a lot done in three periods of hockey, I would find out. I had time to practice pin-curling and back-combing. He would wince if I tugged too hard on those elastic curlers. To my delight, he encouraged my creativity each week. After each game, he would reward me with a big smile in the handheld mirror I proudly thrust in front of him.

One hockey season ended and another began. Dad and I had an ongoing date every Saturday night. I'd like to believe that he enjoyed this time together as much as I did. Two surprising things began to happen. He was an excellent color commentator and soon I had a good understanding of the game and a repertoire of favourite players. We always cheered hardest for the Toronto Maple Leafs. After a couple of seasons, I became more enthusiastic about watching hockey than I did about curling his hair.

On Sunday mornings, Dad's hair always looked great in church. It became commonplace to hear "Jules, you sure have been blessed with wonderful hair" or "I wish I had those curls." Dad would wink at me. He recognized a win-win situation.

Now married with a family of my own, Hockey Night in Canada is an institution in our household. I didn't become a hairdresser but I continue to cut and curl family members' hair as a hobby. During the Olympics, I was contracted to work with Hockey Canada. My father proudly took the credit for that accomplishment. My early training, perched on the back of the sofa and watching the game over my dad's head of pink curlers, had taken me a long way.

Over the years, we fondly reminisced about all the hockey

seasons we had watched together. In our joint venture of pink curlers and pucks, we had forged a strong father-daughter relationship. At Dad's funeral, it blessed my heart to overhear a woman say, "He always had such a good head of hair." And, Dad, that's an accomplishment for which I proudly take credit.

~Sally Walls
Calgary, AB

A True Canadian!

Canada is hockey.
~Mike Weir

I'm Canadian, but as life happens I've lived a large chunk of my life overseas. Regularly, though, I bump into fellow Canadians in my work and travels. There may not be all that many of us, but we sure do get around!

During the summer of 2002, I travelled to New Delhi, India for a conference, which is where I met David. The Soccer World Cup was in full swing, hosted that year by Japan and Korea. As a child, my family lived in Italy for several years, so I'm a bit of a soccer buff. Though India is, of course, partial to cricket, the World Cup was getting a lot of coverage there as well. Local restaurants played the games live, and newspapers printed the highlights of the latest games and speculated on those to follow.

David told me his fiancée was from Germany, and that as he'd never been to Europe, he was trying to learn more about the country. "My ancestors are from there as well—and we might want to live there someday."

"Well," I told him, "here's some information for you: your gal's country just creamed Saudi Arabia 8-0 a couple of days ago."

David's response was instant: his face lit up as he exclaimed — "At what — hockey?"

A true Canadian!

~Evangeline Neve
Canadian living in Belmont, MA, USA

Where There's a Wheel There's a Way

A pessimist sees the difficulty in every opportunity; an optimist sees the opportunity in every difficulty.
~Winston Churchill

Even though I loved a good snowball fight or the stinging frost ricocheting off my cheeks as I picked up speed on the toboggan hill, growing up in a farming community in east central Alberta just made "winter" synonymous with "hockey." The fact that I was a girl and didn't play on an organized team didn't matter. At least twice a week most of the town would gather at the local arena, clamouring for the warm seats under the heaters, to cheer on the hometown team, from the little Mighty Mights to the Old Timers. My brother was a goalie, so through the years I regularly heard the plea, "Take shots on me." Whether it was a makeshift goal on the farm with a tennis ball or playing street hockey in town with a "real" net, I soon became adept at mixing it up between glove hand, stick side and five-hole shots.

Saturday night would find us sitting around our little nineteen-inch TV taking in the latest NHL match-up. Our favourite clash was between our beloved Toronto Maple Leafs and those pesky Montreal Canadiens. From the first note of the Hockey Night in Canada theme song, you could feel the energy level rise in our home. Enthusiastic cheers and homemade replays just added to the excitement.

Intermission meant time for a quick round of hand hockey on the living room floor… until Mom told us to "quit before we wrecked something." As the expansion teams began making their way into the league, my loyalties shifted west. Despite several moves throughout western Canada I have remained a die-hard fan of my hometown Edmonton Oilers—in their dynasty years as well as their dismal ones.

Now, years later, my brother coaches his boys' hockey teams and the tradition continues with regular trips to the arena for practices and games. However, as an adult, I had thought that my connection with grassroots hockey was pretty much over. You see, our daughter is an accomplished musician and our son has cerebral palsy. While our son loves hockey and cheers with exuberance, his body does not cooperate with his mind, so his physical limitations made the idea of playing hockey all but impossible… or so I thought.

When he was twelve years old, we were introduced to power wheelchair hockey, and hockey was revived as part of our family's life. For the past few years, every Saturday during hockey season, we join the small army of wheelchair-accessible vans at one of our city's rec centres for the next match-up. There are four teams in the league, each coached by one of the dads, or someone from the community with passion and heart for both the players and the game. The players' combined fervour and grit are reminiscent of the Original Six. They play on a full size basketball court bordered with custom covered foam "boards" to keep the ball in play. The league is open to both males and females twelve years and older who require a wheelchair, regardless of their diagnosis. Some players are able to hold their stick in one hand and use their wheelchair controller in the other. Others strategically tape or bolt the stick to the side of their chair. Despite the type or severity of their disability, they arrive ready to play. Some are able to speak clearly, others not. Some are able to use two hands, some can only use one. One player even uses his chin to manoeuvre his chair. For some of them, this is the only sport they can play and they live for Saturdays and "the game."

Now, lest you think this is a nursing home league, do not be fooled. They play with the same rules as able-bodied hockey, with one exception. Cross-checking penalties have been replaced with ramming penalties. In typical hockey a fight often gets fans on the edges of their seats or up on their feet. However, in wheelchair hockey, on the rare occasion when two chairs collide and a chair goes over, both the sidelines and the stands empty as they scramble to set up the chair and make sure the player is unharmed.

Not only were we introduced to power hockey but also to the power of belonging to a community. With approximately thirty-five players in the league, it's a pretty close-knit group. Cheers from the stands often go both ways, acknowledging great plays at either end. Whether it's needing assistance getting their gear on, mounting their stick, or helping players with any number of problems with their wheelchair, capable and compassionate help is readily available regardless of which jersey a player is wearing.

Just like the NHL, the playoffs bring a new round of intensity. The stands are fuller, the stakes are higher and everyone has their "game on." As the intensity increases, so does the commitment to each other and the game. Duct tape solutions and bungee cord quick fixes are freely shared with whoever needs them, as resources are pooled in a collaborative attempt to limp the wheelchairs through the rest of the game until more adequate repairs can be made later.

Perhaps this community is felt the strongest as wheelchairs line the aisles of churches and funeral homes in a statement of solidarity for a lost comrade. As players and those associated with the sport succumb to disease, complications or the simply unexpected, there is an overwhelming sense of community that rises up within the league. At each funeral we've had the sad privilege of attending, I am awed at the number of players and their families that come to show their support.

Indeed, this is a remarkable group of people. Week after week I marvel at the stories behind each of the players and their families—stories of daily struggle and realities that are foreign to many. They are stories that most people would characterize by limitation. Yet, the players and their family's collective tenacity and commitment to the game and to each other demonstrate their ability to live far beyond their limitations. When life would say no, they say a resounding yes. Where there's a wheel, there's a way.

~Cindy Martin
Delacour, AB

Once a Canadian...

Hockey is like a disease, you can't really shake it.
~Ken Wregget

"Offside!" my husband shouted, throwing his hands in the air.

I looked up from the counter where I was making salads for dinner. Our kitchen and family room are joined, so it was easy for me to see Roger in his recliner with the big screen TV in front of him.

"Come on, ref, that's cross-checking. He didn't even have the puck!"

I knew Roger liked sports. I'd catch him eyeing games on televisions in restaurants when we were dating. But since we were married, it seemed to be one game after another, nonstop. Particularly his beloved hockey. He used to play when he was in college in Montreal, but a knee injury sidelined him. Roger often regaled me with stories of his dad hosing down the backyard in winter to form a makeshift ice rink. When his career took him out of Canada and all the way to California, Roger's love for the sport stayed with him.

"Boarding!" he yelled one day, then jumped out of his chair.

"Why do you watch if you get so worked up?" I asked.

"I love hockey. It's how I relax."

"Relax?" I said under my breath. "It doesn't look like relaxing to me."

Then one day in the summer of 1993 Roger came home with something in his hands. "Look what I got for us," he said with a broad smile. "Season tickets to the hockey games." He brought out the brightly coloured tickets showing players in their jerseys.

"Season tickets?" I asked incredulously.

"Remember Southern California just got a hockey team? I told you. They're called the Mighty Ducks of Anaheim and they'll be playing at the Pond."

That's right. He did tell me.

"Now we can actually attend games. There'll be teams from all over that come here to play, even from Canada."

Ahhhh... so that's why he wanted season tickets to see this new fledgling team.

Many of the teams that came all the way out here that first year included the Oilers, Maple Leafs, Canucks, Flames, and Nordiques. The Montreal Canadiens, Stanley Cup Champions the prior year, came only once, on March 2, 1994. We were there. Roger loved every minute of the action, and since we attended almost every game, and sat in the same seats in the same section, he got to know many hard and true hockey fans who loved talking stats and player trades. From preseason September into April, I huddled in a jacket, mittens, boots, scarf and hat while jumping up and down when a goal was scored. I could tell it was hard for Roger to root for two teams: Montreal, the team of his heart, and Anaheim, the team of his city.

Named after the Disney movie *The Mighty Ducks*, this new team became stronger each year. They changed their name to the Anaheim Ducks and re-designed their team logo and colors. The team morphed and grew, and if it was at all possible, Roger's passion grew right along with them. In the 2006-2007 season they were in the playoffs and in contention for the Stanley Cup. They advanced from the first round into the second and seemed to grow more motivated as each game was played. Even though my fingers were still cold inside woolly mittens, and Roger sometimes took off his outer jacket and wrapped it around me for warmth, I did get excited as we watched them battle it out.

Like all hockey teams, they worked hard. Blood was often spilled during cross-checks and boarding, and broken noses were common. Nevertheless, they skated with enthusiasm, showed up for extra practices, and stayed long after the games were over to discuss strategy. Players gave 110 percent and often relinquished their place in a coveted line in order to help the team to score and win. Like all who battle for the Stanley Cup, they overcame injuries and suspensions to reach their common goal of hoisting that beloved prize.

But no one thought this fledgling hockey team would be contenders. Everyone expected one of the Original Six to win: Montreal, Toronto, Boston, New York, Detroit, or Chicago. But the Ducks had spirit, pluck and determination. One day the team was seen at practice wearing a T-shirt designed by one of the players. It was black with white letters across the front: Destiny = Heart, Sacrifice and Passion.

Roger possessed those same qualities. He had room in his heart for both the Canadiens and the Ducks. His passion never ebbed for the sport he loved so much. Even after being sidelined with that knee injury, he still loved the game and supported it wholeheartedly. And Roger sacrificed. There were nights when the ride to the game was long, in backed-up traffic, or we were tired after a busy day at work, but we navigated our way there, parked the car, sat among the diehard fans in our section and rejoiced when our team made a goal.

The Anaheim Ducks won the Stanley Cup in 2007 and we attended the huge rally to celebrate the victory. With that win there's always hope they'll win again. We stand proudly before the start of every game with our hands over our hearts and sing along to the U.S. National Anthem, but while Roger already knew the words to the Canadian National Anthem, I have learned them, and we sing "O Canada" when a team from Canada is here to play.

I love the country my husband was born in because I love my husband. I may never understand or even love sports as much as Roger does, but I love sharing his passion.

You can take the man out of Canada, but you can't take the Canada out of the man. And I wouldn't want to. Bring on those awesome Canadian teams. I can't wait to attend our next game.

~B.J. Taylor
Wife of Canadian living in Huntington Beach, CA, USA

He Shoots, She Scores

People didn't know the difference between a blue line and a clothes line.
~Al Michaels

When I was seventeen, Hockey Night in Canada was not the best warm-up for a romantic evening. In fact, it left me cold. But that didn't stop me from having a little fun before getting my "just desserts."

It all started with a call from my boyfriend around dinnertime. "Harriet, what are you doing tonight?"

"Nothing," I said, thinking a movie would be nice. Cozy dark theatre, light romantic comedy, maybe a bit of lip-locking.

Simon had other plans. "I scored great seats to a Canadiens game. They're on a roll. Couple more wins and they'll clinch a playoff spot. Maybe even the Stanley Cup." He paused to catch his breath. "I can pick you up in ten minutes."

"Slow down. What game? What cup?"

The sigh on the other end of the phone should have told me this wasn't the best idea. "A hockey game," he said. "None of the guys could make it, so I called you."

I was not about to let that comment slide. "Let me get this straight. You only invited me because no one else could go. I was your last resort."

"Uh," he stammered, "I just figured, well, you know, that the guys might enjoy it more than you would. Look, forget it. I'll go by myself."

"No way. You invited me and I'm going. I've never been to a hockey game. It might be fun."

"Okay, I'll be there soon," he said, his voice sounding a little strained. "Dress warmly. Our seats are practically on the ice."

I told my parents where I was going, had a quick bite, and put on a warm sweater under my jacket. Thirty minutes later Simon and I were sitting on very hard metal seats a couple of rows from the ice. I kept shifting, trying to get comfortable, but I couldn't. My jacket didn't cover my fanny and the cold from the seats quickly penetrated my jeans.

He stared at me. "What's wrong?"

I squirmed. "These seats are really uncomfortable. And cold."

He sighed—a long, drawn-out sigh. "You'll be fine. You won't even notice it once the game starts."

It was my turn to sigh, very loudly, and glance at my watch. "Speaking of games, how long does it last?"

"There are three periods of twenty minutes each."

I brightened as I did the math. "One hour. That's easy. Maybe we can catch a late movie afterwards. You know, in a nice warm theatre."

This time Simon squirmed. "Well, actually, it's not exactly an hour. There's a short break between each period. And the game clock only runs when the puck is in play, so the actual time..."

Before he could finish, the players skated onto the ice and we all stood for "O Canada."

As we sat down again, I poked him. "So how long are we really talking?"

He shrugged. "Usually about two and a half hours. More if they go into overtime."

I groaned.

He patted my hand. "Just watch the game. Once you get into it, you'll love it. I promise." Then he leaned forward to watch the action, forgetting all about me.

With nothing else to do, I turned my attention to the game. Because I didn't understand the rules, it was just a bunch of guys skating and fighting, with the ref blowing his whistle while the fans alternated between cheering and jeering. Not exactly my dream date.

I wrapped my scarf tighter around my neck. Within a few minutes, my toes started to tingle. I poked Simon again. "Has anyone ever gotten frostbite at a hockey game?"

"No," he said, gaze glued to the players, "you'll be fine. Just watch the game. You might even end up being a hockey fan."

Like that's ever going to happen, I thought, trying to imagine myself in a warm movie theatre rather than in a freezing arena. Unfortunately, my imagination wasn't up to the job. I rubbed my hands and tapped my feet, trying to get the blood circulating. It didn't help.

Bored, half-frozen, and frustrated, I figured it might help pass the time if I understood a few of the rules. "Simon, what's the blue line for?"

He waved his hand in the general direction of the ice and muttered, "Divides the rink into zones. Defence, neutral and offense."

Having no idea what that meant, I waited a minute before coming up with another question. "Why are the blue lines solid while the centre red line isn't?"

He shrugged, still focused on the ice, not me. "I don't know. It just is." The words came out clipped and I could see his jaw clenching.

That's when I realized I had found the perfect way to be entertained. I surveyed the rink. "Simon, what are the circles for?"

"Face-offs. When two players fight for control of the puck." He paused, turned to me and spoke very slowly, enunciating each word, the way people speak to children or dummies. "You know, the round black thing that the players push around the ice."

Now I had his attention. "I do know what a puck is. I am Canadian, after all."

"If you're Canadian, then love of hockey should be in your blood."

I shivered. "The only thing in my blood right now is icicles.

Remember, you're the one who invited me, after none of the guys could go, that is."

"As if you'd let me forget," he murmured, half under his breath. "Any other questions?"

"Not just now, but I'm sure I'll come up with something." Warming up to the task, I learned forward for a closer look at the rink. "Here's one. Why is the centre circle blue, but the other ones are red? Did they run out of blue paint?"

He slumped in his seat. Then straightening up slowly, he faced me, a half-smile on his lips. "Do you really want to know or are you just doing this to bother me?"

I grinned.

"That's what I thought," he said. "Here's the deal. If I promise to take you out later for a really great dessert, will you stop asking questions?"

"Deal."

So ended my stint as a hockey fan. But there was a happy ending. Simon watched the rest of the game in peace, the Canadiens won and I got my favourite dessert—mile-high lemon meringue pie—and a cup of hot chocolate to warm up my fingers and toes.

Our next date? A movie. My choice.

~Harriet Cooper
Toronto, ON

O Canada

Slice of Life

A lot of funny stuff happens in Canada.

~Samantha Bee

Storm Chaser

Sunshine is delicious, rain is refreshing, wind braces us up, snow is exhilarating; there is really no such thing as bad weather, only different kinds of good weather.

~John Ruskin

Everybody has a weather story—I just have more of them and mine tend to be more extreme. As a storm chaser, I go out of my way to get close to some of the wildest weather in the world, and Canada certainly has plenty of it.

Weather is the one subject that anybody can talk to anybody else about. Think about it. It's not political or religious so nobody gets too offended when you talk about it, yet the weather affects every aspect of our lives from what we wear to what kind of food we grow to how we build our homes. Who hasn't experienced the situation when you step into an elevator with a stranger and you need to break that awkward silence with some chitchat? "Sure is warm out today, isn't it?" or something like that.

There are a few things that we, normally humble Canadians will openly brag about: hockey, the awesomeness that is Tim Horton's, and how we're able to cope with just about any weather. I must admit that I sometimes consider myself a "bad Canadian." I don't like beer and I even spelled "hockey" wrong the first time I typed it out in the last sentence, but what I lack in Canadian cultural stereotypes, I more than make up for with my love of all things involving the extremes of weather across this vast nation.

Because I specialize in documenting the extremes of weather, it's been my mission to put myself in harm's way to show people how bad things can be when they get REALLY bad. I never started off thinking that I was going to have my own international TV show chronicling my adventures, but looking back I can see how I got my interest in nature and weather.

Growing up in Hull, Quebec, I was always fascinated with the natural world. I fondly remember being twelve years old and riding my bike through a hailstorm. It was so incredible to see ice falling from the sky in the middle of the summer, feeling the stones hit me as I rode around the neighbourhood. It's a good thing they weren't too big! I guess that was the first storm I ever "chased." Evening thunderstorms became a family event, especially if we were lucky enough for the power to go out. There were times when I'd hear the rumble of approaching thunder and we'd get the candles out and have them at the ready just in case, disappointed every time the lights remained on.

That flicker of a candle may have been the tiny spark that eventually led to my passion for getting up close to nature's fury. There's something extremely humbling about being in the presence of a tornado, or feeling the raw power of the wind in a hurricane. It puts me in my place, never letting me get too comfortable or cocky.

When I was twenty, I moved to the big city of Toronto and it wasn't until after I'd already been living there for a few years that I really kicked my passion for the weather into high gear. My mother had given me a waterproof camera as a gift and I loved experimenting with it, finding new ways to capture unique images. It helped me hone my photography skills, especially since back then there was no digital photography, so I had to wait for every roll of film to be developed before I could see the results of my latest experiments. Eventually I upgraded to a more sophisticated camera and that notched up my interest even more. I could open the shutter for longer periods of time and attempt to catch lightning images as these storms scribbled their high voltage signatures across the sky.

I had no car at the time, so I would run out in the rain and set up my camera in any dry spot where I had a clear view of the CN Tower. Not only is it one of the tallest structures in the world, it's also one of the world's tallest lightning rods. The tower gets struck between seventy and one hundred times per year (and you thought lightning never strikes the same place twice!).

Harkening back to my childhood years in the hailstorm, I bought a mountain bike and thus had even more mobility. My reach was extending and I found myself heading out into more storms, sometimes getting my tripod caught in the spokes of my wheel, sending me flying over the handlebars into a puddle. I didn't care though. I just got right back on and continued heading off into the rain. Even today, I sometimes shake my head thinking about it.

When I eventually bought my first car (which I still drive today some thirteen years later) I filled it with all the gadgets and equipment that I needed to travel across the continent, chasing tornadoes in Kansas, hurricanes in Florida, or whatever weather I could find closer to home in Ontario. By now, there was no turning back. I was a fully addicted nature junkie.

Here in Canada we're exposed to almost every weather extreme imaginable. The east coast gets hammered by hurricanes like Juan, which did tremendous damage to Halifax in 2003 with 160 kilometre per hour winds and twenty-metre waves.

The coldest temperature in North America— -63°C (-81°F)— was recorded in Snag, Yukon back on February 3rd, 1947. We also have two "Tornado Alley" regions in Canada, one in the Prairie provinces and another in my stomping grounds of Southern Ontario. Then there are the blizzards, avalanches, heat waves, ice storms... We get it all and this variety helps define us as a people. How many times have you heard the old saying: "If you don't like the weather, just wait five minutes, it'll change"? Well, many places make that claim and in all my world travels, I've discovered how true it really can be at times in Canada.

Because I spend so much time in disaster zones, it sometimes becomes difficult for me emotionally. These weather events can bring widespread destruction, injuries and loss of life, but my being there to capture it on camera as it happens won't prevent any of it from happening. Nevertheless, if I can show the world what these storms are capable of doing, then perhaps some people will sit up and take notice, get prepared in advance or get to safety when the next one is knocking on their door. I never wish for communities to be impacted by these natural events, and that's exactly what they are: events. They only become natural "disasters" when they affect people or property.

Even in a country as vast, rugged and wild as Canada, we all are more separated from the natural world than ever before. We wake up in our air-conditioned homes, drive our climate-controlled vehicles on paved roads to our equally air-conditioned offices. So we forget that we are as much a part of the natural world as any other species on the planet until Mother Nature gives us a wake-up call, usually without much warning.

Because we have so many different terrains and climate zones I'm convinced that I'll never run out of unique weather phenomena to document in Canada. I'll keep doing it until my final breath.

Thank you, Canada.

~George Kourounis
Toronto, ON

20

Chicken Soup
for the Soul

The Tim Hortons Lady

Canada is not a country for the cold of heart or the cold of feet.
~Pierre Elliott Trudeau

When I was working, the first stop I made each morning was the same place most Canadians make their first stop each morning—Tim Hortons for their first cup of coffee. Without Tim Hortons, Canada would grind to a screeching halt, which is why I maintain that their employees are definitely not paid enough. A few years ago, as I went through the drive-through, radio on but only half awake, the lady at the window said to me: "You must like country music also. I love country music!" Delighted to discover another country music fan, our morning conversations, albeit very short, usually revolved around the same theme. "I just love that song!" the server would say. "One of my favourites…" I'd respond.

One day I drove up to the window and told my friend I'd heard on the radio that Randy Travis was coming to Ontario. "Randy Travis!" she exclaimed. "I would absolutely love to go see him!"

"Me too," I responded. "Bet the tickets will be sold out as soon as they're on sale."

"Yeah, you're right," she agreed. "But imagine seeing him live!"

"I sure wish I could," I said, pausing for a second before remembering I was late as usual and needed to get moving.

A few days later a plan began to hatch in my mind. Over the months of going through the drive-through I discovered that my country music friend was a single parent living in a small basement apartment with her young daughter. She had no vehicle and had to use the bus for transportation. Anyone who has taken the bus consistently through a Canadian winter will understand why I am mentioning this. The woman's life was difficult but she worked hard and didn't complain, trying to make the best of things.

My plan was to purchase two tickets to see Randy Travis and then ask her if she would like to attend the concert with me—that way transportation wouldn't be a problem. She had also mentioned that her ex-husband took their daughter occasionally on the weekend, and fortunately I was able to purchase two tickets for a Saturday evening show.

Driving up to the window the next morning I could barely contain my excitement. "You look happy today," she commented.

"Remember the Randy Travis concert?" I asked. "Well, I have two tickets. So why don't you come with me—your ticket's already paid for." At that point I had to drive on because the traffic was piling up behind me. "See you tomorrow!" I said, but the look on that young woman's face as I drove away was absolutely priceless.

Every morning afterwards we spoke about the concert with great excitement. The details were worked out one by one, coffee by coffee. Like most things, waiting to see Randy Travis was almost as enjoyable as seeing him. We had so much fun anticipating the songs he'd sing, the things he'd say (he's quite the comedian) and how long he'd sing. Our friends and the people we worked with must have been tired of hearing us rant about our concert.

The night of the concert I arranged to pick up my friend. I hardly recognised her out of her Tim Hortons uniform, with hairnet off and make-up on. Because we arrived before the "appointed time" I had the opportunity to take her out to eat. It was nice to sit and relax, as opposed to our one-minute drive-by conversations. When the great moment came and it was time to find our seats, we were thrilled they turned out to be excellent, not far from the stage. In addition to this there were giant screens on either side of the stage for people to see Randy perform up close.

It seemed like a long time until the curtains drew back, and a few moments later, there he was, black cowboy hat and all. As he sang his first number we were absolutely mesmerized. This voice that we had listened to so often was singing to us live from the stage. What a difference! I don't believe our eyes left that stage for the next two hours as we listened to song after song from that deep, melodious, unforgettable voice. There was much laughter also as Randy told stories of some of his "kinfolk." One cousin was so ugly that people used to make fun of him all the time. "My cousin can't help that he was born ugly," he said one time to his grandmother. "No he can't," she said. "But that doesn't mean he has to go out in public so much!"

We laughed, we cried, we heard songs that had lightened our days and been with us through the darkest of nights. All too soon it seemed, the concert was over. He wasn't going to get away without an encore of course, but this was quickly over also. With glorious memories we left the theatre and found our way back to the car, reliving all the moments of the concert.

The Bible says that if you give something to someone who can repay you, it doesn't mean anything, but if you give to someone who cannot repay you, you will be blessed. I was blessed beyond measure to give to someone who could not repay me. I later found out that the apartment my friend and her daughter lived in had serious mould issues, forcing them to move. I sometimes wonder what became of them and am thankful our paths were destined to intersect—albeit at a Tim Hortons drive-through.

~Elizabeth Young
Barrie, ON

21

Where Ye To?

The Canadian dialect of English… seems roughly to be the result of applying British syntax to an American vocabulary.
~Lister Sinclair

I sat with my little family in a roadside restaurant within view of a towering metal statue bent and welded into the form of an enormous corn stalk. We were on the lower edge of Canada's Great Plains, in southern Alberta. I leaned forward in my seat, toward my beautiful little son, and started chattering to him in baby talk.

"You some cute," I told him in my happiest mommy voice.

That was when the woman from the table next to ours caught my eye, smiled, and politely asked if I was originally from the east coast. It took a moment for me to figure out why a stranger would ask me such a thing. She wasn't exactly wrong about me. But I certainly didn't recognize her from anywhere and I hadn't lived in the east since I was a teenager. And I wasn't exactly sitting there in rural Alberta wrapped in the Nova Scotia flag.

Then I knew what had given me away. It was my choice of adjective for my baby. For most people on this side of Canadian Shield, the word "some" is not used as a superlative. Those of us who do use words like "some" and "right" where most English speakers would use "really" or "very" usually have some connection to Atlantic Canada.

In the new world mobility of the twenty-first century, it's not uncommon to hear Canada's regional accents spoken in every quarter of the country. And they're not just collecting in the big metropolitan areas like Toronto, Vancouver, and Calgary. Canada's northern boomtowns—like Fort McMurray and Yellowknife—are also great places to learn about the dozens of accents and dialects that make up Canadian speech.

Personally, I think this little diaspora of accents is fantastic. And I was always touched every time the nice Newfoundlander ladies who work at the grocery stores in Fort McMurray, Alberta, addressed me as "my love" while they totalled up my order.

Maybe I like this outpouring of regional accents because my own regional identity is fairly muddled. When I was a child in my parents' home, my dad worked for the federal government. Every promotion meant a move. In all, I attended eleven different schools before graduating from high school. Some were on the west coast, others on the east, and many were in between. On bad days, I feel like nowhere in Canada is my home. And on good days, I feel like everywhere in Canada is my home.

Despite the Maritime accent that seems to have crept into my baby talk, I wasn't born in the east. I arrived there as a kid when I was still linguistically pliable and, within one summer, I had made the Nova Scotian accent my own. My western Canadian born siblings and I were all merrily pronouncing "out" like "oat" and "pants" like "pay-ants" while my parents shook their heads and wondered what was going on.

Of course, it's important to recognize that there is no single, monolithic Atlantic Canadian accent. It doesn't take a very practiced ear to hear the clear differences between accents from places like Newfoundland, Cape Breton, the Miramichi, North Preston, and Prince Edward Island. There is even a little influence from New England accents that sneak over the border, mostly through American network television affiliates, to infiltrate Maritime speech.

In my late teen years, my family moved west again. We arrived in Alberta with all the high vocal energy of our Maritime accents—talking quickly and loudly. Even though we had lived here as small children, it was like we were hearing the western Canadian accent for the first time. To us, it sounded long and drawly—almost American.

People were wearing cowboy boots and hats on a daily basis, not just on Halloween. And all the guys who would have been called "buddy" back east were known as "dude" instead.

The differences in my accent were obvious in my high school French classes too. I hadn't known it before our move west, but I had been taught to speak French with an Acadian accent. It was nothing like the throaty Continental chit-chat of my Alberta French teachers.

Once I left my parents' home, my days of annual moves were over. I settled down with my lifelong Albertan husband and hardly noticed my manner of speech being assimilated back into a western accent. It's now my natural speaking voice—most of the time. But as soon as I say hello to an Atlantic Canadian, my old accent comes rushing back. All of a sudden, I'm calling inanimate objects "she" and making sure to inhale instead of exhale when I say "yeah." And for a little while, it's as if the last twenty years—and those five thousand kilometres—didn't matter at all.

~Jennifer Quist
Lacombe, AB

22

Crossing the Line

The Americans are our best friends, whether we like it or not.
~Robert Thompson

For years Canadians and Americans have crossed the International Windsor/Detroit border with no problem. The two cities have always felt more like family than neighbours. When my daughter, Miriam, took dancing lessons in Michigan I knew the names of the Customs officers, the names of their kids, and they knew us. A talk with a Customs officer went like this:

Customs officer: "You're wearing your pretty pink leotard. You must be going to dance class tonight."

Miriam: "I'm learning the Dance of the Cygnets!"

Officer: "Cygnet, huh?" Then he would turn to me. "Anything coming in?"

"No, sir."

Officer: "All right, you're set to go. Have a good class, sweetie."

Yup, we were very friendly.

Then the unthinkable happened. September 11th.

Because Ambassador Bridge is part of the NAFTA Superhighway and thousands of trucks cross it every day, no one got into the U.S. without an intense interrogation and scrutiny of the vehicle. It was a minimum wait of four hours to cross the border.

The people of Windsor and Detroit stopped crossing the border unless it was an absolute emergency. For my daughter, it meant the end of dance classes. For many Canadians and Michiganders it meant the end of careers.

Customs officers had an almost impossible job to do. Happy talks about dance class were replaced with terse and probing questions.

To add even more tension, several members of Hezbollah and Hamas openly declared that they were in the Windsor/Detroit area. No one disagreed with how border crossings were being handled. Inconvenience hardly seemed too steep a price to pay for security and peace of mind.

Thankfully, we have not had a major incident here. Canadians and Americans cross the border again, but it's not like pre-9/11 days. It has turned into a surreal gauntlet of bureaucratic red tape. Here's what happened recently...

"Okay, you're ready to go. Have a good time shopping," said the U.S. Customs officer after handing back our passports. We knew each other from Miriam's dancing days and I had told him about my excitement at receiving a Macy's credit card.

"It looks like a great day to use that card of yours," he said.

He suddenly held up his hand. "Uhhh, wait. You have to go in for a random agricultural survey. Should only take a couple of minutes."

Miriam worried as I drove to the inspection area. "This never goes well," she groused. "Something always goes wrong."

"Not always," I said as I parked. "Remember that time we went to Henry Ford Museum? It only took ten minutes."

"Yeah," said Miriam. "But they took our cookies. We had bananas in them. And when I was in the *Nutcracker* with the Detroit Symphony they accused you of child slavery and threatened to take me away. That was in '97, Mom. Before 9/11. Imagine what's gonna happen now."

I sighed while waiting for a burly officer to further direct us. "We got through, Miriam. And we haven't had any problems like that since then."

"Except for right after 9/11 when the National Guard pointed their guns at us while they stripped the car. If I hadn't started to cry they would have arrested us. My adolescence would have been spent in jail!"

"You're being melodramatic."

"No I'm not. I had to stop taking dance lessons in Detroit."

"Ma'am, you and your passenger step out of the car."

I felt relieved that I didn't have to get into the "dancing career was ruined" discussion for the billionth time. "Sure thing," I said.

Once outside the car, Officer Burly looked in my purse.

"Are you bringing any horses or cattle into the country today, ma'am?"

I nearly choked. "You're kidding, right? I'm driving a Honda."

Officer Burly didn't crack a smile. "Answer the question."

"No," I said. "No horses or cows, today."

"Where would we put them?" asked Miriam.

Officer Burly grunted with annoyance. "Any sheep, goats, or pigs?"

"Come on," I said. "This is a joke, right?"

"Turkeys, chickens, or any kind of fowl?"

"No," I said more seriously. Officer Burly had a snarl on his face. Every Canadian who has crossed the border since 9/11 knows to never mess with the guy wearing that snarl.

"I have to search your car. Follow that yellow line inside the building and register. I'll get you when I'm done."

"Fine," I said.

"Follow the yellow brick road," sang Miriam.

"That's not funny!" shouted Burly.

"I thought it was funny," said Miriam with an indignant air. "Didn't you think it was funny?"

"No," I muttered.

We hurried into the Inspections building. "I've got a feeling we're not in Kansas anymore," said Miriam.

"Quiet, brat."

We headed for a man sitting behind a desk. "Hi," I said. "We're here for an agricultural survey." I read the scribble on the yellow paper. The agr looked more like age.

"Looks like AGE, don't you think?" I said.

The man chortled. "It does, but it's agricultural. Just sign in here. It won't take long, I hope."

"Thanks for the warning," I said.

Another officer approached us. "I'm the head of the Agricultural Department, if you'll sit over there——"

Officer Burly charged into the room just then, brandishing a puppy biscuit in his hand as if it were a kilo of heroin. "You have a dog biscuit in your car!"

"Yeah," I replied. "I have puppies. Obviously, one of them dropped a biscuit."

"They're not in the car. Where are they?"

"I keep the biscuits at——"

"Not the biscuits," he snapped. "The dogs!"

"Oh. At my home."

"Why aren't they with you?" said Burly.

"I don't bring dogs shopping," I said.

Burly pondered this for a moment and then narrowed his eyes. "I'm stripping the car. Sit down."

Miriam groaned. "Aw, man! I'm naming him Krupke."

"Easy, Action," I said.

The head of the Agricultural Department cleared his throat. "Come with me."

"He didn't smile at the Krupke thing," humphed Miriam. "Maybe I'm not funny. I thought I was."

"They'll take care of you in here," he said.

I smiled at an officer while pointing at the writing. "I want to complain about this agr survey you're doing. Since when can't a lady cross the border to go shopping? Doesn't it mean anything that I have a brand new Macy's card I want to use? Macy's! That's almost as good as having an American Social Security card."

"And you guys owe us some cookies," Miriam averred.

The officer raised an eyebrow and Miriam mumbled something under her breath that sounded like "Completely unappreciated..."

The officer stamped my yellow paper and handed it back to me.

"Go use that Macy's card. My wife thinks a Macy's card is better than a Social Security card."

After we bid farewell to Krupke, Miriam sighed. "It took us two hours to cross the border. If people had any sense, we'd act as if nothing ever happened on 9/11. We'd show terrorists we're not afraid."

Sometimes pearls of wisdom come from the mouths of babes.

~Pamela Goldstein
Amherstburg, ON

Green Card for Sale

Vive la Canada. This country is not for sale.
~Don Sweet

First of all, let's be clear. I am not a Canadian. While it is true that I was born just five miles from the Canadian border, in the Upper Peninsula of Michigan, I never in my wildest imagination thought that I'd ever marry a Canadian. I mean, come on. They say "eh" at the end of every phrase, they sit on Chesterfields and they are so irritatingly... polite. Who can live with that?

Once I graduated from Michigan Tech, I headed west and eventually found myself in Salt Lake City, Utah, out of money and in need of a job. I was fortunate to find employment, and began dating and looking for Miss Right. Who could have imagined that I would find a Canadian girl? I mean, I had Idaho, Wyoming and Montana in between Canada and me, and those are very large states!

It started one Saturday with my joining several young men and women for a day of cross-country skiing. Out of nowhere, this little fireball plowed into me and knocked me down in the snow. "Are you are alright, eh?" she said. Did she say, "eh?" I must have had too much snow in my ears. As I brushed myself off and stood up, I found myself looking at her startling blue eyes and crooked smile. I was a dead man!

When I got up on Monday morning for work, and found my apartment door and my whole car bound in plastic wrap, I'll admit

I was intrigued. This girl was enticing, even if she was nationally challenged.

I found out that she was teaching elementary school in one of the rough parts of town, and that she had a tremendous love for her students. Wow, I thought. Depth and those blue eyes. Did I say I was a dead man?

I'll admit that I was very interested, but I wasn't ready to get too serious with any girl at that particular time. That is, until I found out that she was about to walk out of my life forever. As it turned out, she had a work visa to teach school that never should have been granted to her. About the same time that I found her, Uncle Sam also found her, and decided it was time to send her back across the border. That is, unless she could get her hands on one of those green cards.

I'll be honest—I had to do a lot of soul searching in a big hurry. Should I take a leap of faith with this girl I had only know a few months? And a Canadian at that? My head was swimming... don't rush things... but those blue eyes... there are plenty of other girls... what a sweet smile... she's older than me... what a caring heart... but... but... she's a Canadian!

So we made a deal. She would give me $10,000 to marry her. Then she would get her green card, allowing her the ability to live in the USA, we would get the marriage annulled, and I could use the money to buy a really nice new car. Perfect plan, eh?

So here we are twenty-nine years later in Boise, Idaho. She's got her green card, but I'm still waiting to get my $10,000! I'm not letting her go until I get every penny! Through the years I've grown to truly love this wild Canadian woman, with her pretty eyes, big heart, and her patriotism—for Canada! She refuses to take out American citizenship, because, of course, she's Canadian.

However, there are some perks. I'm one of the few people who get to celebrate two Thanksgivings each year, and she makes a great stuffed turkey! Our two children have dual citizenship, and hey, she's still so darn... polite!

So a few years ago, I quit fighting it. I bought a large Canadian flag to fly from our house for those holidays from up North. I've learned to love vacations in beautiful British Columbia, and we love the traditional music of Cape Breton. I'm still not convinced that Smarties are better than M&Ms, but she is.

So hey, Blue Eyes. Slide on over next to me on the Chesterfield and I'll put on some Celine Dion, eh?

~Bruce Mills
Husband of Canadian living in Eagle, ID, USA

Canada Is So Big

Under this flag may our youth find new inspiration for loyalty to Canada; for a patriotism based not on any mean or narrow nationalism, but on the deep and equal pride that all Canadians will feel for every part of this good land.
~Lester B. Pearson

I grew up in a large family with seven siblings. I am the third oldest and have had the privilege of watching my younger siblings grow, struggle and learn for many years now. I consider all of my siblings a blessing in my life but one in particular has really filled my life with laughter as of late.

My youngest sister, aptly named "Treasure," has been reminding me of childish enthusiasm, innocence and naivety all four years of her life. There is one day that will stand out in my memories for the rest of my life though. It is the day that she taught me that Canada encompassed more than just land, water, and people.

One day, while walking down the main drag of our little city of Portage La Prairie, Manitoba, Treasure and I passed an establishment that proudly displayed a large Canadian flag on its flagpole. This was a common sight for me so I barely made note of it but it definitely caught Treasure's eye.

Grabbing the leg of my pants eagerly, Treasure stopped walking and a big grin settled upon her face. She pointed to the Canadian flag and shouted with excitement, "Look Jazmyne! It's Canada! Wow, Canada is sooo big, eh?" I burst into laughter but decided not to burst her bubble; I will leave that up to her future geography teacher!

I very much believe that I have learned a lot from being an older sister but what I took from that day was momentous. Now every time I look upon a Canadian flag, a new sense of pride and admiration fills me. Canada is large in mass, population, culture and freedom but Treasure taught me that it is also largely filled with the love, laughter and enthusiasm only a child can teach.

~Jazmyne Rose
Portage la Prairie, MB

A Matter of Opinion

When I am right, no one remembers. When I am wrong, no one forgets.
~Elizabeth Arden

Rural Manitoba is dotted with stone cairns marking the spot where old schoolhouses used to stand. These one-roomed schools were a big part of our prairie life until consolidation sent our farm kids bussing into town. Now, the old schoolhouses have disappeared from the landscape. The few that remain have been transformed into granaries or sheds or even homes, and have been carted away from their original sites.

My Aunt Ethel attended one-room country schools for the better part of her life—first as a pupil, then as a teacher. After decades of boarding with local families, or living in teacherages, she finally retired to her home area and bought a little house.

Aunt Ethel was one of the few alumni still living when the cairn was dedicated to Sunny Slope School. She was also the oldest, now in her early nineties. As such, she was asked to attend the ceremony and had her picture taken standing beside the cairn.

This picture appeared in the local weekly paper, along with one of the original school and a description of the event. In the story my aunt was mistakenly identified as Miss *Edith* Sherson, instead of Miss *Ethel* Sherson. Now, my aunt was not one to make a fuss. She was a retired teacher, never married and quite content to live out her days quietly in her small house on a corner lot with her garden and flowers. So, although a little annoyed, she would never have contacted the paper to point out the mistake.

My Aunt Shirley, her sister-in-law, on the other hand, felt no such compunctions. She phoned the editor of the weekly paper to let them know the name should be Ethel, not Edith.

The paper did the honourable thing and printed a correction the next week, "We are sorry for the printing error. The identification should have read Miss *Elsie* Shearson, not Miss Edith Shearson."

Well, they still didn't have it right. Aunt Shirley contacted the paper again.

Once more, the paper printed the apology and correction. "The third time is the charm. The name of the oldest student has been reported erroneously in the past two issues. Our apologies to *Mrs.* Ethel Sherson, not Elsie or Edith."

Well, now the names, first and last, were both correct. The only problem was that the paper had conjured up a husband, past or present for my aunt, something she would have had no truck with. She tolerated men, as long as they were someone else's husband and didn't smoke in her living room, but taking one for herself had never been in her plan. She had been an independent woman with a very strong mind of her own in the days when women were encouraged to echo their husbands, whether they agreed with them or not. It just wasn't her style.

Still, she didn't believe in creating a scene and kept her opinions to herself. It was Aunt Shirley who again contacted the weekly.

Finally, they got it right. The final version got both the names right, as well as marital status. They could have worded it a little better though. The correction read, "We've finally got the name right, and we are sorry that Miss Sherson never married."

Somehow, I don't think she would have looked at it that way.

~Sharon McGregor
Brandon, MB

Titched?

*You will find as you look back upon your life that
the moments when you have really lived are the moments when
you have done things in the spirit of love.*

~Henry Drummond

I stacked the dinner plates and carried them to the kitchen where my mother was hefting the kettle from the wood stove and pouring steaming water into the tin dishpan. Setting the table for dinner and washing the dishes after the meal were two tasks that I was considered old enough to do.

It was mid-July, and we were visiting the family farm in Nova Scotia. Mom spent her days cleaning the house and stripping wallpaper as she prepared to repaint my Uncle Byron's bedroom. Dad was using his vacation to help Byron bring in the hay. I spent my days talking to the swayback horse in the pasture or fishing in Lamb's Lake.

"Great Uncle Midge could use a little cheering up," Mom pleaded. It was clear from her tone of voice that my boredom was showing.

The thought of visiting my great-uncle in a stuffy nursing home seemed dreary. I imagined the smell of disinfectant and the sight of shrivelled faces. Besides, I had never met this man, although I had heard stories about him.

The winter before, at the age of ninety, Midge had been in a fistfight over a woman. He and one of his neighbours had each wanted to shovel out the snow in front of a widow's home.

"Titched in the head." Aunt Ola rolled her eyes as she told me the story.

So when I learned that Great-Uncle Milledge had recently fallen off his horse-drawn hay wagon, I wondered if Aunt Ola had been right. Midge was raking the tower of hay in the wagon with the pitchfork when he fell from the heap onto the ground. Now Midge was in a nursing home, recuperating from his injuries.

The bed Great-Uncle Midge lay on was in the far corner of the sunroom at the nursing home. Daylight illuminated the room that had once been the front porch of a large Victorian house. The tall glass windows looked out on the town centre. Vibrant gold, green, red and blue crocheted afghans covered the beds in the room. I sat down in the chair beside Midge, his crispy sunburned face relaxed into a smile.

"You're Linda, Horace's daughter, aren't you?" I nodded shyly. I had not introduced myself, and he had remembered my name and my place in the family tree. He went on, "I'm old and probably going to die soon, but I don't mind. I've lived a great life." Drawing in a small gasp of surprise at his frankness, I could think of no response.

Midge quickly changed the subject. "You know," he said, "we've got a lot of ministers in our family, but it's not our fault." I giggled, but he seemed quite serious and continued.

"Take Kenneth, who was Ernest's son. He took after his mother, you know." He followed with, "We aren't to blame for Bill either, Blanche's son, because he always favoured his father."

One by one, he named each relative who had joined the clergy. He was right; there were a lot. In each case, he ruled out our family's responsibility for the individual's vocation. I wasn't sure whether to giggle or appear shocked. When he was done he seemed content.

As the conversation ended, he thanked me for coming and announced that his lady friend was about to arrive. He had won more than a fistfight in the snow. Bluntly, he indicated that he wanted me to go. As I was leaving his bedside, in walked the widowed woman. She wore a printed cotton dress, which I guessed she had made herself.

When she saw Midge her mouth opened into a big grin, displaying that she had lost most of her teeth.

I never imagined then, that forty years later, when it became legal for two women to marry, I would wed a minister. I think my Uncle Midge would understand why I chose love over convention. He would certainly understand why love is worth fighting for. However, he might not understand why I brought one more minister into our family!

~Linda A. Wright
American of Canadian descent living in Tallahassee, FL, USA

Travelling through the "Axis of Evil"

Wherever you go in the world,
you just have to say you're a Canadian and people laugh.
~John Candy

I was travelling solo through the Middle East, and all my family and friends were worried about my travels to Syria. They had all read about Syria as "the axis of evil"—a place of horrors. But from my travel book's description of ancient fortresses and markets set in secret passageways, the allure of adventure was too exciting to give up. Danger or not, I was going to Syria.

Leaving Turkey by bus I had travelled all day to finally arrive in an ancient Syrian town set in the middle of the desert. The region was experiencing a heat wave in the middle of what was already the hottest time of year. As I stepped out of the bus the humidity stopped me dead in my tracks and I struggled to put on my oversized backpack.

Within seconds a large crowd of anxious taxi drivers surrounded me—all vying for my business. One driver was pulling my knapsack off my back, while another was tugging at my sleeve, guiding me in the direction of his car.

In the distance I noticed a minibus waiting for customers. It looked like the same type of white minibus that I had been taking in Turkey. It was an extremely convenient system—one simply waved one's hands to be picked up and then yelled "stop" when one wanted off. It was cheap, safe, and best of all—hassle-free.

I gently pushed past the taxi drivers, walked in the direction of the minibus and jumped on. A couple of passengers were already seated, waiting for the driver. I threw down my huge backpack and took my seat. As time went by a few more customers got on, and eventually the driver finished his break and started the engine. The girl beside me spoke English and asked where I was going. She translated the location to the driver—and with no more than that we were off.

As I had just arrived in the country, I didn't have any coins, just bills that I had exchanged in Turkey. When I handed the bill to the driver he didn't have enough change, and no matter how much I insisted he refused to take the money.

About ten kilometres later the minibus slowed to a full stop as we reached the base of a very steep hill—and the young girl told me we were close to my hotel. The young girl took my bag and told me we should get off because the vehicle could not make it up the hill.

As she climbed out of the minibus with me, the driver said something to her. She turned to me saying, "My father is very pleased to have met you."

Apparently I was not on a minibus at all—but riding in the family vehicle! As it turned out, everyone was too polite to tell me.

What's more, the family lived in the opposite direction from my hotel and had just driven ten kilometres out of their way. But the hospitality didn't stop there. They insisted their daughter accompany me to the top of the steep hill.

The young girl explained that her family had company arriving so they had to take their leave, but that she would be pleased to stay with me until I found my hotel. No refusal on my side would be listened to—and she didn't seem to mind in the least to take on her new assigned duty.

With the persistent heat and the weight of my backpack it was a breathless journey up the hill, but the young girl insisted on helping me carry it, all the while smiling.

As the only traveller in the area, people along the route would stop to inquire if I needed any help—and all offering me their telephone numbers in case I needed something during my stay.

When we finally found my hotel about forty minutes later, the young woman refused my offer to bring her to dinner or pay for a taxi to bring her back home. She simply hugged me goodbye, and with a smile turned the corner and disappeared.

If this was the "axis of evil" I was anxious to experience a lot more of it!

~Melissa Valks
Ottawa, ON

28

A Small Start to Something Big

It's important to give it all you have while you have the chance.
~Shania Twain

When Nathaniel, my older son, was eight years old, he was eager to perform in the Kingston Buskers Rendezvous. Years before, I toured my one-woman clown, mime and mask children's shows in many types of venues throughout Ontario, so to appease his interest I agreed to apply to this buskers festival. If accepted, I promised to choreograph a mask piece for the two of us.

Kingston, Ontario, twenty minutes south from where my family and I live, is where we venture for work, school, supplies and most of our live entertainment. A slew of festivals take place every summer in this historic city, providing the locals and tourists with lots to enjoy. Our favourite, and one of the main attractions, has always been the Kingston Buskers Rendezvous.

My husband and I, accompanied by our four children, would frequent this international festival faithfully, arranging our summer around this not-to-be-missed weekend. After packing lots of healthy snacks, we would make sure that the excited children were lathered up with sunscreen before heading off "into town." The children knew that once the "bagged food" was eaten, they would be rewarded with ice cream and popsicles from the bicycling vendors so they were agreeable to this plan.

Walking towards the hub of the festival from where we parked the car, we could hear the performers appealing to the audience and the crowds responding with enthusiastic cheers. There were many interesting acts from musicians, balloonologists, magicians, jugglers on six-foot-high unicycles, skate boarders, tightrope walkers, fire breathers and even a trampoline team. The city would close off a few streets to the traffic during the afternoons and evenings, allowing the entertainers large performance spaces in the middle of the road. We would weave through the mob, find an act that caught our collective eye, then assemble behind the circular chalk-marked areas and watch the performers in awe. As the sun beat down on this mid-July, hottest weekend of the year, our children were so caught up in the entertainment they never complained about the sweltering heat while the performers carried on unfazed, though sweating, as the sun beat down on them.

Humour was an integral part of all the acts, especially when they included audience volunteers. One time a female clown asked for a male volunteer and my husband, a burly six feet two inches tall, tried desperately to hide behind my five foot two frame so as not to be singled out. I'm sure his veiled attempt made him even more obvious, which resulted in him being picked. We cheered him on as he clumsily tried to imitate the dance steps requested by his clown partner in this very silly but comical number.

At the end of each act, the performers would solicit money from the audience or have a hat placed in front of their act to collect funds. If we liked the act, I'd give a loonie or even a toonie of my saved stash of coins to one of my children who would proudly drop it into the hat. Other audience members would give quite generously as we watched the hats fill up with many five- , ten- or even twenty-dollar bills.

"I can't wait to be in the show and make tons of money!" exclaimed Nathaniel a couple of months later when I read him the acceptance letter. I was thrilled at this wonderful opportunity to perform with my son.

For days, Nate and I rehearsed our act as he learned how to manoeuvre his body and gesture with ease while wearing a mask which restricted his view. I was impressed by what a natural performer he was, practicing tirelessly and giving it his all.

On the first day of the Kingston Buskers Rendezvous, Nate and I were excited, almost giddy, on our drive to Kingston. After we checked into the festival we found our designated performing spot and were delighted with this ideal location. It was in front of a church which was set back from the road, allowing us a fair amount of performing space and some grass around for the audience to sit.

I set up my stereo, props and masks and waited for the audience to gather on the sidewalk and lawn around us. Nathaniel placed our collection hat down on the sidewalk in front of us and threw in a couple of quarters to start it off, as planned. When there was a large enough crowd gathered around us, I signalled to my son that it was showtime. I started the music and we began our act. Nate wasn't intimidated by the audience and followed through with all the choreography like a pro, moving, gesturing and keeping in sync with the music. At the end of our performance we both took off our masks, as rehearsed. Nathaniel glowed as he bowed to the audience, then smiled with confidence while soaking up the applause. It was heartwarming for me to witness his enjoyment and initiation into my world.

After the crowd dispersed and Nate stared into the collection hat, he was saddened by our meagre earnings. He expected that everyone watching or passing by our performance would give us some coins or even bills. I encouraged him to keep going, stay positive and hopefully the situation would improve.

By our third show my husband arrived with our other children to support us and float around the festival. Nathaniel told his dad that he really enjoyed performing but he was disappointed with our lack of earnings. My husband smiled proudly and said to his son: "It's not about the money. Just have fun. You guys are doing great!"

"Okay," Nate answered, trying to keep focused on his performance and glad that his dad and siblings were there to watch.

Once our show was finished, my husband proudly ran over to us with our collection hat. Nate beamed when he saw the hat filled with coins.

"Great," he exclaimed. After tallying up the coins my husband announced "Twenty-five dollars and thirty cents."

"Wow," Nathaniel answered. We could tell by his expression that he felt our professional endeavour was well worth the effort.

It wasn't until a few days later that my husband confessed to me that he had put all the money into the hat. I laughed at his good nature. "You're a good dad," I said, smiling. We didn't have the heart to tell Nate, not wanting to crush his little heart, until years later when we could all laugh about it together.

Nathaniel's professional debut at the Kingston Buskers Rendezvous began his thirst for live theatre and as a result he started focusing all his free time on learning magic and juggling. Years later, an accomplished juggler and an international award-winning magician, he continues to tour with various circuses and theatres throughout Europe and North America.

~Dalia Gesser
Battersea, ON

29

Nothing Short
of a Miracle

Miracles come in moments. Be ready and willing.
~Wayne Dyer

People often think miracles happen only to other people. Sometimes when miracles happen we overlook them, just as I did.

When I was in my twenties, I had the oddest and most dramatic experience.

At the time, my friend Della and I didn't see it that way. I didn't tell anybody what happened. More than thirty years later, as I was writing miracle stories for my Angel Scribe "Angels and Miracles" e-newsletter, I suddenly realized that we had witnessed a colossal miracle all those years ago. To confirm it, I telephoned Della who said that she, too, had never talked about the incident with anyone. At the time, she was dumbfounded and questioned the experience, but now we both realized that what happened was indeed a miracle.

I met Della, a beautiful and kind Cowichan's First Nation young woman, when I worked at Mercia's Health Food Store in Duncan, British Columbia. One day, she walked into the store with such a welcoming smile that it was impossible not to become her friend. We began discussing herbs and I asked her if she had any stinging nettle in her yard. Stinging nettle has healing qualities and I wanted to plant it in my yard. She broke into laughter. "Stinging nettle is a nasty weed; it grows all over our reservation. We are trying to get rid of it, not plant it!" she said. We became friends, soul sisters joined in the love that we both had for herbs, their medicinal qualities, and our desire to help others.

Shortly after we met, I dreamed that Della phoned. At the time, Della had three small children and no phone, running water, or car. The dream was so unnerving that as soon as I awoke, I dressed and drove over to the Cowichan Reservation to see if Della needed something. This was totally out of character for several reasons: First, it was before 8:00 and I don't get dressed until well after 10:00 most mornings; second, I had never before had a prophetic dream; third, I had never been to her home before. But this dream left me with an odd feeling and an urgency that lingered after I woke up.

As I stood knocking on her unpainted front door, I felt uncomfortable. What would I say when she opened the door? It was so early, and I had not been invited. How would I tell her a dream had sent me?

Della opened the door with a look of happy surprise. She was thrilled to see me, and it was plain she was deeply agitated about something. Even at this early hour, she had a house full of people. She turned to them, reached for her purse, and said, "Good, I have a ride now." She grabbed my arm and pulled me out the door toward the car, saying, "Let's go."

Della explained that the much-loved minister of their First Nation Shaker Church was found outside his home in a coma. Doctors had informed his family and church members that he was not expected to live. Because of Della's healing skills, several of the tribe's members had suggested that she visit him. But she had no car and no idea what she would do when she saw him. She was feeling helpless and frustrated. When I miraculously landed on her porch first thing that morning, she knew this was a sign from Spirit that she was meant to go to the minister.

We drove to the hospital, neither of us knowing what we would find or what we were supposed to do when we arrived. At the hospital we found the corridor outside the minister's room was filled with his family and friends. Nearly one hundred First Nation people silently sat in chairs or stood along both sides of the hall. The silence was eerie in its intensity as the minister's family and friends mourned and waited for word.

Della and I quietly entered the hospital room of the dying man. It was startling how young and good-looking he was. He appeared to be in his late thirties. In the tiny room were about thirty concerned and upset members of the First Nation tribes silently sitting or standing.

A few stared at me. I thought, "Gosh, why am I here, the only non-native?" I felt both privileged and unsettled. Della walked over to a church elder and asked if we could stay to help. She told him that a dream had brought me to her, and we were here for some higher divine reason. The elder gave us permission to approach the minister.

Della ran her fingers over his head and found a large lump. Thinking about a reflexology class we had taken, Della did a gentle manipulation of his head and then showed a respected Native healer how to do it. According to reflexology, the brain reflex is in the ball of the big toe, so I hesitantly pulled the bed sheets back to reveal the comatose minister's feet as I wondered if it was legal to do reflexology in a hospital. Taking his foot in my left hand, I used my right thumb like a wrench and pushed my thumb deeply on the brain point on his big toe three times. This is when things took an unexpected turn!

The dying man sat straight up in bed and yelled "HI! HI! HI!"—once for each time that I had pushed on his big toe. Della said he was saying, "STOP! STOP! STOP!" His friends out in the hallway rushed into the room. When they asked him what happened, he said something about a "stake." His friends and family thought he was hungry and wanted a "steak," so they all rushed out. It was mayhem! We knew we were no longer needed, so we backed out of the room. We were both in shock! We had effectively just woken up an almost dead man! We did not talk on the way out of the hospital.

I lost contact with Della, but after thirty years I located her new phone number and called her to get her side of the story. She said she had not shared that day of her life with anyone because she was just as startled as I was. Then she talked fast, like a river that had been dammed up. Della said that when the dying man woke up so abruptly from his coma and mumbled something about a stake, he was telling everyone that he had fallen off his back porch and hit his head on a stake.

The minister remained fully alert the rest of the day and late into the night. He talked to his son, from his heart, apologizing for not being there for him, and told him he loved him. He told his wife he loved her. He laughed, told jokes and shared his precious time with his many friends. Then, just as unexplainably, he died the next morning, after having the chance to explain what had happened to him and to say goodbye to his loved ones.

Dreams are often precursors of miracles, such as the one that indicated Della needed me. That dream literally drove me to her home and to a miracle.

Della is a respected healer in the Cowichan tribe, and I grew up to be an author on miracles. It appears that we had a date with destiny all those decades ago!

~Mary Ellen "Angel Scribe"
Canadian living in Cottage Grove, OR, USA

O Canada

The Cultural Mosaic

Canada has never been a melting-pot; more like a tossed salad.

~Arnold Edinborough

"Do Your Thing"

From the CD *The Return* by Liona Boyd

Lyrics courtesy of Liona Boyd ©2011

Mid-Continental Music SOCAN

He grew up in a city in northern Spain
An idyllic life til the Civil War came
Under Franco's gaze there came darker days
And life was never quite the same

He met my mother on a London bus
They married at a registry without any fuss
His Air Force days passed, he found love at last
And soon there were three of us

Just do your thing, whatever life should bring
Accept what will be will be
Help your fellow man, do the best you can
My father would say to me

With a few hundred dollars and no guarantee
We sailed from England across the sea
Though we struggled alone, Toronto soon was home
To my mother, sister, brother and me

He painted on a rooftop in Mexico
A year long sabbatical we loved it so
We went along with all those sixties songs
And his philosophy we'd come to know

Just do your thing, whatever life should bring
Inner peace will set you free
Never be afraid of the mistakes you've made
My father would say to me

He lectured on art and creativity
And lived his life with humour and dignity
He made his own plan, he was a Renaissance man
His family would all agree

As he lay on his deathbed I whispered a prayer
And cut a small piece from his long silken hair
I knew he would be forever part of me
And the memories we'd shared

Just do your thing, whatever life should bring
Accept what will be will be
Help your fellow man, do the best you can
My father would say to me

I Am Canadian

There isn't any one Canada, any average Canadian,
any average place, any type.
~Miriam Chapin

As an English as a Second Language teacher for adult newcomers to Canada, I am one of the first "Canadians" my students have sustained contact with. As their unofficial ambassador to Canada, I see my job as much more than teaching them grammar and vocabulary. I teach them about Canada and Canadians, beginning with myself. I talk about myself and my family and invite my students to ask questions, so they can see how a fairly typical Canadian lives.

One of the first questions they ask is: "Where are you from?"

"I was born in Montreal," I say, "but I've lived in Toronto for years. I'm a third generation Canadian of Eastern European descent."

The European students pick up their heads. "What country?" they ask.

"From several," I say. "My father's parents were from Romania. My mother's mother was from Austria, but her father was from Lithuania. They met here in Canada. So, I'm a mixture—a bit of this and a bit of that."

The Europeans smile.

Then I add, "My sister's husband is from China. One of my nieces married a man whose family was originally from The Netherlands; the other is dating someone from Peru." I pause to let them take in all the names of the countries, before continuing. "We are definitely a multicultural family."

Now it's the Asian and South American students who are smiling.

The questions come faster. "Are you married? Do you have any children?"

"No, I'm not married, like about twenty percent of Canadians. I don't have any children, but I do have several cats." This information often leads to spirited discussions on the pros and cons of marriage, divorce and having children.

On another day, we talk about food and cooking.

"What's a real Canadian food?" they ask.

"You mean apart from hamburgers and pizza?" I think for a moment. "I'd have to say maple syrup, all kinds of berries, and salmon."

A woman calls out. "What's salmon and how do you make it?"

I smile. "Salmon is a fish. As for how to make it, first you open a can."

"But canned food isn't fresh," they say. "You should shop and cook every day."

"If I had to eat what I made, I'd starve. Most of my cooking goes right from the stove to the garbage can. For me, it's easier, cheaper and much better tasting just to open a can of something."

Laughter greets my comment.

Then I describe the food my grandmother used to cook. "She used every part of the animal, from cow's tongue to chicken feet. None of which I'd eat, but my mother still eats those foods." That sparks a discussion about what people eat or don't eat in different countries and why.

For major holidays, I bring in the traditional foods—pumpkin pie for Thanksgiving, candy canes for Christmas, hot cross buns for Easter, and unleavened bread for Passover. "You don't have to like the food," I tell them, "but you do have to try it."

I invite students to do the same with their holidays and associated foods.

By the time they leave my class, my students have had a chance to get to know at least one Canadian. In comparing themselves to me, they learn about the similarities and differences between Canadian culture and many other cultures. For these students, I am Canada—something I consider both an honour and a privilege.

Although I take my job as teacher and role model seriously, I'm not above having some fun. If you ever meet a new immigrant who thinks salmon grows in cans or you can't become a Canadian citizen until you own at least one cat, the chances are I was his or her teacher. Say "Hi" for me.

~Harriet Cooper
Toronto, ON

Reaching for the Stars

Canada is not a starting point, it's a goal.
~Jean-Claude Falardeau

Hockey night in Canada. It didn't mean anything to me, except to spend my evenings away from home. The hospital where I worked as a radiology technician was across from the Forum, home of the mighty Canadiens. When they played in town, a doctor and a technician had to sit by the fiberglass and go back to the hospital when a player got injured. I gave my seat to my younger son Robert, barely eight years old, while I sat in the hospital knitting and waiting for the game to end. Once in a while, muffled cheering vibrated through the walls, breaking the silence. I smiled, knowing it meant the mighty Montréal Canadians, the Habs as they were called, were winning again.

In Hungary, I grew up with soccer, cheering on our national team when they won gold at the Olympics. It was the time when the names of Puskás and his teammates were held in high esteem in the world of soccer.

But the revolution changed all that.

Escaping from the communist regime that ruled my country, my husband and I and our young son became refugees. Then, Canada opened its borders and hearts to us. It took a while to assimilate into our new environment, but we had freedom and countless opportunities.

Robert was the first Canadian in our family, born and raised in

Montreal. His brother was the best student in his class; Robert was the most popular one. Every Saturday night, as a true Canadian boy, Robert watched hockey, and with the many young boys in his class, he dreamt of becoming a star.

One Saturday evening, while Robert was sitting in the Forum cheering for his team, he met the Terrebonne Park's hockey coach. And that's when it all started.

When I picked up Robert, he could hardly contain his excitement. "Mother! I can join a hockey team!"

"But you don't have skates," I reminded him. "You can't even skate!"

"I can learn, Mother." Robert pushed my concern aside. "Can we buy skates on Monday? Right after school?" I couldn't refuse his shining, pleading eyes.

"Okay, we will get you a pair of skates on Monday."

Monday came, and after work we went to a sports store. Robert wandered around, looking at the pictures of his favourite players smiling down on him from every corner of the store. The shelves were packed with skates in different sizes and colors. Robert couldn't make up his mind. Finally, he said to the young salesclerk who waited on him. "I want skates like Yvan Cournoyer has."

"Good choice, young man," the salesperson smiled as he pulled down a box from a shelf. "He is the fastest on the ice. Let's see how these fit." Robert took off his shoes, and with great concentration he watched while the clerk laced up the skates.

"Okay, boy," the salesclerk tapped on the skates, "stand up."

Robert tried to stand, then looked around and a small cry slipped out of his mouth. I hurried to his side holding out my hands and Robert, on shaky legs, grabbed my arms and stood up.

"I see." The clerk shook his head. "You still need more practice before you can play in the Forum."

Then, he turned to me. "How about a hockey stick?"

Robert, forgetting his precarious situation, plunged forward, pointing to the rack holding the hockey sticks. "I want that one!" he shouted, while falling on his tummy. We left the store with a pair of skates, a brand new hockey stick endorsed by Béliveau, and with bruised hands and knees but without a scratch on Robert's spirit.

The next day, Robert, with his brand new skates dangling over his shoulder and swinging his hockey stick by his side, hurried to the local arena. The dressing room was filled with boys of all ages.

"Put your skates on!" the coach yelled while he rushed by. Robert, with clumsy fingers, started to lace up his skates. It took him a long time before he got it right. When he tried to stand up, he had to lean against the wall to hold himself up.

By the time he wobbled out to the rink, bigger boys were on the ice. One of them pushed him aside. "Go to the bench before you get hurt!" he bellowed at him. Robert sat down in a daze. He managed to find his way back to the dressing room where he took off his skates and left.

He cried all the way home.

He locked himself in his room and threw himself on his bed. When he composed himself, he turned on his back and stars twinkled at him from the ceiling. His face broke into a grin remembering the time when I, reluctantly, helped him to put them up there.

"I will be a star!" He whispered to himself. "I can't skate, but I can be a goalie; they don't have to skate that much." And without his supper, he went to sleep.

Five years later he became the first string goalie on his high school's hockey team, and they travelled to Nova Scotia to the Nationwide High School Tournament. Their first competition was against bigger and older boys, some in their late teens. It was a rough play, but by the end, the score was still a tie. That's when the shoot-out started. The crowd, with great enthusiasm cheered for the young goalie, shouting his name after each save he made.

"Robby! Robby!" His name vibrated through the arena, and although they lost, Robert became a star.

In the spring, the team toured the U.S. prep schools. As a parent I joined the many hockey parents travelling with the troupe. In Exeter, they were out-shot by 64 to 12. Robert kept his team in the game and it ended with a tie. That year, Exeter was undefeated; their coach couldn't accept a tie to blemish their record. He asked for a sudden death overtime.

"Boys," Robert's coach gathered his players around him. "You don't have to do it." He looked over his squad. "It's up to you."

A dozen tired eyes stared back at him. Suddenly Robert jumped up. "We'll do it!" and as in the past when faced with a challenge, he transferred his desire to his teammates, who jubilantly joined him. They won the game.

A year later, his unshakable determination earned him a hockey scholarship to Exeter, a prestigious prep school, and two years later a scholarship to an Ivy League university.

Thank you, Canada, for giving us the opportunity and freedom to reach for the stars. We are proud to call ourselves Canadian!

~Gemma Tamas
Surrey, BC

Nothing Would Remain the Same

It is in our nature to travel into our past, hoping thereby to illuminate the darkness that bedevils the present.
~Farley Mowat

"Taliban" is a word I will never forget. Every time I hear the name, sweat comes down like an endless river; my entire body starts shaking like I have no control. Often when sleeping, images come back again and again.

We were playing soccer in a playground when someone yelled, "Taliban is taking over our country." Back then I had no idea what that meant. In fact I did not care what it meant until it started affecting me and my family.

Soon everyone was disturbed by this horrific news. Likewise my family was very concerned about our future. Therefore, we decided to emigrate to Pakistan, which is on the northwest side of Afghanistan. However, it was not as easy as we thought it would be. Civilians would be slaughtered, beaten, imprisoned or raped if they were caught escaping.

To escape such circumstances, my family decided to travel at night. My father went to find a taxi for us. However, he did not come back for the whole night. Everyone in the family was concerned.

The next day we found out that they had taken my dad away, along with many others. My mom, who now was the head of the family, went looking around for our father, sometimes waiting outside the Taliban's offices for days and nights. Unfortunately, we were unable to find any information. Therefore, our trip to go out of the country was rescheduled until we found out about Dad.

Days passed, months went by, fear started taking over us. The situation was getting worse and worse. We had no news of our father. Every day, there was something even more horrific we had to live with. Women were forcibly taken away from their houses. They were raped and there was no one to make any justice. Even God had turned his back on us.

People were starving, children were dying of hunger, because the heads of their families were killed or forced to go to war. You would be lucky to have a meal a day. Often, when Dad was no longer with us, we had to manage with one meal a day because no one in our family worked out of the fear of the Taliban. If my brothers were caught working or seen outside the house, they would kill them right away or send them to the prison where they would eventually die. Therefore, it only left Mom to take care of the family. Along with many other widows, she would be sitting outside the Taliban offices under the burning sun begging for pennies.

Eventually when matters got worse, my mom decided it was time to move on and get on with the plan. At night we had to be really careful, because we could not afford to let our neighbours know of our plan. They would be the first ones to send the Taliban after us. Therefore, we left the house almost untouched, taking only the valuable things with us. We got on our horses and travelled through the dark until we found a taxi. We drove for the whole night. Finally when we got to the border, the security guards were unwilling to let us cross the border. They were convinced that we were escaping from the Taliban. So they decided to hand us over to the Taliban, who might kill us all.

I was really scared because I knew what they were going to do us. Before Dad's disappearance, the Taliban had invited us to take part in the trial of a woman in the same soccer ground where we used to play before their arrival. She was believed to have walked out of the house without her husband and without her burka, a piece of cloth that would cover a woman from head to toe. When they brought her for trial, the Taliban decided to shoot her in the head in front of thousands of people. I could not see it because Dad had his hands on my eyes to stop me from witnessing this brutal injustice.

Finally, after convincing them with money and other valuables, the guards opened the gate and allowed us to cross the border. That was the day when I got my freedom and my life back from the Taliban.

Nevertheless, life in Pakistan was not easy because we were new there, and we had to start over. My brothers and I found a job in a carpet factory, where we made carpets from five in the morning until nine or ten at night. We could not attend school. Finally, when we settled in, my brothers thought that I should start going to school. I was really happy that everything was getting back to normal.

After seven years in Pakistan, we applied to emigrate to Canada. Eventually, we got accepted and we were on our way to the most beautiful country in the world. After so many years of struggle, we finally found a place to call home, where everyone is equal, and most important of all, you feel safe. However, every now and then when the word Taliban is mentioned, those horrendous memories flash in front of my eyes like it all happened yesterday.

~Asmatullah
Coquitlam, BC

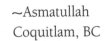

Walking the Tartan Road

We have it all. We have great diversity of people,
we have a wonderful land, and we have great possibilities.
So all those things combined there's nowhere else I'd rather be.
~Bob Rae

I feel like the clichéd tourist as the plane descends towards Edinburgh. No camera hanging around my neck (it's tucked into my carry-on), but a lot of mental baggage. Maybe it's a symptom of encroaching middle age, or a recent and unexpected fork in my career path, but I've been thinking about roots lately.

As an army brat, I never had a hometown to call my own. People ask where I'm from and I'm not sure what to answer. Brandon? Calgary? Toronto? Germany? I've lived in them all. With no answers in my past, I'm looking further back. Edinburgh, Scotland, where my maternal grandmother's family lived in the 1800s.

I climb down from the plane and take the bus to the terminal. Like every other airport in the world, it's currently under construction, ceiling beams exposed, tarps hanging everywhere. If all goes well, my husband will be joining me here from Paris in an hour, and we can start exploring.

Of course, all doesn't go well. His flight is delayed an hour, then another half-hour to twelve o'clock. I groan in disbelief as the ETA is updated to three o'clock. Five minutes later, the screen changes again. The plane has arrived and we head into town.

Edinburgh's history, and the city itself, is centred on its castle. So that's where we start, even though I have no royal connections. It's well worth it, too, especially as the afternoon darkens into evening. The combination of massive stone buildings and dim lighting is quite spectacular. I can almost hear the clatter of hooves on the cobblestones, picture a torch-lit procession of laughing gallants on their way to the Great Hall.

Leaving the castle, we enter a tartan shop. The lady behind the counter asks if we have any Scottish roots. I admit to it, wondering if they ever get tired of the endless tourists. After all, there are more people of Scots descent outside Scotland than in it.

"Tell me the name, and I'll look up your tartan," she offers.

"You won't find it," I tell her. "It's not a common name and it's not in any of the books."

"We can try."

"Carphin," I say, and sure enough nothing comes up. Still rootless.

"Perhaps you have some Irish connection," she says. "There are Irish tartans, too."

I want a piece of history, not a piece of fabric. I'll have to look elsewhere.

The next morning, we're out before sunrise. Of course, the sun doesn't rise until nine or so in December, but I'm feeling virtuous about our early morning as we look for the address where my great-great-grandmother lived in 1881. So much for virtue. Like many buildings in Edinburgh, there are stores at street level and flats above—above a bookie's shop in this case.

We continue our mission to find another of my family's old addresses. Address number two is more respectable—a building full of university offices. It may have been a student residence, my husband and I agree. We've seen enough of them to know. I pose for a picture on the steps, wondering how much things have changed in five generations.

Address number three is in New Town, filled with Georgian architecture, wide, straight streets, and former banks and insurance offices that have been turned into pubs. Some of my family were insurance agents and chartered accountants (no romantic smugglers or courtiers in my background) so they probably worked here as well as living here.

There's number 26, across from us. A white panelled door in a stone façade, topped with a fan skylight and—a Scottish Tourist Board sign? We can't believe our luck when we discover the place is a bed and breakfast.

We explain that my family used to live here. They invite us to have a look at the sitting room on the second floor. We climb a graceful circular staircase rising through the middle of the house. The sitting room is magnificent, with high ceilings and plaster mouldings, long narrow windows, and a fireplace with a mirror. I picture myself as a Jane Austen heroine, peeping through lace curtains for the arrival of my beloved's carriage.

On to St. Cuthbert's, the parish church where family births and marriages had been recorded. We soon discover that the present church (with the exception of the bell tower) was built after my family had left the country, although there's been a church on this site for 1,300 years. By now it's late afternoon and already dark. Standing in the graveyard, we're just steps away from the holiday shoppers on Princes Street, but it feels quiet and isolated, and, with the rows and rows of graves under winter-stripped trees, more than a little spooky. Behind and above loom the stark lines of Edinburgh Castle.

Two days later I enter the ancestral home once more, this time as a guest. We follow our host up the wrought iron staircase to the top floor, where we're established in the yellow room. I'd like to think the room belonged to one of the family, but given its location, it's more likely to have been used by the servants.

We look around, wondering how much has changed. The bathroom's certainly not original (though it might as well be, I decide the next morning, when I get nothing but cold water for my shower), but the blocked off fireplace behind the bed might be. The long, narrow windows looking on to the street two floors below might be, too. Time to write out the last of my postcards and try to get a good night's sleep before leaving for the airport in the morning.

As we head to the airport, I realize how comfortable I feel here. Race memory? I play with that idea, but don't really believe it. It's not the look of the place—too European. And to my surprise, my red hair stands out more here than on the streets of Montreal. The language? Perhaps, but I always feel like a stranger when I visit the States.

I think it's the people. The ones we've spoken to seem a lot like us. They worry about education and health care and the government. They live from contract to contract, never knowing if their funding will be renewed. They're polite and friendly, but not pushy and in-your-face. I can easily picture them living down the street from me in Canada, selling me my groceries, sitting beside me in church.

After a long day's travel, we walk out of Dorval airport to find a foot of snow on the ground. I find it cheering, exhilarating, more normal than Edinburgh's short, mild days and rainy nights. As we wait for the bus, we're soon joined by a trio of Spanish/English speakers.

The bus is full of the usual West Island mix of French and English, chatting away energetically as the snow melts off their boots. The heater runs full tilt to counteract the cold draft gusting in each time the doors open. Outside, most of the houses are bright with Christmas lights. I feel myself relax, realize how much I've missed the casual interplay between cultures.

I may not have much history here, but it sure feels like home, and I am glad to be back.

~Kate Tompkins
Pointe Claire, QB

The Home Child

You look at the history — the aboriginal people welcomed the first settlers
here with open arms, fed us and took care of us ... that continues today, we
welcome people from all nations to come in and share.
~Peter Stoffer

Dromore County, Northern Ireland. It was February 11, 1903 — bitterly cold. But even more so for Alec Kerr and his brother Samuel as they listened to the minister read their mother's last rites before her simple pine coffin was lowered into Irish soil. Alec would be eleven in two days, a grim birthday gift for him. Samuel was sixteen. Their father was gone — to war, in search of work, perhaps dead himself. No one knew.

Times were hard for many in Ireland. The streets of Belfast were already crowded with children: orphans begging for a coin, working in the steam and sweat of factories. Something had to be done with the boys. The decision that was made would send Alec across countries, oceans, and cultures.

There is a picture taken of Alec in July of 1903. Alec has his blond hair sheared close to the head. His face is long, still chubby at the cheeks from boyhood. He wears a simple black jerkin that looks like he might bust a button at any moment. Alec isn't smiling. There's a look in his eyes that contradicts his boyish features. It's old, knowing.

The picture was taken by Dr. Barnardo's after he was admitted to

Leopold House, a boy's orphanage in the East End of London. Alec and Samuel were separated.

Alec spent a year in orphanages in London. It was not an easy year. Dr. Barnardo's was a charitable organization that took in the unwanted children of the poor. Alec ate what little was given him, slept in cold rooms, and worked for his keep.

On July 21, 1904, Alec, along with hundreds of other Barnardo children stepped onto the deck of the S.S. Southwark. Samuel had gone on the same voyage ten months earlier. Alec felt alone, frightened, yet expectant too. Something waited for him at the other end. A new home, and a chance to find his brother.

Each child carried a trunk made by the children at Dr. Barnardo's. It carried what little clothing they owned and a few cherished mementos, a photograph, a letter from a loved one. All Alec carried was the image of Samuel's face the last time they spoke. He would embrace this new land, work hard, and by God, he'd find Samuel!

Ten days later, the S.S. Southwark finished its slow wind along the mighty St. Lawrence River to land in Quebec. Alec felt displaced and very much alone. Still tired from his long journey, he was herded along with the others into cramped railway cars for the next leg of their journey.

The train puffed great clouds of black smoke as it chugged along through fields, forests, and towns. It was green here too. Not the deep blanketing green of Ireland, but wilder, with more forests and lakes. And it was huge!

Alec let the wonder of it fill him. It was almost enough to quench the fear. Almost. The train finally stopped in the city of Toronto, where Dr. Barnardo's kept its Canadian head office. There Alex was processed one more time. He was weary of this—weary of the time ticking past when he wasn't looking for Samuel.

Alec was now twelve, becoming an adolescent. He stood solemnly as he was introduced to Mr. Long, a farmer from Huntsville. He swallowed back the fear and extended his hand. Alec had heard the tales. This man could be friend or father, taskmaster or jailer.

Home Child. That's what they called him. The orphan from

Ireland who'd come to Canada to work in exchange for his shelter and passage.

Years later a secretary at Dr. Barnardo's head office would write down this report:

"His conduct was said to be satisfactory and he did well. He had several moves and throughout was said to be a trusty, truthful, and well behaved model boy."

What they didn't write about was Alec's vitality, his zest for living every minute to its fullest. He worked harder than any twelve-year-old should have to. But he put his heart into it, and earned the respect and love of all who knew him.

There is another picture, this time taken at a vantage point in front of Niagara Falls. Alec's hair has turned grey. He's wearing the clothes of a working man; white shirt, no tie, dark pants held up with suspenders—his Sunday clothes. This time he is smiling. His right hand is blurred as he waves to his wife, Gertie, who's holding the camera. To his extreme right is Samuel, also smiling, and his wife, Berdie. Samuel's daughter and her husband are in the centre.

Alec was a man many years before he and Samuel finally met again. It was a joyful reunion with happy and sad tales to tell.

Alec Kerr was my grandfather. He adopted my mother. I've been told that many of the home children who came to Canada adopted children—their way of giving back. It is estimated that ten percent of Canada's population, some three million people, are descendants of these home children.

What continues to impress me today is not just the journey made by such a young boy, but the way that he faced life head on, regardless of the obstacles fate set in his way. It would have been easy to be bitter. But Alex greeted each problem with a smile, each obstacle with determination. It was a testament to him and to the welcoming country he now called home.

~Debbie Ouellet
Loretto, ON

Hundreds of Flags

[The] Canadian flag which, while bringing together but rising above the landmarks and milestones of the past, will say proudly to the world and to the future: "I stand for Canada."

~Lester B. Pearson

It was a warm day. So warm, in fact, that the beach was exploding with people. I was there with a group of friends. We're not particularly beach people, but it was in the high thirties, and it was Canada Day. For some reason, we chose to go to the beach. It's an athletic group, so we always spend some of our time competing. This time it was a competition to see who could hold their breath and swim the furthest completely underwater.

Coming back out of the water, we grabbed a Frisbee and a football, claiming a spot on a reasonably large field at the park. Five of us tossed them around, chasing them when the throws occasionally went out of control. I started out on the beach side of the field, but eventually rotated around towards the side that lined some taller trees and brush. This is where the story begins.

Well, actually, it begins long ago. I was born in Canada. Grew up playing hockey on the street in summer and on a sheet of ice in the backyard in winter. We had a Canadian flag in the backyard, and watched the Olympics, anticipating the gold medal match. When Canada won in 2002, we screamed so loudly we nearly lost our voices. When, in 2010, we set a new record for the number of golds in an Olympic games, we were ecstatic. I was always proud to be Canadian.

But I didn't know why.

Jump back to today. My friend throws the football towards me. I follow its arc and, realizing it's not coming directly toward me, I start running. I take off towards my left, barefoot and trusting that the ground won't suddenly twist my ankle. There's a garbage can on the field and I know it's coming, so I avoid it. I jump to reach for the football and miss. It rolls off my fingers—I couldn't quite make it in time.

I land on my feet and slow down, turning to follow the bouncing ball. I chase it down to where it has rolled—within feet of a group of people. I look up from the ball and take in my surroundings. I had noticed that they were having a picnic, but I hadn't seen. It was a family gathering of East Indians. There were about fifty of them, only half the size of my own large family. Someone in the group sees the football and tosses it back to me, a smile on his face.

On his right cheek is a maple leaf.

On his left cheek is a maple leaf.

On his forehead is a maple leaf.

On his shirt is a Canadian flag.

On the tree behind the group is a Canadian flag, draped and fluttering in the wind.

In that one glimpse I saw between two and three hundred Canadian flags. On the trees, on shirts, on faces, on hats, on towels, on chairs, on tables, on just about everything and anything with a surface.

In that moment everything came crashing down. I threw on a Canadian hockey jersey during the Olympics or the World Juniors. I cheered when Sidney Crosby scored in overtime. I laugh at the Canadian jokes and the beer commercials. But I never understood what it meant to be Canadian.

I complain about the roads. I complain about the weather (though I love winter). I complain about the government. I complain about so many things.

All it took for me to see reason was an East Indian family celebrating a new country. Celebrating the things that Canada offers that I take for granted. The wonderful things that make this country a great place to live.

I grew up here, so I don't see them. But they're there. I don't even need to list them. I can leave that up to you. But I hope it doesn't take a mis-thrown football and hundreds of Canadian flags for you to see what I saw.

~Paul Loewen
Winnipeg, MB

36

Flight AC7485

Give your head a shake. This is the greatest country in the world.
~Curtis Sanderson

"Oh no!" I grumbled to myself. I was waiting at Pearson International Airport in Toronto for a flight to Saint John, New Brunswick and after three jam-packed days of lectures, story-telling and late nights all I wanted to do was get on the plane, plunk myself in the seat by the window, close my eyes and grab a nap. But when I read the departure board, I knew things weren't going to unfold in such a timely manner. My plane, already scheduled to arrive home after midnight, was delayed for another hour.

Somewhere between my disappointment over the delay and my longing to get home, I was reminded of the closing remarks Dr. Joel Freeman had made to the more than 200 authors and editors gathered at the Write! Canada conference. "Look at travel delays and unexpected events as an opportunity to study people and perhaps discover something to write," he had said, but I was in no mood to follow his advice.

Sometime after midnight I boarded the plane and made my way down its narrow aisle. Perhaps I'm mistaken, I thought, as I searched the numbers overhead and matched them to the ones on my boarding pass. No, I'm right. Someone is in my seat.

"Excuse me, I think you're in the wrong seat," I said after I'd stuffed my backpack in the overhead bin. The occupant, a heavyset, middle-aged man, glared at me. I pointed to the number on my boarding pass, and the oversized man heaved a sigh. I always get the best nap on the plane when I'm by the window and by now I really felt the need of some sleep as I had to drive for another hour after the plane landed.

With slow, deliberate movements, the gentleman moved to let me in. "Thank you," I said, but he didn't acknowledge me. Instead, he fastened his belt, lowered the armrest between our seats and folded his arms across his chest. His attitude and body language seemed to confirm that he was a non-talker. Good, I thought. Perhaps I really will be able to catch the nap my body craves.

As the plane took off and reached for the sky, my seatmate kept staring out the window. I turned away, pretending I hadn't noticed him but before I could close my eyes, I heard him say, "It's so beautiful!" The lights of the city dotted the night sky like the lights on the game of Lite-Brite my children played with when they were small.

"Yes, it is," I agreed, all the while keeping my head turned to the window.

"I don't speak very well when I'm tired."

"A long travel day?" I asked, turning to look at him.

"Twenty-five hours," he said. "I'm so excited to go to Saint John."

I was torn between wanting to know why he was excited and wanting to sleep. Conversation would be a challenge because I could barely understand him. I closed my eyes and was relieved when he settled back in his chair. Silence hung between us. The plane rose higher and I heard him say, "Like someone lined the lights up with a ruler."

I squelched the long sigh that threatened to escape my lips. There was no mistaking it, I was seated beside a talker, not just any talker but one who had such a heavy accent that I had to concentrate in order to understand him.

"Do you know New Brunswick?" he asked. "Would I be able to find work there? What is it like?" While the plane soared through the night sky, I answered his questions about the cost of housing, the weather, the Fundy tides, the schools and our health care system.

When a new set of lights appeared, much smaller than those we'd seen at the beginning of our flight, I was amazed at how agitated my seatmate became. "Is that Saint John?"

"Yes, the lights of the runway are over there to the right."

"I'm so excited." And as the plane began its decent, he continued, "Could I find a quiet place for my family?" Throughout our last moments of conversation he shared he was leaving a war-torn country, one where bombings were becoming a way of life.

The pilot brought the plane down with a gentle landing. "Oh Canada," I heard my seatmate say. "I can't wait until tomorrow morning to see what my new country is really like."

As I saw again my great country through the eyes of my seatmate, a newcomer to Canada, I was reminded just what a wonderful nation I call home.

~Elaine Ingalls Hogg
Smiths Creek, NB

37

Manitoulin Connections

If it matters at all, it's because we know who we are. I'd never leave Canada.
This is my home and I got to be everything I am right here.
~Sarah McLachlan

One fall morning, surrounded by empty cottages and bronze maples, I perched on a picnic table at Lake Mindemoya's vacant beach. Quiet waves nudged my thoughts back to childhood memories—swimming for hours with my sisters, sunning ourselves crispy, then years later taking our babies for their first beach experiences. Dad's freshly caught lake trout dinners, Chinese checkers and visits to relatives' homes on rainy days. Memories of these warmed my heart while my body shivered in cool October breezes. It was time to let go of the cottage and that wouldn't be easy.

Nine years a widow, cottage-owner responsibilities had become a burden for Mom. My husband and I had come to the cottage on one last vacation. On arrival, we hammered a For Sale sign into the ground. It'll go fast, passersby said. Three bedrooms, attached garage, indoor plumbing, a short sprint to the beach, someone will snatch up your four decades of memories in a hurry.

If not for a small island blocking my view from the picnic table, I would see a hilltop log cabin across the lake. Built by my great-great-grandparents, John and Sarah Galbraith, when they were newly married Scottish immigrants, the stone foundations of the cabin are a monument to their determination to carve out a homestead in a new country. They and other pioneer couples seeded central Manitoulin Island with their offspring.

My parents, both children of pioneers with farming in their veins, moved to a nearby booming paper town because it promised a better and more regular paycheque than life on the farm. I was four, my sister three when we left what citizens call The Island.

Once a month, on Dad's long weekends, we made the seventy-mile trip back to Manitoulin to visit grandparents, aunts and cousins. When our family's number reached seven, fitting us into a relative's already full household wasn't easy. So, my parents built the cottage, our Manitoulin home.

When the cottage sells, my identity here disappears. People here know where I come from — "That's Bill and Millie's oldest girl," the folks used to say when I visited the general store near my grandmother's house.

Another would nod, "Yea, she's a McCormick alright."

Whenever our toes touched the Island, the local paper added the event to its social column. Even now, mysterious forces report our visits. The following appeared recently — "Doug and Rose Brandon and family visited Evelyn Pattison [my aunt] and had lunch with Ted and Georgeanne Legge [my cousins]."

Friends who also visit but don't have roots on the Island wonder why our names, and not theirs, appear in print. "You're not connected," I say. My husband's not connected either but he caught onto the importance of connections on his early visits. Other fishermen, recognizing him as a non-local, would ask how he knew where to fish. That was another way of asking, "Who are you and where do you come from?" Curiosity is an Island pastime.

His answer was always, "I'm married to Bill McCormick's daughter."

"Is that a fact? That means you're related to the Galbraiths too." He was in, connected, almost as good as homegrown. Son-in-law status became his calling card. Few people know his actual name.

These connections made me reluctant to sell the cottage to strangers. As I gazed at the water, I wondered if I should heed sentimental memories and buy the cottage. Were my memories getting in the way of a common sense decision—letting go?

In the end, I decided that my memories are more than sentiment, that it really matters to me, my children, and their children, that we maintain our connection to Manitoulin Island. We are people who care about treading in the footsteps of our forefathers. I've shown my children John and Sarah's original home. We can envision their tired, scorched bodies dunking in the waters of our lake after a hard day of gathering stones.

That day at the picnic table I decided to buy the cottage. My two grandchildren have become the sixth generation to connect with our Island. I know my Scottish and Irish pioneer ancestors would be pleased that I've decided to keep my Manitoulin identity.

~Rose McCormick Brandon
Caledonia, ON

Chapter 5

O Canada

Wilderness and Wildlife

It is wonderful to feel the grandness of Canada in the raw, not because she is Canada but because she's something sublime that you were born into, some great rugged power that you are a part of.

~Emily Carr

"Silver Birch"

From the CD *The Return* by Liona Boyd

Lyrics courtesy of Liona Boyd ©2011

Mid-Continental Music SOCAN

Silver birch
Scent of pine
Lakes and forests
Land of mine

Silver birch
Cedar nights
Rocky islands
Northern lights

Silver birch
Eagle's cries
Raging rivers
Painted skies

Silver birch
Harvest moons
Golden maples
Call of loons

Nehiyawaskiya
Nehiyawaskiya
Nehiyawaskiya

Silver birch
Morning haze
Flaming sumach
Summer days

Silver birch
Winter night
Crystal snowflakes
White on white

Silver birch
Scent of pine
Lakes and forests
Land of mine

A Cave with a View

*Nature reserves the right to inflict upon her children
the most terrifying jests.*
~Thornton Wilder

The United States is known as the melting pot of humanity. Canada, on the other hand, is called the mosaic of cultures. Is there a difference? Yes. In the U.S., people who immigrate try to blend in and absorb that wonderful American heritage of baseball, apple pie, picnics and July 4th.

We Canadians love being Canadian and we're proud of our country, as well. But we've never given up the culture from our previous homes. So, for example, when you go into the Grey-Bruce peninsula of Ontario and visit towns like Kincardine and Lion's Head and Tobermory, you find men looking as if they have just walked out of eighteenth century moors. And often wearing kilts.

When my boys were five and three, and I was pregnant with my daughter, we went camping in the peninsula.

Joshua, my eldest, had learned about caves from a TV show and desperately wanted to see one. Much to his delight just "a wee bit east of Lion's Head" were the Greig's caves.

It turned out that "wee bit" meant forty-five minutes. No matter, we made it.

"Hallo, lass!" said a kindly elderly gentleman in a red plaid kilt. "What brings ye to my woods?"

I told him we wanted to see the caves.

With a twinkle in his eye he said, "It'll cost ye two dollars a head."

I paid the man.

"Just follow the path down there a bit. It'll take ye around the mountain and into the woods on the other side. 'Tis a small hike, shouldn't take ye but an hour."

Forty-five minutes into the walk and we came to the first bend on the path. It was then that I noticed we were very high up and overlooking a lush green valley with ribbons of yellow wheat and wild purple lavender trailing through it. The morning mist was just clearing and the remaining glistening threads gave this pastoral scene an ethereal quality.

"He's so pretty," whispered Josh. He was staring into the face of a huge harrier hawk, not even ten feet away from him.

"Yes," I murmured as I slowly moved between Josh and this magnificent bird of prey that was eying his blond hair.

Now, I suppose at this point another more observant person would have noticed that there were no safety fences or guardrails along the way, but hey, this is Canada, the rough and wild country. It didn't even occur to me to question this.

After a while, the wide path suddenly turned into a ledge that was eighteen inches wide if we were lucky. I debated going back but reasoned that we only had a few more minutes to go. After all, the man had said it was only an hour's hike.

We put our backs to the wall and inched our way along. This wasn't a problem until I foolishly looked down at the tree tops a hundred feet below. I gasped with terror.

Did I mention I'm afraid of heights?

"It's okay, Mom," said Josh. "I know being high up scares you, but I'm not afraid. It's a good thing I'm leading."

Right. Being led by a five-year-old made me feel a lot better.

Another ten feet and we almost fell into an enormous cave that had partially collapsed.

"Whoaaaaa! This is awesome!" shouted Josh with glee. "Look at all those rattlesnakes. They look like Mississaugas. They're so cool."

Cool? Are you kidding me?

"Where did you learn about snakes?"

"The Discovery Channel," Josh replied. "Cartoons are boring."

He immediately started throwing stones into the cave.

"What are you doing?" I asked.

"Scaring them away. See? They're slithering to the back of the cave so we can go along the front."

Well, God bless the Discovery Channel.

We forged across four more gigantic caves, every time throwing stones to clear the way of snakes. At one point I forced myself to look at the view and I stopped moving. Now that the mist had evaporated I could see the vastness of the tranquil blue water of Lake Huron.

"It's so still," murmured Josh. "I never saw somethin' so pretty."

"Me neither, sweetie."

Finally, the path widened again. I could see a forest in the distance. A small glen nestled in front of it.

We were going to be okay.

Just had to get by the adolescent black bear that stood a hundred feet away.

"What'll we do?" whispered Josh. "I didn't see any shows on bears yet."

"We're going to sit behind this rock until he moves on," I replied, sounding braver than I felt.

"Awwwww, bear!" shouted Ben, my three-year-old.

"Shhhhh!"

At that moment I heard voices coming from the woods. Frantic men.

A large Scotsman in his kilt suddenly strode out of the forest and onto the path. Not a man to reckon with that was for sure. The bear seemed to agree. He scurried away when the Scot bellowed at him. At that point I think I was more afraid of the man than the bear.

He spotted us sitting on our rock.

"Oh glory be, praise God!" he cried. "I found them!" he shouted to the other men who were now entering the glen.

I smiled at him as he rushed over to us. "Good morning," I said as cheerfully as I could. "Lovely day, isn't it?"

I rose to my feet to shake his hand.

"Oh mother of God she's with child!" he cried. Then he noticed Josh and Ben. "Ach! And she has wee bairn with her! I'll kill him for this."

The man was nearing seventy and he was out of breath. I began to worry that he was having a coronary. "Are you all right?" I asked.

"Am I all right?" he shouted. "Jeezus, Mary and Joseph!"

He finally calmed down enough to speak to me. "I was scared out of me wits. No one has taken that trail for years. Since the side of the mountain sheared off. Are you sure you're all right, miss?"

"We're fine," I replied with a grin. "We had a great time."

Just then the elderly gentleman arrived. "It was a grand view, wasn't it?"

I noticed some of the other men mopping their brows with handkerchiefs. They had been terrified for us. "Indeed it was, sir," I said. "Worth every penny."

"I knew you'd fancy it," he chortled.

"What?" cried his son. "You charged her money for this torture?"

"Of course I charged her. Two dollars a head."

"I swear I'll be putting you in a home if you do anything like this again!"

Sean, the son, insisted that we all had to have tea and baps to make up for his ninety-four-year-old dad's "error" and listen to a few tunes from the bagpipes. (He was the leader of the town's pipe and drum band and they had been at practice.) Then we bid farewell.

T'was a grand day, indeed, in the Bruce Peninsula of Ontario!

~Pamela Goldstein
Amherstburg, ON

Of Masks and Mountain Lions

My face is my mask.
~Lorne John (Gump) Worsley

One of my neighbours called this morning, knowing my habit of taking an early morning stroll with the dog before tackling the daily grind. He caught me just as I was leaving the door. A cougar had been sighted just down Youngs Lake Road, our usual route. This created a problem. When you live close to nature you expect to see it, even share it. You just don't want to become part of the menu.

Rather than hit the road we wandered round the safer but somewhat duller yard. I check the Internet for cougar factoids. A cougar's favourite mode of approach is from behind, stalking you, then leaping on you and taking you by the neck. Then you are dragged off to some secluded area where the cougar will dine on you. "Cowards," I grumbled, "stalking me from behind." The problem remained though: how would the dog and I enjoy our daily jaunt without turning around every second step to check for golden tagalongs?

Later that night I discussed it with my husband, Richard. "What am I going to do about the cougar situation?" I asked. I wanted to make sure the dog and I got our usual outing, but how to outfox a cougar? Richard pondered for a while, then remembered a documentary he had seen. In India, he recalled, the natives wear a mask on the back of their head. They do this because of tiger attacks. The tiger also sneaks up from behind, but before he pounces he is faced with another face staring him down, which makes the tiger stop and say "Hey, is that human coming or going?" Perhaps I could use the same technique for my situation.

I checked upstairs in the Halloween trunk for a suitable mask, but Cinderella didn't quite cut it. I then recalled my older daughter Amanda had a brief interest in Chinese opera and had collected some masks. Sure enough, in her boxes of goodies left home for Mom to store, was a devilish mask with orange and white markings and bold black eyes. A quick trip to the sewing box for an elastic band and I was set.

Not knowing how the neighbourhood would react to the latest from that "eccentric writer lady" I waited till I was safely off the main road before I attired myself. When you saw me coming, I was mild-mannered and grey-haired, but from behind I was a Chinese demon ready to attack. Take that, you cowardly cougars.

I had it all under control, or so I thought. Kali and I had our jaunt along the road, and it was going so well I soon forgot about the mask. As I turned onto the main road I was met with a sudden squeal of tires. "What the heck are you playing at, lady?" a gruff voice yelled. A truck driver, who saw the back of my head with the Chinese opera mask, screeched to a halt and nearly went off the road. I started to explain about tigers in India, and the traffic began to pile up behind him. The guy shook his head and drove on. In a tangle by my legs, my dog hid her head in embarrassment. I stuffed the mask in my bag and beat a hasty retreat.

For the next two weeks, I still wore my mask when out on lone walks, until word got around. I become a topic for debate, and some people wondered if I had been smoking some BC green, or whether it was just the way prairie people react to the island. In discussion at the local coffee shop I plied the locals for advice. One insisted that cougars move on after a territory is out of food. Another said they are territorial and stick around. I started to dream of cougars in demon masks and wondered if I was going off the deep end.

•••

Time has passed but every now and then in the not so silent woods, I hear a snickering and I wonder if a cougar is having a good belly laugh at my expense. Or perhaps it is my neighbours, who sometimes wonder about that eccentric writer who lives down the road.

~Nancy V. Bennett
Sooke, BC

The Life of a Mountie Wife

We have the Mounties, they have the FBI.
Can you imagine the FBI doing the Musical Ride?
~Dave Broadfoot

"Hang on," my husband said, his large, strong hand tightly gripping my small, shaking hand. "We're not going to sink. Now stop whining."

My Mountie husband and I were newlyweds and new arrivals to the Queen Charlotte Islands (recently renamed Haida Gwaii) off British Columbia's northwest coast. As newlyweds, we just wanted to be together all the time. (Okay, maybe it was just me.)

The headlight of the small police boat we were in barely lit the dark ocean that surrounded us that night. "We'll soon be there," my husband added reassuringly.

I don't like darkness. And that day, in the middle of the night, I was consumed by darkness—the darkness of the Pacific Ocean and the darkness of the sky.

Maybe I should have stayed home. But, no, I wanted to go everywhere with Rick and any time I got a chance to go with him I went—whether it was in the police cruiser, the police boat, or one of the small airplanes he often rode in.

Earlier, my husband had received a call to attend to an incident at a neighbouring island, and that meant getting over there with the small police boat of the day.

"Can I go with you?" I had asked, eager as always, when the call had come in the middle of the night at our house. (In those days police calls that came in after office hours were routinely dispatched to the on-duty policeman's radio, or to his home phone, as had been the case at our house.)

"Sure, but be quick," Rick had said, and together we had rushed to the police car parked in our driveway, and careened down to the police boat at the nearby dock.

Now, the near-dark ocean and the near-dark sky loomed all around me. Great fear overcame great love.

As if in answer to my prayers, the moon, possibly the brightest I had ever seen, broke through the clouds and lit up our scene. The ocean seemed a little less eerie. Now that we had a bright moon to guide us, maybe we wouldn't blindly run into an island.

As my husband continued to steer the boat to our destination—a large swath of land off in the distance—the ocean, unusually calm that night, began to move unexpectedly. Large sea creatures surfaced, gliding effortlessly around the boat.

"Whales," my husband said softly. "Don't be afraid."

Huge whales gently surfaced all around us, their massive bodies softly breaking the water. They were so close I could almost touch them. Great awe overcame great fear. The moment etched itself forever in my mind, a mind that was quickly learning respect for these majestic creatures.

My husband guided the boat to shore, anchored it, then carted my stupefied body out of the boat.

We got into a police cruiser parked there for such calls, and streaked off down the road, the siren breaking the silence of the night.

We spent two years on the Queen Charlotte Islands before moving on to other detachments on British Columbia's mainland.

In time, two of our four children followed in their father's law enforcement footsteps, likely because they, too, felt the gratification and pride that my husband experienced with his career.

Canada is still a land where police officers rank high in devotion to duty, serving in communities that are grateful for their services. They make a difference, risking their lives, and often giving their lives, while regularly dealing with conditions not for the faint-hearted.

My husband, now retired, was one of them. He never flinched in the performance of his duties, regularly going above and beyond the call of duty, typical of many police officers.

It was a unique way of life, not without its worries, though I think I usually did the worrying for both of us.

I don't remember what the call was about the night I accompanied my husband out on the ocean in a police boat many years ago; I just remember the whales.

~Chantal Meijer
Terrace, BC

Roaring, Rumbling, Rainbow

My heart leaps up when I behold
A rainbow in the sky...
~William Wordsworth

"Come visit me in Canada. We'll go to the falls," coaxed my good friend, April. "The Canadian side. I promise you'll see a rainbow."

I adore rainbows. April calls me a rainbow magnet. Since I live in Florida, brief summer showers followed by hot blinding sunshine regularly allow rainbows to grace the suddenly blue sky. I stop to wonder at the beauty of them every time. The opportunity to study a shimmering rainbow cascading over Niagara Falls tugged at my heart. I immediately said yes.

"Besides," I tell April, "I'm part Canadian."

She laughs when I say that.

But I am part Canadian by birth. My grandmother was born in Canada. The family moved to Detroit and continued to regularly make the trek across the bridge to Windsor, Ontario. We spent summers on the Canadian side of Lake Erie frolicking in the ice cold water and dousing our pancakes in pure maple syrup. I hadn't visited Canada in years. Never having seen the falls, this was the perfect time to reconnect with my roots.

"I'm going to see Niagara Falls," I told my seatmate during the flight to Toronto. "And I'm going to see a rainbow."

"There's always a rainbow at the falls," she agreed.

Once in Toronto, April and I spent time doing all things Canadian. I freshened up my high school French by reading the food labels at the grocery store. To escape the cold, we sipped hot, delicious Tim Hortons coffee. I feasted on sinfully rich Nanaimo bars, buying one in every bakery we passed. I embraced everything around me in the not-quite-yet spring of Canada.

April and I planned to make the one-hour drive to Niagara Falls on Sunday. We awoke to a cloudy, grey and drizzly day but even that couldn't dampen my excitement. I was finally headed to the falls to see a Canadian rainbow.

"Don't worry. There's always a rainbow at the falls," April assured me as she drove. "It's how we welcome thousands of visitors to Canada. A sparkling burst of color over the majestic Niagara Falls."

I stared out the window in between the swiping of the windshield wipers.

"Not today. Not a single ray of sunshine is going to make it through those clouds," I whined.

"You've got to have faith," she said, patting my hand.

The car slowly turned the corner. A sweeping vista of water, rushing, pounding, pulsing over piles of rock greeted me. Water flowing from Lake Erie up the Niagara River crashed over the falls before eventually finding its way into Lake Ontario. The sight of this magnificent natural wonder filled me with awe.

April had barely parked the car in its spot when I leaped out, slamming the door behind me. Running across several lanes of traffic, I pulled up my hood, slipped on my gloves and wrapped my scarf a little tighter. I breathed in the mist from the falls, letting it fill my lungs. The sound roared through my ears. The power lit up my soul.

From the Canadian vantage point, the falls are spectacular. All three unique falls in plain view, the flat and straight American Falls, the small and delicate Bridal Veil Falls and the grand and roaring

Canadian Horseshoe Falls. Mesmerized, I couldn't take my eyes off the rushing water.

"C'mon. Let's go behind the falls," April suggested when she finally caught up with me.

"You can go behind the falls? How cool is that?" I asked.

The sign read "The Journey Behind the Falls." We paid our admission fee and got in line for the 150-foot elevator ride down. We smiled for the obligatory tourist photo and I couldn't open my wallet fast enough to purchase a picture of April and me standing in front of the falls, photoshopped or not.

My ears popped as we rode in the elevator. Swallowing hard, I couldn't wait for the doors to open. Once below, we wound our way through the dank, cold tunnel. Seeing light ahead of me, I walked toward it. A barricade stopped me from getting near the white light.

"It's frozen." I shivered. "They weren't kidding when they said behind the falls," as I stared at a block of ice the size of a ten-story building. A dull rumble reminded me that water still flowed on the other side, the ice having squashed my rainbow dreams only for the moment.

Once back above the falls April asked, "What do you want to do now?"

"Can we go on the Maid of the Mist?" I asked like an overly excited schoolgirl. "I've always wanted to ride on the Maid of the Mist."

"Look down there," April pointed.

Leaning over the railing I could see the stairs leading down to the dock. Then I looked toward the river to see the steamship icebound.

"Guess the boat can't run through the ice, huh?"

"No. It can't." April answered.

"For sure I'd see a rainbow down there, if only the Maid was running."

"You'll see a rainbow. Don't worry," she reassured me again.

"So far that's not looking too promising."

The falls were all that I had imagined. They left me speechless.

But I knew my trip wouldn't be complete without finding the elusive rainbow.

We spent the rest of the day leisurely walking up and down the sidewalk. Every few steps I'd stop and snap more photos. I'd taken over 200 pictures, not wanting to miss a single angle. Every drop of water would be immortalized in the yet to be created, treasured scrapbook of my trip.

As I gazed across the river toward the American side, I couldn't shake the thought that they had a monopoly on rainbows today. Half of me wanted to take the bridge across to see. Half of me wanted to stay right there.

The sun never came out from behind the clouds that day. I tried to pretend the joy of finding a rainbow no longer mattered.

April wrapped her arm around me. "The falls are amazing, eh?"

"More than amazing, they're phenomenal," I answered. "Thanks for bringing me to the Canadian side. It's beautiful."

"I'll go get the car. Stay here and take some more pictures." April left me alone with only my thoughts of the day as my falls experience came to an end.

The falls took on a shimmering golden hue as dusk began to fall. Standing at a spot where the water seemed to flow directly under my feet, I leaned over the railing as far as I dared and took a few more photos. The sound of the car horn jolted me back to the present. I quickly snapped one final shot before heading home.

"Let's check out my pictures," I said as April drove and I scrolled through the photographs now stored in my digital camera. As the roar of the falls faded into the distance, I carefully studied each one. After several minutes, I came to the last photo. I gasped.

There it was, curving through the smoky mist across the Canadian Horseshoe Falls. In the corner of the last picture I took as the water hurried by.

My rainbow by the falls.

~Linda C. Wright
American of Canadian descent living in Viera, FL, USA

Digging It

I thank you God for this most amazing day,
for the leaping greenly spirits of trees, and for the blue dream of sky
and for everything which is natural, which is infinite, which is yes.
~e.e. cummings

My son, Joshua, loved nature when he was young. While other kids his age still wondered how many cookies the Cookie Monster ate on Sesame Street, Joshua discussed the eras of dinosaurs and where we could go fossil hunting. He watched the Discovery Channel. A lot.

Windsor had several quarries and beaches and we spent days hunting for fossils from the Devonian era: brachiopods, corals, trilobites. As Josh called them—the cool ones. There weren't too many to be found.

After a little research we learned that one of the best places for hunting fossils from that era was only two hours away from us—the Rock Glen Conservation Area. Located on the outskirts of Arkona, Rock Glen is a unique island of nature within the Ausable Bayfield watershed jurisdiction.

The park is home to the Arkona Lions Museum, which houses an impressive collection of Devonian Era fossils and aboriginal artifacts. Josh and I spent hours there as he drooled over the fossils. Archaeologists and palaeontologists have found many fossils in the exposed beds of the Ausable River, dating back 350 million years.

My son was determined to be one of the ones to discover a "great" find.

"Wouldn't it be awesome if I found something really rare?" said Josh.

"So rare that you would have to give it to a museum?" I asked.

"That would be way cool!"

After pitching our tent and setting up camp, there was still time to do an initial trek down the ravine to the river. We armed ourselves with chisels, hammers and pails. Just in case.

Forty minutes into our descent, Josh suddenly stopped.

"Mom," he whispered. "Look! Deer!"

Not even twenty feet in front of us stood several female deer and their fawns in a broad patch of pure white trillium flowers, Jack-in-the-pulpits, and wild raspberries.

"They smell us," announced Josh. "I knew we shouldn't have taken a bath today." Always an excuse!

One of the mothers moved closer to Josh and sniffed him, then walked back to her babies. We were no threat.

"Gently back away and head down the path," I murmured.

After another twenty minutes we were in the ravine, next to the bank of the river.

"Whoaaaaa, it's a good thing it's summer and the water is so low," said Josh. "Look where the water mark is. How high is that?"

"At least ten feet," I replied.

"Look at the stone in this bank, Mom! It's full of fossils."

"Not just any fossils, lad," said an elderly gentleman. "This is a load from the sea that covered this area... some good samples of horn and colony coral."

It turned out that this man was a palaeontologist and professor from Toronto. He was with some of his students, who were doing research and taking specimens. As is typical of Canadians, he immediately took Josh under his wing and proceeded to teach him all about the fossils they found. He patiently showed Josh how to tap and chisel out a specimen and label it. He also included my son in his discussions with his students and treated him like a young scholar.

Josh was ecstatic.

He continued working beside the professor; I was long forgotten and did my own thing. Josh seemed focused on one section in particular.

"Professor, this doesn't look like the other corals," said Josh at one point.

The man gasped when he saw what Josh pointed at. "Oh, my word!" he shouted triumphantly. "This could be from one of the oldest fungae known to man. I do believe you found part of a stock from a prototaxite. Nothing like this has been uncovered in this bank since 1954."

Together they worked on chiselling around the specimen for another hour. Suddenly, the rock around it gave way and the "specimen" was free. It was over a foot long and at least three inches around.

"It's from the top of the plant," said the professor. "They used to grow several feet high." He examined it further. "We'll have to do a lot of study on this. It might also be from a plant from a later era. Still... Well, no matter. This was very well done, son! Well done, indeed. It's too late in the day today, but we'll have to do a proper setup and carefully go through this area tomorrow."

"Can I help?" said Josh.

"You better. This is your discovery."

After swimming under the river's waterfall and a supper of hamburgers on the grill, we climbed a nearby hill to stargaze, another favourite pastime of my son's. Several people were already gathered.

"We're supposed to be able to see the Northern Lights tonight, after midnight," said one woman.

Josh turned to me. "Do you think we'll really see them?" he asked. "That would make this day totally perfect."

The Northern Lights, or aurora borealis, are caused by charged particles from the sun meeting with the earth's magnetic field. Canada is optimally located within the auroral oval—a ring of electric activity that stretches across most of Canada's North. It's rare to see the lights in Southern Ontario.

We sat on the hill for hours as Josh located constellations. Finally, midnight arrived. No lights.

Josh suddenly grabbed my arm. "Mom! Look!"

A wide ribbon of emerald green had unfurled from the northwest and woven its way through the black sky and stars.

"Wow! It's kind of like a hand," murmured Josh. "Look at how it's moving."

Slowly fingers of magenta, red, yellow, blue, and violet spread across the black. The colours cascaded toward earth until the entire sky shimmered in these rainbow hues.

It was magnificent—ethereal.

"This is one of those gifts from Hashem (God) you talk about, isn't it?" Josh murmured.

"Yes, sweetie, it truly is."

We stayed on the hill until the lights faded. Josh sighed with contentment. "That was an awesome gift, don't you think, Mom?"

"Absolutely."

The next morning, Josh was wide awake and ready to help the professor with the dig. Unfortunately, no other part of the plant was found. By the end of the day, Josh's pail had several brachiopods, horn and colony coral pieces and various other fossils. And his big find.

"Well, Joshua, my boy, what do you intend to do with your discovery?" said the man. "It's yours."

"You can have it for your studies," said Josh. He grinned. "Just put my name on it."

The gentleman chortled. "With pleasure."

Josh smiled all the way home.

"What's got you so happy?" I asked.

"Nothin' much. The Rock Glen and the aurora borealis and how cool it is that we only live two hours from there. It was a great weekend."

He grinned even more. "I'm also thinking how awesome it would be to go fossil hunting in the badlands of Calgary."

"Badlands?"

"Yeah, they had a show on them. You can find bones and dino-saur teeth."

"Let me guess, on the Discovery Channel."

Josh laughed. "No, PBS."

Gotta love PBS.

~Pamela Goldstein
Amherstburg, ON

43

The Case of the Flying Squirrel

You can't be suspicious of a tree, or accuse a bird or a squirrel of subversion or challenge the ideology of a violet.
~Hal Borland, Sundial of the Seasons

Summer had finally arrived, after a long Canadian winter and a wet spring. The only problem was that the summer was looking like "monsoon season" and was putting a damper on my desire to go camping. But my husband had pulled our trailer to the mountains by the middle of June and I had promised that after the first weekend in July, I would join him. Friends that we camped with every year were also at the campground awaiting my arrival. I decided, rather grudgingly, to go even though the skies were dark and cloudy and the weather reports promised more rain.

It was good to see everyone and the next few weeks were a flurry of shared dinners and visits around the campfire. I spent time reading, walking with friends and taking photographs of the stunning mountains, sky and wildlife.

One evening as night closed in, we sat around the campfire laughing and teasing one another. Suddenly there was a crunching sound. We stared beyond the fire, into the darkness. Something was out there.

"Did you hear that?" one lady asked.

"I heard it," I said. My heart began to pound wildly. Maybe the cougar spotted a few days earlier had returned.

Silence prevailed as we strained to see anything beyond the rim of firelight. There was a plopping sound, then a grey creature moved across the gravel, just beyond the light.

What was it? We held our breath as the thing again dropped onto the gravel and scurried out of sight beyond our friend's trailer.

"Maybe it's a flying squirrel," someone said.

There was another plop and disappearance near the trailer. Something seemed odd. What was it?

A friend grabbed his camera and waited for the creature to return. We waited and waited. "I think it's gone," someone said.

But it landed again and just as quickly vanished.

"You'll have to tell me when to shoot," our camera buff said to me. "I can't see it fast enough."

I stood and waited. "Now," I shouted, and he tried but was unable to get a picture of the strange rodent.

He moved to the rim of the firelight, positioning himself for a better shot, then began to laugh. There was a crunching of gravel and from beyond the trailer's darkened end emerged the thirty-something son of a couple who were sitting around the campfire. He carried a fishing rod. On the end of the fishing line was a grey sock, stuffed to give it a head and body. We had all been duped by a flying grey sock!

Laughter prevailed. We sat long into the evening reminiscing of past years and other pranks. I smiled as I pulled a blanket around me to keep out the encroaching night chill. Yes the camping weather differed from most summers but the friendship remained the same. I looked at the faces, with firelight dancing across them, and thanked God for this group of friends. No, I corrected myself, these were more than friends. They were family, chosen summer family. And my heart swelled with love for them. I pulled the blanket closer and smiled. There was no place I'd rather be.

~Christine Mikalson
Taber, AB

44

Chicken Soup for the Soul

Close Encounter

*Last year I came face to face with a polar bear and while I was scared, I also
felt a deep respect for the fact that I was in this bear's territory...*
~Lonnie Dupre

The Polar Rover bounced along the frozen Arctic tundra as the
driver slowly made his way to the icy banks of the Hudson
Bay just outside Churchill, Canada. We'd flown for six hours,
changed planes twice and ridden a shuttle bus, all to experience a
firsthand encounter with the largest land carnivore in existence... the
polar bear.

My mind drifted back to the beginning of my love affair with
bears. At a very tender age, a fuzzy, brown "Teddy" bear, with golden-
orange eyes, was my constant companion. Teddy absorbed my tiny
tears without hesitation, protected me from the bogeyman at night,
listened to all my make-believe stories with a placid grin pasted on
his face, and held me close when I was scared. I loved my Teddy and
could never quite part with him, even though most of his fur was
worn off. Crude, white thread held his seams together and his nose
was permanently crooked.

I came out of my reverie, though, when the Polar Rover rolled
to a stop and the engine hushed. Everyone scurried to the right side
of the vehicle and lowered the windows for our first glimpse of a real,
live polar bear.

Our guide pointed at the furry, potato-chip-coloured bear
ambling out of the willows in a swaggering, pigeon-toed gait. She

said bears were very curious by nature and might come right up to the Rover if we kept quiet. My pulse quickened. I could hear my heart pounding in my ears.

The polar bear's long, black snout twitched back and forth, nosing the air. He came closer, checking out the smells on the door. His jaw dropped open slightly.

He sauntered alongside the bus, then, without warning, jumped up on his hind legs and put his front paws against the Rover, his sharp, black claws clicking on the white metal siding.

His massive head was now only four feet from the open windows. He gazed up at the faces staring back at him. His thick fur and gentle demeanour made him look almost cuddly for a thousand-pound carnivore.

I jockeyed for position to take a photo, then remembered there was an outside balcony on the Rover.

I carefully closed the balcony door behind me and leaned over the wall. The bear had moved towards my end of the Rover, but his head was under the balcony, leaving only his rump exposed.

My heart was banging now. If he would only back up, I could get the perfect photograph. I waited, not making a sound. Snowflakes drifted by in the air.

Then I heard a loud, snorting noise, but it wasn't coming from my side of the balcony. It was coming from underneath my feet. I looked down. In my haste, I had failed to notice the floor was a see-through metal grid. The polar bear was sniffing me.

I froze, not in fear, but in amazement. His wet nose almost touched my feet. He wanted my scent. He gazed up at me with chocolate-brown eyes, ears pointed forward, as if he wanted to say something. But he didn't have to. Instinctively, I knew.

I waited in the chill Arctic breeze, watching him lumber away. Just before he disappeared behind the snowdrift, he paused and looked back at me for one final farewell.

~Carolyn T. Johnson
Houston, TX, USA

O Canada

Absence Makes the Heart Grow Fonder

There's something romantic about being Canadian. We're a relatively unpopulated, somewhat civilized and clean and resourceful country. I always push the fact that I'm Canadian.

~k.d. Lang

"Home to the Shores of Lake Ontario"

From the CD *The Return* by Liona Boyd

Lyrics courtesy of Liona Boyd ©2011

Mid-Continental Music SOCAN

I'm coming home to the shores of Lake Ontario
Home to the place I left so many years ago
The world has been my playground, but how was I to know
I'd left my heart beside the shores of Lake Ontario

I'll see the magic in the maple leaves and beauty in the snow
And watch the monarch butterflies when autumn breezes blow
I've been to seven continents, but how was I to know
I'd left my heart beside the shores of Lake Ontario

Oh that special feeling I have always known
Oh that special feeling, I'm coming home

At times in life it seems that dreams make circles like a song
If home is where my heart is, it's home where I belong

I'm coming home to the shores of Lake Ontario
Home to the friends I left so many years ago
I've flown ten times around the world but how was I to know

I'd left my heart beside the shores of Lake Ontario

Oh that special feeling I have always known
Oh that special feeling, I'm coming home
At times in life it seems that dreams make circles like a song
If home is where my heart is, it's home where I belong

I'm coming home to the shores of Lake Ontario
Home to those dear places that I left so long ago
The world has been my playground, but how was I to know
I'd left my heart beside the shores of Lake Ontario
The world has sure been good to me, but now I really know
My heart is here beside the shores of Lake Ontario

Coming Home

Home is a name, a word, it is a strong one; stronger than magician ever spoke, or spirit ever answered to, in the strongest conjuration.
~Charles Dickens

It was 2004... and life was great. Business was good, and my husband and I had a gorgeous house in the Hollywood Hills, with plenty of room, a pool, and lots of trees. Our two children were going to one of the best private schools in Los Angeles. Some might say we "had it all" and, and yet, for me, something was missing.

I had grown up in Ontario, Canada—born in Kingston, raised in London and Toronto. I realized that what was missing was simple. I missed my home. I missed my parents, I missed the seasons, I missed the kind of green that southern California just doesn't have; in short—I missed Canada.

We had been seemingly happy in Los Angeles, and we were... just not completely. As our children grew up, we had been feeling increasingly disenchanted with their environment. The constant scheduling of time with playmates, dealing with nannies more than parents, and just the general pace of the culture there for kids. Meanwhile, my darling father, with whom I had been extremely close, was not doing very well. Though the doctors didn't really know what was happening to him and nothing was life-threatening, I knew that if he were to pass away, and I wasn't there, I would regret it for the rest of my life. When my husband and I added it all together, the answer was obvious.

We were moving back to Canada.

Normally, this kind of move would have been impossible because of work, but being in the entertainment and toy industry my husband and I were flexible. We had always said that if we didn't need to be in L.A. we wouldn't. So we said goodbye to our beloved circle of friends, packed up our wonderful home with only our essentials, leaving everything else, and moved to Toronto. Our intention was to rent out our house, and stay up north for two, maybe three years, allowing our children to experience the charms of Canada, and giving me some much needed time with my mom and dad. Well, over seven years later we are still there, having sold our L.A. home in the summer of 2007, just months before real estate in the States started its spiraling free fall.

Soon after we moved, we found we had traded freeway gridlock for supermarket gridlock. Supermarket gridlock is when two shopping carts bump into each other at the end of an aisle and the "drivers" end up chatting with each other, whether they are friends or sometimes have never met. We found a house in a wonderful Toronto neighbourhood where our children walked to school, came home for lunch and where we suddenly knew dozens of parents. Quite a switch.

Now don't get me wrong. Los Angeles is an amazing place with many, many wonderful and truly genuine people. We'd loved it there when we were younger, but raising kids, well… it just wasn't exactly working for us. I wanted my kids to experience what I remembered: riding your bike to the corner store for a Popsicle, and your next door neighbour's your best friend simply because… he's your next door neighbour. Our house in L.A. was behind a gate, and while it was safe and lovely, it was not the spontaneous social childhood we wanted for our children.

Whenever we would tell people in Toronto that we had moved from Los Angeles, their first response was always the same incredulous, "WHY?" Why would anyone leave Shangri-la for Canada? For them, the visions of swimming pools and movie stars (cue *Beverly Hillbillies* soundtrack) had been implanted from an early age. I guess the "grass is always greener"—and *warmer*, and the whole concept of leaving such a fabulous place for "boring old Canada" seemed absurd.

To be sure, once we'd made the move, we did find ourselves missing certain aspects of L.A. life: the sun, the beach, Trader Joe's, and especially our friends. However, what we got almost instantly from Canada was an increased sense of intimacy and connection with our kids.

For one thing, as most people already know, Canada is hockey crazy. So when my ten-year-old son, who had only been on ice skates once at a birthday party in Burbank, announced to us after just one practice—where he fell more than he skated—that he had "found his game," we knew that we had truly arrived in Canada.

Everywhere you go in this world, children love to play sports. Los Angeles is no different, but in Toronto, we found that fathers and mothers drive their children all over the city to play hockey and stay to watch the games. And it is during those car rides to and from the various arenas that the children, especially the boys, tend to open up. While their minds are preoccupied with the impending practice or game, and without the pressure of the parent's wanting to "talk" I found that they would just start talking on their own. My husband is fond of saying, "Forget quality time, it's *quantity* time that counts," and I must say I agree. The more time we spend with our kids, the better, and not just for the good times but the bad ones as well.

The organized "play dates" were now replaced with our children spontaneously bringing various kids home after school, for sleepovers, or calling us to ask if they could go over to their friend's house. All but gone too were the cliques, so common in the private school scene we had been part of. In Los Angeles, sadly, most of the public schools are not so great. Not true for us in Canada. The schools are wonderful and because Toronto is such a huge melting pot, our children found themselves in class with kids from all over the world, which was fun for them. Our son just graduated from four years at an amazing performing arts public high school. Our daughter, meanwhile, was treated to an incredible three years at a newly created integrated arts middle school where the children are taught all the subjects through the arts. They might learn a math lesson by doing dance steps, or French by writing and performing original songs. We are so grateful for these experiences.

Then there is my time with my dad. I had always been the apple of my father's eye, and had known how sad he was to lose me to Los Angeles. He was getting on in years and his health was failing. He needed me, but would never have said so. My parents' joy at our arrival cannot be overstated. Not just seeing more of me, but having constant access to my kids made their hearts soar. They were so happy. And my kids got to be around their grandparents so much more too. Even if nothing else good had come of our move, just what I was able to do for my dad and mom made it all worthwhile. I think this is part of the wonder of Canada for me—the strong sense of family values that just seems to prevail.

Do the crazy winters chill me to the bone and make me want to jump on a plane? Does the slower pace sometimes bore me a little? Do I miss the excitement of the "biz" and my great friends in L.A.? The answer to all of these is "yes." Will I stay in Canada forever? It's hard to say, but even if I ever do move south of the border, I will never truly leave again. It is real, it is genuine and the people are truly warm, welcoming and friendly.

After all, it's Canada.

And it's home.

~Laura Robinson
Toronto, ON

Proud Canadian

Where we love is home,
Home that our feet may leave, but not our hearts.
~Oliver Wendell Holmes, Sr., Homesick in Heaven

Growing up I never felt proud to be Canadian. While my friends came from diverse and glamorous backgrounds like Ukrainian and Polish (you might guess that I grew up in Western Canada), I had the unfortunate peerage of being distinctly Canadian. Thirteen generations had settled between these rocky shores on one side of my family and, even less impressively to me, eleven on the other.

While my not-so Canadian friends got to go on exotic holidays to Hawaii or Disneyland, our family vacations only took us across Canada visiting relatives in one province or another. Not only was my family boring and unsophisticated, but we had to visit them too! My childhood was spent firmly planted in Canada with escapes to exotic destinations only occurring during long stints of daydreaming.

Graduating from university with an Arts degree changed all that, not so much because I had loads of options, but because so few of them were in Canada. I gamely followed the trail of unemployed art students before me who signed up to teach English overseas. I was in my early twenties and eager for adventure, and Japan sounded like just what I'd always yearned for.

It was there I would learn firsthand the old adage that you don't know what you've got till it's gone. I ended up in a small town not all that different from my own hometown (the one I left just as soon as I was able). In fact, one could even describe where I lived in Japan as the Canadian equivalent of Northern Saskatchewan. There, you couldn't find much that was Western save a few classic movies at the video store or the spongy white bread similar to the Wonder loaves of my childhood.

Ironically, it was in my new setting of backwater Japan that I cultivated my inner Canadian-ness. I stayed, or should I say survived, four years by tricking myself into believing I was still in Canada. I begged my mother to send anything related to Canadian pop culture. And so, each month a box arrived with things like Longview Beef Jerky, scented hand sanitizer and video tapes filled with the *Anne of Green Gables* TV movie, an unfortunate Rita MacNeil Christmas concert and commercials advertising the arrival of the Sears Wishbook.

I re-read her dog-eared copies of *Canadian Living* and would make those recipes as best I could for a taste of home. Homesick one holiday season, I succumbed to making Christmas Morning Wifesaver, that breakfast casserole every family in Canada seemed to prepare on Christmas Eve.

With scant Western ingredients available, I became a member of the Foreign Food Buyers Club, racking up the points ordering cases of Ragu and packets of basil. Naturally, each annual trip home required a pilgrimage to the Real Canadian Superstore, dropping enough Yen to fill a hockey bag with necessary supplies. I would be fully stocked for the year with Hawkins Cheezies, Old Dutch Dill Pickle chips, real maple syrup and Montreal steak spice.

With these rations, I hosted what would become an annual Thanksgiving party for the local expat community. It didn't matter that the majority of expats were American, the event would be held the second weekend in October to coincide with our Canadian celebration. Apple pie and marshmallow-topped sweet potatoes were banned in favour of pumpkin pie, traditional stuffing and plain mashed potatoes. Canadians are humble folk after all, and our feast reflected this.

Taking advantage of being able to finally travel where I wanted to, I explored most of Southeast Asia during those years. Fellow Canadians were always easy to spot with our uniform of Tevas (white runners were part of the American uniform), The Band watchstrap and of course, that ubiquitous Canadian flag sewn proudly on all our backpacks. Though I was never a fan of country music, I embarrassed myself by turning to the country music station to remind me of home each time I stepped on an airplane.

The years in Japan flamed the wanderlust of my daydreams as a child. It's something I've never outgrown, spanning several decades and culminating in travel to over fifty countries and counting. I even had another two-year stint abroad, one that I was able to enjoy without needing Canada shipped to me in a box. But I always come home.

John Ed Pearce said, "Home is a place you grow up wanting to leave, and grow old wanting to get back to." And so it was for me. It took four—sometimes long—years in Japan to finally understand and relish my Canadian roots. I now appreciate what these mean, no matter where I am.

~Jody Robbins
Calgary, AB

Four Strong Winds

Above everything, we are Canadian.
~George Etienne Cartier

"I f you don't get goose bumps listening to this song, your Canadian citizenship should be revoked." It was January 25th, 2005, and the voice on the radio was introducing Ian & Sylvia's song "Four Strong Winds." Instantly I was back in August 1975, in a little pub in Bermuda with Daniel, my first husband.

Daniel had insisted we go to Bermuda for our honeymoon. He'd been there once before and was eager to go back. From the way he spoke of it, Bermuda was a paradise, and he would be happy to live there.

When we arrived, I could see why he was so enthusiastic. Bermuda was gorgeous—warm, verdant, sunny and full of hospitable people. Except for a trip to Niagara Falls on the American side of the border, it was my first time outside Canada.

It was also my first experience of the tropics. I'd never been in a place where orchids and banana trees grew in people's yards instead of sheltered in greenhouses. On the way to and from our guesthouse in Hamilton, we passed a yard where a frangipani tree dropped fragrant white blossoms into our hair. The hedges were hibiscus, and I watched in disbelief as one man, squaring up his hedge with trimmers, unconcernedly clipped flowers in half to keep the sides straight.

The first day we strolled into downtown Hamilton for lunch. The restaurant was deserted, except for us. The streets were quiet, too. Nobody else was out, except for the traffic policeman in his white uniform and helmet, standing in his white-domed kiosk. We took the hint, and thereafter spent from noon until two dozing, just as everyone else on the island did.

I loved it all—the pink coral sand beaches, the ocean, the tropical plants. I loved the tiny, bright green lizards sunning themselves on the tops of walls, and the peeping frogs whose chorus filled the air every evening, and all the birds I didn't recognize.

We ate seafood every day—fresh-caught red snapper, crab, whatever was on the menu. One evening at dinner I ordered lobster for the first time. When it arrived on the plate, it was immense.

"What if I don't like it?" I asked Daniel.

"You will," he said. I did.

There are no cars for rent in Bermuda; all the cars belong to citizens. Tourists can rent motor scooters to drive around the island. On our second day, we rented a little red one from a lot in Hamilton.

"Don't look behind you," the man at the scooter rental said to us. "You don't look out for the cars—they look out for you." He was right; they did look out for us. We never had a moment's worry driving, even the day we went from one end of the island to the other and back—a roundtrip of forty-two miles.

We toured three of the four sunken caverns, caves that had once been dry, but were now flooded by the ocean. Limestone columns, joined stalagmites and stalactites that had formed millennia earlier, drop by drop, stood now in ninety feet of crystal clear water. The bottom of the cavern was as visible as though the water had been air. We visited Devil's Hole, where a collapsed cave had trapped ocean fish, even sharks, in what was now a huge saltwater pool.

And, of course, we swam. I'd never even seen the ocean before. Daniel grew up in Halifax, and knew the Atlantic Ocean that beat on Canada's east coast. This was a gentler sea, warm to swim in, washing up on miles and miles of pink sand beaches. "Bermuda is another world," says one of the island's songs. It was true, and it was a beautiful world. I began to understand how Daniel felt. I thought that maybe I could happily live there forever, eating lobster, swimming in the ocean; I might even learn the names of the birds.

Bermuda clings to its British heritage. They drive on the left. The policeman, but for the fact that his pants were Bermuda shorts and his uniform white instead of navy, looked like a bobby. The hotels served afternoon tea. On our fourth night, we went out to a British-style pub.

The room was all dark wood, with small tables, and "snugs" — little enclosed booths — along one wall. There were dartboards, although nobody seemed to be playing. There was a choice of beers I'd never heard of before and the barmaid called us "luv" in an English accent.

Half an hour or so after we arrived, the live music started. The duo looked like typical folksingers. She had long, straight blond hair; he wore sideburns and played guitar. They performed a few folk songs, then invited the pub patrons to join in some music hall sing-along numbers. After a few raucous rounds, the woman adjusted her microphone and waited for the crowd to settle down.

"I'd like to do a song for you now," she said, "that was written by Ian Tyson. It's called 'Four Strong Winds'."

I was fine until she got to the line "Think I'll go out to Alberta." At that moment, a wave of homesickness washed over me. My throat closed, my chest ached, and tears welled up in my eyes. I missed Canada desperately. I wanted to be back in that wide land, a land of distances that could create such a lonely song. I'd never been so homesick in my life.

I looked around and thought, "Does anyone else here even understand what it is to be more than a day's walk away from somewhere?" I looked at Daniel, sure he must be thinking what I was, but he seemed simply to be enjoying the music.

I wiped my eyes with my napkin and swallowed the rest of my tears. By the time the song ended, I had managed to get my breath back, and could clap and smile as though nothing were wrong. But the spell was broken; I couldn't live in that other world, and I knew it. The only place I could live was in my own country. I enjoyed the last three days of our time in Bermuda, but I didn't regret leaving.

It's still that way for me. I live now in Northern Ontario, in the foothills of the Laurentian Mountains on the Cambrian Shield. We measure distance in hours driven, and there's hardly anywhere I could walk in one day. I've travelled to other countries over the years, and enjoyed my travels, but I know that there's nowhere else I could live.

If I ever doubt it, all I have to do is listen to "Four Strong Winds."

~Elizabeth Creith
Thessalon, ON

The Cost of Freedom

When a soldier steps on foreign soil in a high-risk environment, every single
Canadian should be walking with him or her.
~Rick Hillier

I n the spring of 1991, I was a young Canadian in a strange land. After months of discovering Europe with a backpack and a student rail pass, I paused in Italy and fell in love with the Italian people and culture. A glorious month of fabulous adventures and delicious cuisine sealed the deal and I decided to settle in Pescara, a beach town and fishing port on the Adriatic Sea. I started a job teaching English and found a cozy apartment overlooking the long stretches of sandy beach and aquamarine sea.

My idealistic dreams of settling into Italian culture proved more difficult than I anticipated. As a social, talkative person, my inability to communicate effectively in Italian was frustrating. Sometimes I would get lost in the city, or have uncomfortable misunderstandings with people. Because of the language barrier, I felt like my new friends didn't know the real me. I couldn't converse or joke around with them the way I wanted to. I laughed along but missed most of their Italian jokes. Not being able to contribute to conversations made me feel awkward and quiet. Because this was contrary to my nature, I felt very alone as I struggled to learn Italian as quickly as possible. Besides all this, I missed my close family and friends in Canada.

One morning when I was feeling exasperated and homesick, an Italian friend announced he had a special place to show me. We drove for over an hour south of Pescara, passing through several small towns along the Adriatic coast before arriving in the town of Ortona. It was a quaint town of 20,000 people with some stunning beaches. I assumed that we were on our way to a unique beach to sun the day away. But as the car slowed down and pulled into what looked like a park entrance, I realized we were driving into a cemetery, unlike the other Italian cemeteries I had visited.

Rows of evenly spaced identical white headstones stretched as far as I could see. Beautiful red flowers grew beside the stones on perfectly maintained grass. A white marble cross towered as the pinnacle in the centre of the cemetery. Fabrizio led me to one of the tombstones, and I noticed it was engraved with a Canadian maple leaf and a Christian cross below it. I was confused. I looked at the gravestone beside it, and it had the same carvings. They all had the Canadian maple leaf at the top and a cross carved below it. Then I read the engraved words: L. 2382 Private W. Harrington, The Saskatoon Light Infantry, 29th December, 1943, Age 24. He was a Canadian soldier from WWII!

"Are all of these Canadian soldiers?" I asked Fabri, surprised at what I was seeing.

"Look," he said, pointing to the next gravestone. Again I read the name on the stone: F 97977 Private E. Smith, Royal Canadian Army Medical Corps, 29th January, 1944, Age 31. At the very bottom of the tombstone, these words were engraved: May His Soul and All the Souls of the Faithful Who Departed Through the Mercy of God Rest In Peace.

I walked to the next gravestone and the next, reading each name and the personalized memorial at the bottom. I wanted to read them all but Fabrizio beckoned me to a small white pavilion decorated with flowers. In the centre of the pavilion was a large book with the names, ages and hometowns of every soldier. Most of the men were from Ontario and Quebec and most of them had died before reaching the age of thirty. In total, 1,375 Canadian soldiers were buried there.

A homesick pain struck my gut and tears began to stream down my cheeks. I sat on the bench in the pavilion and put my head in my hands. Fabrizio sat beside me and put his arm around me.

"I didn't know so many Canadian soldiers were buried in Italy!" I thought about all the men who had come here to fight for our freedom, who gave their young lives so that we could be free. I imagined the mothers, fathers, friends and loved ones they had left behind. I envisioned their last moments in battle, fighting for their lives with bombs exploding and guns firing all around them. I pictured their relatives back in Canada collapsing from sorrow after receiving the news of their death. And finally, I cringed at the thought of them being buried in this graveyard, so far away from their homeland, thousands of miles from Canadian soil. How heartbroken I would feel if one of my three brothers, my father or my friends died in battle, never to return home!

Fabrizio and I continued to walk amongst the graves of the soldiers again. So many men had died here. I realized this was only one of many cemeteries throughout Europe that are filled with Canadian men and women who died during WWI and WWII. My mind wandered to the poem, "In Flanders Fields," written by Canadian Lieutenant Colonel John McCrae during the First World War, "…the poppies blow, between the crosses row on row, that mark our place…"

My difficulty fitting into Italian culture now seemed trivial compared to the horror these men had endured. As we drove away from the cemetery, there was one important thing to do before leaving this place forever. I turned my head towards the tombstones and whispered a quiet "thank you" to the soldiers who gave their lives for me, for the freedom to visit this beautiful country, Italy, and to live in a free homeland, Canada. I knew that one day I would be going back to Canada to see my family and friends. These soldiers came to Europe knowing they might never see their loved ones again. And with that knowledge, they laid down their lives for our freedom. Their bodies never made it home, but their memories endure. I felt a sense of peace knowing that their lives are remembered and honoured in an obscure little town in Italy. Thank you my fellow Canadians. Thank you for my freedom.

~Kathy Linker
Canadian living in Kailua-Kona, HI, USA

My Canada

You can never go home again,
but the truth is you can never leave home, so it's all right.
~Maya Angelou

I never knew I had a home until it was gone. I was born in Montreal, Quebec, in 1951, to English-speaking parents, the oldest of five children. By the time I started grade one, we had moved to the small town of Saint-Jean-sur-Richelieu just south of Montreal.

My best friends through grade school, in the English Protestant school I attended, were all English-speaking. There was a separate English school for Catholics, as well as at least one French school. French was a subject taught from grade one until graduation. Stupidly, I was never interested in a second language and did not apply myself, which I regret to this day.

In grade six, my best friend was French-Canadian. We were inseparable, and one would think I would have learned some French from her, but I didn't. Michele was also fluent in English, so she didn't need to speak French with me.

When I was sixteen, my father moved the family to the United States. At that time, the Quebec nationalist group, the FLQ (Front de Libération du Québec), was coming to a head, and I guess my father thought we, as English-speaking Canadians, needed to leave. As a result, my last two years of high school were spent in Pennsylvania.

I had a rude awakening.

I had left a small school, with fewer than five hundred students from grades four to eleven, and enrolled in a senior high school with more than two thousand students. I was lost, alone, scared. Not to mention that teachers, once they found out I was from Canada, thought I should be proficient in French. I felt like an idiot, a dunce.

I also felt out of place. Americans did not seem to know anything about Canadians or Canada, whereas Canadians were well-versed on Americans and their country. My classmates, and even some teachers, thought I was an Eskimo. They thought all Canadians lived in igloos and wore fur hats and deerskin coats to keep warm. They thought all of Canada, all year round, consisted of sub-zero temperatures; they were amazed we existed in that frigid cold. They also thought we all spoke French. Obviously they had never heard of the Inuit language, or they would have thought that's what was spoken. Even at my age, I couldn't believe their ignorance.

Luckily, I made friends with Patricia, who was also new to the area, and the two of us made friends with another student, Cheryl, who had lived in the area since birth. The three of us became fast friends, and still are today, even though many hundreds of kilometres separate the three of us.

I still felt lost, however. Classes were totally different. In Quebec, we stayed in one classroom for the entire day; in Pennsylvania, each subject meant a move to a different classroom. The building was huge, several stories, and I was always lost, literally. The grade system was different, and I graduated a year later than my friends in Canada. I yearned for my old school, where everyone knew everyone, where I knew where I was, where I knew where I was going. Ironically, I didn't appreciate my previous school at the time.

I graduated from school and enrolled in an out-of-state college. The summer after graduation from high school, I had met my future husband. I went ahead with my plans for secretarial school, but I managed to graduate a year ahead of schedule so we could marry that same year. After marriage, we moved to another state, where my husband had joined the Armed Forces. In the meantime, my parents moved the family back to Canada. They built a new home in Ontario, with bedrooms for everyone—everyone but me. That house was never my home. Ontario was never my home. I felt lost, again.

After a few years, my American husband and I moved to Canada; however, we moved to the east coast, two thousand kilometres from my parents and siblings. By that time, I had an American son. I was happy to be moving back to Canada. I felt like Canada was my home, would always be my home, even though I didn't have a house of memories to return to.

However, I had another rude awakening, even in my home country.

Prince Edward Island was—and is—a great place to live. We bought a house in the country and neighbours welcomed us to their community. But, at a social gathering one night, someone asked me, "Are you a PFA?"

PFA? What the heck was that? I was confused and showed my ignorance when I questioned the individual. "PFA" means "person from away." Apparently, if one is not born on Prince Edward Island, one is a PFA, one will always be a PFA, one is never truly an Islander no matter how many years one lives there. We were welcomed, yes, but I'm not sure we ever really fit in. I was starting to wonder if I would fit in anywhere.

Fast forward thirty years later, after two more children and two divorces: my husband of ten years and I are living in Halifax, Nova Scotia.

I actually have roots here in Nova Scotia, something I discovered when I began genealogical research a few years previous to our move. I found that my great-great-great grandparents on my father's side came over to Nova Scotia in 1803 from Scotland and settled near Barney's River, Pictou County. The area they resided in was named after them—"Kenzieville"—a small community which still exists today. The generations branched out over the years, some to other counties in Nova Scotia or to other parts of Canada, others to the United States. My father's parents made their home in Bridgetown, Nova Scotia, eventually moving to Halifax, and my grandmother remained there after my grandfather died. I had visited her numerous times when I was single and living on Prince Edward Island, so I was familiar with and loved that great city. It had always been my dream to live in Halifax, but I never dreamt it would actually happen.

Today, I feel like I finally have a place to call my own. I finally feel like I fit in. There are old family homesteads I've been able to visit, cemeteries I've roamed through searching for ancestors, and living relatives I've connected with.

Two of my children live with their families about thirty minutes away from me. My older son, the American, lives in Calgary, but we manage to visit once a year at least. I didn't have an extended family nearby when I was growing up, nor did my children, so this has been a new experience for all of us, and we relish being able to get together on a whim.

This is my Canada. I'm glad I'm finally home.

~Catherine A. MacKenzie
Fall River, NS

There's No Place Like Home

As for my country, I don't live there,
but obviously I'm very proud to be Canadian.
~Mike Weir

I no longer take being a Canadian for granted. You see, I now live in the USA. Don't get me wrong. I love the reason I am here. As a widow in my fifties I was fortunate enough to find the love of my life, get married again, buy a house, and start a whole new life. Who wouldn't love a fairy tale like that? I live in a city that I adore, enjoy wonderful new friends, and have the career for which I always pined. In fact, I'm living the life of my dreams. I know I am because I have a "wish box" into which for years I stuffed little slips of paper. Onto each scrap of paper I faithfully scribbled my hopes and dreams. Almost all of them have come true. But one thing happened that was NOT on my wish list—leaving behind my family, my friends, and my beloved Canada.

Growing up on the streets of a very cosmopolitan Toronto, I considered the Canada/U.S. border to be an unnecessary inconvenience. I figured that for the most part we enjoy the same culture, the same pastimes, the same music, even similar politics, so what's the big deal? We may as well be the same country. Living beyond the borders of Canada I now realize it is not as simple as that.

What I didn't understand was that the world is a different place when you live in a country other than that of your birth. I guess I am experiencing what millions of immigrants all over the world already know—that no matter how generous and welcoming your new country, there's still no place like home. And for me, no matter where I live, Canada, forever and always, will be my home.

Since living in the U.S. I have met the most wonderful, warm Americans who opened their hearts and their homes to me. They have made me feel comfortable here, helped me find my place, definitely making my transition from hometown girl to immigrant much easier to take.

Circumstances vary across the U.S., as do laws and politics, but the longer I am here the more I appreciate what being a Canadian means. I am not going to get political, but my heart is warmed to know that every Canadian has access to topnotch affordable health care. That's certainly not true in many countries across the globe, even those close to home.

When I take a job in Canada, I am guaranteed a minimum wage, no matter who I am, no matter where I'm from. Free of charge I can visit any of the many world class libraries and avail myself of rich stores of knowledge so great that I will not be able to absorb even a fraction of them in my lifetime. And I can share them with my children. We have millions of acres of national parks to enjoy with our families, and I've never once seen them close their gates due to lack of funding or political disputes. Just a short walk or drive from almost any home in Canada we have parks, parkettes, conservation areas, and massive forests for our enjoyment. Our neighbourhoods are relatively safe. We don't have to worry that the guy next door might have a handgun tucked into his belt, so our kids are free to play outside without fear.

These are just a few of the privileges of living in Canada that we may have come to take for granted. I know I did. It's easy to gripe about high taxes and funding cuts because no one likes them, but let's face it, no system and no country is perfect. But our precious Canada comes pretty darned close.

It took me leaving my own country to realize just how fortunate

I was to be born a Canadian, and how I failed to appreciate it. I guess you could say I had to go away to really come home.

~Ruth Knox
Canadian living in Meridian, ID, USA

Two out of Forty

Canada is an interesting place; the rest of the world thinks so,
even if Canadians don't.
~Terence M. Green

In September of 1997, I e-mailed my friends letting them know that in July of 1998 I wanted to go to Europe. If anyone was interested they had to start saving their money. I was a twenty-three-year-old Canadian ready to have a European adventure.

When it was time to book the trip I was disappointed that only my mom had saved the money to go. I decided to make the best of it. Plans for the great adventure began. We chose a tour that started in England, took a hovercraft to France, then continued on to Belgium, Holland, Switzerland, Germany, Italy, and finally returned to France. We were going to be jet setting in fabulous European countries for close to a month. I made it my mission to try wine and chocolate in every country I visited. As we were packing, Mom handed me Canadian stickers and pins to put on my backpack and luggage. I was going to die of embarrassment. How dorky is it to travel with your mom and wear Canadian flag pins too? Europe was high fashion, not cheesy pins. I reluctantly stuck one of the smallest stickers on a hidden spot of my backpack and tucked the rest into my suitcase. I wasn't a full-blown rebel yet.

The first of July marked Canada's birthday and the beginning of our European tour. Loaded down with very heavy suitcases and full backpacks, my mom and I headed to the airport to start our five-hour flight to Heathrow airport in England. We went to our hotel in a cab and were to meet up with our tour bus the next day at the hotel. The next day all the tour participants loaded onto the bus. Freda, our tour guide, decided we needed to introduce ourselves. My mom and I sat near the middle of the bus and as the first half of the bus made their introductions they realized they were all from the United States. That was the ingredient for instant friendship. As the introductions moved down the bus to my mom and me, there were no other Canadians. Mom was the first of us to speak, "Hi, I'm Chris and we live near Niagara Falls, Canada." I could hear murmurs going around the bus and wondered what they were saying.

We were delighted to learn that the back half of the bus was from various parts of Australia. We were the only two Canadians on the whole bus. Two out of forty!

While I enjoyed the scenery and all the tour stops I noticed we always had people around us. At different rest stops our fellow European travellers wanted to talk to us. They wanted to know all about Canada. The people from down south in the States wanted to know about igloos.

Soon everyone on the bus knew our names and had talked to us about Canada. Many didn't realize that Canada is actually big. They thought it was possible to drive from the Rockies in British Columbia to Niagara Falls in Ontario in just a day. I told them it would take more like a week. The strangest thing is that I started to feel an inkling of pride to be Canadian. It was a strange feeling that I had never felt before. Honestly, I never thought about it really at all.

As the trip moved from England to France and then on to Belgium people noticed my mom's Canadian flag pins. They would say, "Canadian? Yes?" Then when we agreed they would give us nice warm smiles and work hard at speaking English to us. I had a few pats on the arm and back when people realized we were Canadian. Maybe, there was something to wearing those Canadian pins? I just wasn't ready to change to the bigger stickers just yet.

Once we arrived in Holland, the reception was very pleasant everywhere we went: the hotel, the shops, the Klompenmaker (the wooden shoe maker), and the cheese farm. I thought everyone on our tour was receiving this extra warm reception, but talking at dinner we found out they were not having the same experience. Maybe there was something to this Canadian thing. Before leaving Holland I was proud to wear one more sticker on my purse. Only one more though. I still wasn't ready to cry out on the rooftop that I was Canadian.

This special treatment continued throughout Switzerland, Austria, Italy and back around to France. While in a Paris subway my attitude towards being Canadian took a serious turn. I became proud to be Canadian. My grade school French classes suddenly became very useful. I took the required French classes up to grade nine and then continued with an extra year in grade ten. I could actually use my French when I really needed it. One of our new American friends wanted to ask the student rate for the subway and the teller could not understand English. I offered to help. The man was able to understand me and told me the amount. I felt proud to be Canadian and to be part of a country that required students to learn French.

I did add another Canadian sticker to my luggage and my backpack after that subway trip. I could have even worn red and white and painted a Canadian maple leaf on my face. I realized I lived in a great country. We are bilingual, have a huge beautiful country, and we are known for our friendliness. By the end of the trip I was proud to walk around with those pins from my mom. I never did thank my mom for giving me those pins. I have to remember to do that. Oh, and I did have a great time on the trip with my mom. We had our moments but in the end we grew closer and have our European adventure to look back on fondly. I'm proud to have travelled with my mom and the trip helped me realize I'm proud to be Canadian. After all, being Canadian is eh okay.

~Leslie Czegeny
Beamsville, ON

O Canada

Holidays and Traditions

Cultures grow on the vine of tradition.

~Jonah Goldberg

51

Why I Wear a Poppy

Patriotism is not dying for one's country, it is living for one's country. And for humanity. Perhaps that is not as romantic, but it's better.
~Agnes MacPhail

In 1919, the year my father was born, the first Remembrance Day was observed throughout the countries of the British Commonwealth. Originally called Armistice Day, this day commemorated the end of the "war to end all wars" on Monday, November 11, 1918, at 11 a.m. — the eleventh hour of the eleventh day of the eleventh month. Remembrance Day is a day when "Canadians pause in a silent moment of remembrance for the men and women who have served, and continue to serve our country during times of war, conflict and peace."

Dad was twenty when Canada went to war again. He was drafted into the army, but spent his years of service on Canadian soil, as an officers' chauffeur on the west coast. Although he never saw battle, he hated every minute of his time there. He missed home, he missed his family, he missed his own mother's funeral. When he returned, he married and settled down to raise a family and rarely spoke of his years in the army. My father was not your typical, flag-waving veteran. Dad never joined the Legion, never made a speech about being proud to serve his country, never spoke of how privileged he felt to wear the uniform. I wear a poppy one day a year to honour him, regardless.

Some time ago I spoke with a fellow Canadian who refuses to wear a poppy on Remembrance Day. "War is against my religion," was the explanation. I said nothing, partly out of cowardice but mostly out of surprise, knowing this person's ancestors had fled from a land of bitter religious persecution to the relative safety of Canada. I wondered how those same ancestors would feel about this stance? Had no one fought for their freedom, those who fled to Canada would eventually face the same thing all over again—with nowhere left to flee. Is it really too much to wear a poppy one day a year to honour that dedication, regardless of one's point of view about war?

In 2008, I saw my young friend James go off to Afghanistan. He called me a few times from that desert land, just to unload some of the horrific experiences he was facing. Each Sunday, I'd see his parents and his wife in church and wonder how their hearts could bear it—the worry, the wondering. We all breathed a sigh of relief when he returned safe and sound, knowing others had not and would not. It doesn't seem too much to wear a poppy one day a year to honour James and his comrades, regardless.

Remembrance Day is not about condoning war or glorifying weaponry or celebrating death. It does not make a statement about your politics or your religion or your conscience. More than 1,500,000 Canadians have served our country in this way, and more than 100,000 have died. They gave their lives and their futures so that we may live in peace.

That's why I'll be wearing a poppy on November 11.

~Terrie Todd
Portage la Prairie, MB

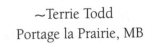

On the Hill

Canada is our country. It belongs to us and we belong to it.
Let us join together, in our time, and make history once again.
~Paul Martin

Canadians have a reputation for being reserved, for being a society of people who do not wave their banner high. Not me, eh! I stand at attention for the national anthem and sing loud enough to deafen the people around me. I display the easily recognized red and white maple leaf flag whenever I travel to foreign destinations and I consider Canada Day on Parliament Hill an annual pilgrimage. Ah, but I do not stop there! I impose my patriotism on everyone I can.

Whenever I learn that friends or acquaintances have never been to the Hill on Canada Day, I go out of my way to get them there. Since moving to Ottawa in 1972, I have shuttled my family and numerous guests to my favourite parking spot at the National Library. Armed with folding chairs they are then marched along Wellington Street to the Hill where I promptly settle them on the lawns in front of the Centre Block to enjoy their celebration of being Canadian.

Over the years and through changes of government I've heard different Prime Ministers recounting our short history and praising the future of this young country. I've helped welcome dignitaries with my loud yahoos and waving flags. Governor Generals have come and gone, each delivering well thought out words to Canadians across our land, those on the grounds and those sitting at home watching the celebrations on television. In 2010, Queen Elizabeth II's visit found me and a friend crushed and sweating, pressed against a barrier for a glimpse of her. Uncomfortable as we were, we wouldn't have missed the experience for anything. Canada Day on Parliament Hill is, for me, a time to publicly celebrate being Canadian.

All this festivity takes place on July 1st and was originally called Dominion Day. I remember those days when I marched in small-town parades proudly wearing my crisply pressed Brownie uniform. Those celebrations still take place in nearly every town across Canada but you'll find me on the "Hill" now. Fond memories of my children, my mother and my friends who have done the trek with me flood back on that special day. However, my most memorable foray to the Hill was in 2005.

During a winter visit, I learned that Carol, my friend of some fifty years, a consummate world traveller, had never celebrated Canada Day in Ottawa. I was aghast, then adamant, and would consider no alternative; she had to come that summer. Carol is an expat, choosing to live in a kinder climate in Palm Springs, California. Originally from Manitoba, she has however, always remained a proud Canadian. Convincing another friend from Picton to join us, the trip was planned. Carol and Mary arrived on the VIA rail train the day before.

Carol, Mary and I fall into the category that is labelled "Seniors," but we are still kids at heart. That being said, we allowed lots of time to navigate the streets and the crowds. Since I know the drill (the program is similar year after year) I positioned us close to the centre of the cordoned off area of the centre lawn in front of the west block. From there we would have a perfect view of the RCMP Musical Ride.

Sixty-four Royal Canadian Mounted Police, dressed in their famed red uniforms and mounted on sleek black steeds, performed their precision choreographed manoeuvres back and forth in groups of four and eight right in front of us. We cheered and clapped as they formed wagon wheels, filed past in crossovers and galloped by with lances lifted high. The performance lasts more than half an hour and the grand finale is always a dynamic crowd pleaser. Charging the full length of the parade square, the horses come to an abrupt halt and the Mounties jab the lances in a forward thrust. I tore my eyes away from the thundering four-times-sixty-four hooves to watch Carol. She was transfixed until a lance point stopped only metres from her face. She flinched, sat paralyzed for a moment, then broke into "bravos" louder than everyone's.

We watched the changing of the guard, cheered the Kilty bands, then quietly listened to the Prime Minister speak. It was a special year as the original maple leaf flag was returned to Canada after it had mysteriously disappeared forty years before. As I listened to the story of its journey and how it came to be returned to Canada, I felt a gripping in my chest. I watched the flag being handed over, swallowed, and held my hand over my heart. Tears fell shamelessly down Carol's cheeks—her pride in being Canadian was written all over her face.

Following the formal speeches, performances by exciting Canadian talent delighted the crowd. Knowing what was ahead on the program and how emotional my lifelong friend was, I watched Carol closely and was not disappointed. Surprise, then elation, spread across her face as the cannons loudly reported, followed by our famed Snowbirds soaring over the back of the Peace Tower, a jet stream of red and white behind them. All eyes were riveted to the sky to see them fan out over the wildly cheering crowd, then disappear over the city. Thirty thousand people stood silent, holding close the moment. Then babble returned and chairs were folded.

As the masses emptied into the streets, we watched a sea of revellers in red, waving flags and wearing crazy patriotic hats. Children and adults were singing "O Canada" and we joined in. Full of warm fuzzies, with arms draped around each other, we headed for the car.

Carol and Mary insisted on thanking me over and over again but I countered that we were not finished celebrating yet. The morning on Parliament Hill only began the day. Leaving downtown, we picked up my friend Polly and headed over the Alexandra Bridge to the Quebec side to board the Senator, one of the Ottawa River cruise boats. The plan was to take a tour down river, have dinner on board and return beneath Nepean Point by dark. However, we were minutes onto the river when the captain announced there were weather warnings and we would be returning to the dock. The blackening sky and rocking boat confirmed he was right. Disappointed we missed the cruise, we were appeased when dinner was served on board dockside. The short downpour and black clouds gave way to a fading sky that darkened and cleared simultaneously; passengers flocked to the ship's railing. No celebration could be complete without fireworks and in Ottawa there is no better place to watch them than from the river.

Brilliant flashes rose high over the parliament buildings, erupting into a blaze of sparkling bursts filling the sky. Cascading like waterfalls they fell toward us, faded and disappeared. Oohs and aahs, clapping and joyous cheers mingled with the noise of the fireworks. Then all was quiet, penetrated only by a lone voice. "Happy Canada Day!" I think it was me.

Yep, we north of the 49th parallel are said to be a reserved society of people who do not wave our banner high.

Not so on Canada Day, eh!

~Molly O'Connor
North Gower, ON

53

Chicken Soup for the Soul

Beyond Beer

There is a Canadian culture that is in some ways unique to Canada,
but I don't think Canadian culture coincides neatly with borders.
~Stephen Harper

"Since you're Canadian, you should fit right in," my Czech driver announced. "We like hockey and beer, just like you guys."

I winced and paused with my hand on the car door. A gust of cold wind rushed in. "Actually, I don't like any of those things," I confessed.

Carl turned to look me over, concern creasing his young brow.

I smiled wanly. "Is that going to be a problem?"

I'd taken a leave of absence from Canada to teach at a language school in Prague, and my new employer had sent Carl to pick me up at the airport. I was hoping for cultural immersion, but living abroad was like walking through a room filled with circus mirrors. I was constantly faced with everyone else's perceptions of what a Canadian looks like.

"Is it true that you have six months of winter?" "Canadians are so nice. They're so easygoing." "Has a moose ever crossed through your backyard?" "There is no Canadian cuisine, is there? You just eat everything."

Apparently then, we are happy creatures who lumber through the snow foraging indiscriminately for anything that looks edible. No wonder we make good travellers.

I tried to draw a less Palaeolithic-sounding national portrait, but I couldn't even fall back on our most cherished national symbols. As a child, I had always heard that nobody does autumn like Canada. Yet I saw hundreds of red maple leafs, our most recognizable ambassadors, lying wantonly on the Czech ground, apparently unconcerned about diluting our national identity. What next? A beaver on Czech currency?

As the trees began to lose their covering, so did I. The old hand-me-downs didn't fit anymore, and by spring, I had to update my national wardrobe, especially when it came to holidays. Easter scrambled our national identity the most.

My Canadian colleagues and I decided to invite a few of our adult students over for Easter brunch at our friend Dennis's apartment. Perhaps our species would seem less strange at this close range. As the teachers and hosts, we provided several courses of food that we might have eaten at home. While reaching for another hardboiled egg, my student Miroslav hypothesized, "Back home in your country, everyone is having eggs for Easter Sunday today, yes?"

My Greek-Canadian colleague, Nick, corrected him. "Actually, it's not our Easter yet."

"Canada celebrates Easter on a different day than us?" asked Miroslav.

"Well, my family does," explained Nick, "but they're Greek."

"But I was asking about Canada, not Greece," said Miroslav.

"Well, my family doesn't celebrate today either, and I'm not Greek. If I were home, I'd be asking for Easter Day off next week," added Nathalie, my Romanian-Canadian colleague.

"Does anyone in Canada actually celebrate Easter today?" asked Miroslav, desperate for cultural enlightenment.

"Oh sure, lots of people do," I answered, trying to smooth over the semblance of national incoherence. "My aunts make this wonderfully fluffy Easter bread."

"Oh, so Canadians also have a special bread for Easter, like us," said Ivanka, one of our other Czech guests.

"Well, Linda's family does. They're Eastern European. Mine

are more into ham with maple syrup," explained Marie, a French-Canadian colleague.

"Yeah, we like Easter ham on the Rock too," announced Tim, who was from the Maritimes.

"You cook on a hot rock?" Ivanka's eyebrows grazed her hairline.

"No," laughed Tim. "That's just a nickname for Newfoundland."

"What about the Easter Bunny?" asked Ivanka. "Where did that idea come from?"

"Uh, the chocolate companies?" suggested Susan, my English-Canadian colleague. "Actually, my family organizes an Easter egg hunt, for the kids, and we pretend that the Easter bunny hid the eggs. Of course, some years there's still snow on the ground, so that complicates the hunt."

"We'd be painting, not hiding the eggs today," I added.

"Oh, we do that too," Ivanka said hopefully.

"Actually we'd be breaking ours," said Nick. "I mean, you're supposed to tap your hardboiled egg against another guest's egg until one of them breaks."

"Are you sure that you're all from the same country?" asked Miroslav, wide-eyed. "What do you actually have in common?"

We paused, forks at half-mast. There is nothing like an attack on our borders to unite Canadians. Ivanka tried to tame the silence. "It's probably the love of nature, of the outdoors, of the mountains..."

"Actually, I'm from Saskatchewan," Dennis explained. "Flat as this table."

"I feel parched when I don't see hills and trees. I'm so glad that we have a mountain in the middle of downtown Montreal," I said.

In an attempt to bring the provinces together, Dennis cleared his throat. "That's just it! We're as different as our landscapes, but the country is big enough to hold all of them."

"It's big enough that we can give each other space to be different," I added. "Maybe that's what many of us have in common. We think it's important to protect those differences."

"Well, your Christmas party should be interesting," said Miroslav. "You do all celebrate it on December 25?"

"Actually,… never mind, we'll talk again next winter," suggested Nick.

~Linda Handiak
Montreal, QB

54

Cops and Mummers

Tradition does not mean that the living are dead,
it means that the dead are living.
~Harold Macmillan

Christmas traditions can vary depending upon where you live. On the west coast of Newfoundland, traditions are pretty much the same as anywhere else, with one minor exception. There's this thing called "Mummering" that up until the time I was ten years old, I'd never even heard of. My Irish mother grew up with this strange tradition in a small village on the east coast of Newfoundland. But I remember the night I discovered mummering had begun to spread to the west coast of the island.

Mummering consisted of adults dressing in costumes on Christmas night, covering their faces and going from door to door visiting neighbours. At each house they were welcomed to enjoy a drink of Christmas cheer, play a few tunes, perhaps dance a few jigs, and have the people who lived there try and guess who they were. I'm sure it was great fun for the adults! However to me, a ten-year-old with a vivid imagination, an encounter with adults completely disguised at Christmastime was an experience I'd never forget!

That year, our family of nine had shared the usual warm family traditions, from finding the perfect Christmas tree, to mother's annual reading of *The Night Before Christmas*, to finally waking up on Christmas morning and discovering Santa had once again surprised us with presents. Although we didn't usually get all of the things we wanted, there were seven of us children and Santa was a busy man, so we were happy with whatever we got. After all there were millions of children in the world so how could everyone get exactly what they asked for anyway?

Mom and Dad always spent Christmas Eve and Christmas Day at home with us, but after supper in the evening on Christmas Day they took a little time for themselves, visiting friends to play cards and perhaps enjoy a few seasonal spirits. My oldest sister, who would have been sixteen at the time, usually remained at home to babysit.

But that year, my sister wanted to visit her friends, so Mom and Dad left my other sister, who was two years older than me, in charge. We spent the evening playing with our games and things from Santa, but around 9:30 my sister tried to make us go to bed. The younger ones listened to her and went off to their beds, but my brother and I decided to defy her and stay up. After all, she was only two years older than me!

It was around ten o'clock when I heard a car door slamming outside our house. Since we lived at the end of a quiet lane on the outskirts of town, there was very little traffic on that dirt road, especially in wintertime. As it was much too late for Christmas visitors, I stood at the living room window, wiping frost off the pane, straining to see who could possibly be coming to our house at that hour.

It wasn't until the two very tall figures reached the stairs leading up to our front door that I was finally able to clearly see who was coming. Fear sent shivers down my spine as I jumped back from the window. In a voice choked with fear I said, "There's a mummy and a zombie coming up the steps."

Laughing, my sister pushed past me to look out the window. Her face turned completely ashen, and she fled the room as fast as her feet could carry her, hiding under the bed in our bedroom. So much for her being in charge of things! Meanwhile, my little brother ran into the kitchen, grabbed the bread knife off the sideboard and hid behind a big chair in the living room, carefully staying out of sight.

Thump, thump, clump, the footsteps drew ever nearer, while I stood there alone, frozen with fear, unable to run. The telephone was on a little table right next to the front door, the fairly thin directory beneath it. Grabbing the phone and directory, I did the only thing I could do. Hiding next to my brother behind the chair, I looked up the number of the local RCMP station.

By this time the monsters had reached the door and were banging on it, turning the knob back and forth. I knew at any moment they were going to get in and we'd all be dead! The phone at the police station only rang once. "Sir, there are two very big scary creatures at our door, and they're trying to get in and kill us."

The officer on duty was a good friend and hunting buddy of my father, and when he identified himself and asked for my name, intense relief washed over me at his familiar voice. "Are your mother and father home?" he asked.

"No, they're playing cards at Mr. and Mrs. White's house," I said, my throat constricted with abject terror.

"Listen to me now. Don't open the door," he said. "Stay where you are and we'll be right there." Hanging up the phone, I silently said the Our Father and Hail Mary over and over again, praying God wouldn't let those monsters get in the house.

After what seemed like an eternity of knocking and shuffling outside the door, we finally heard the sirens and saw the blue and red flashing lights on the living room ceiling. That was when the uninvited guests started slowly retreating down the stairs.

Unbelievable relief washed over me! We were safe and the monsters were going to jail. For a split second I imagined the ghouls overtaking the police and then coming back for us because we called the cops in the first place. But sneaking over to the window, I watched the two RCMP officers talking to the strangers.

And then the strangers removed their masks and I stared openmouthed at two of my parents' best friends. Wanting to surprise my mother with a little touch of her east coast tradition, the two mummers had promised my dad they'd stop by that evening. Apparently Dad forgot!

Needless to say, I didn't get into any trouble for calling the cops on the mummers that night, but that was the last time mummers came to our house at Christmastime!

~Annabel Sheila
Moncton, NB

Thanks, Canadian Style

Small cheer and great welcome makes a merry feast.
~William Shakespeare

I was born and raised in Vancouver, but I have lived in Seattle, Washington, for more than forty years. During that time my American husband and I have made many trips through the Peace Arch border crossing. He learned early on that chesterfields were sofas and serviettes were napkins and that Hockey Night in Canada was as important as Monday Night Football in the U.S.

But there was one time he forgot an important Canadian tradition.

It was a cold, rainy autumn day as he drove home from one of his weekly trips to visit my mother in the hospital in Vancouver. Widowed, alone, and recovering from a string of surgeries, her prognosis was not good. In order to monitor her progress and keep things running with our family at home, the two of us alternated trips to stay with her, switching mid-week.

As he headed south from Vancouver, traffic was light. He was surprised to see his usual fast food stop closed. Hungry and with two hours of driving still ahead, he took one of the last exits before the border. A billboard directed him to a restaurant in White Rock where he assumed the nearly full parking lot meant great food. Inside, customers in heavy coats, carrying dripping umbrellas, lined up waiting for tables.

A smiling, middle-aged woman with a clipboard gently pushed through the crowd toward him. "How many in your party, sir?"

When he said "one," her expression changed.

"Sure thing, dear." She touched his arm, flashing a concerned look, then whisked him to the front of the line. "We'll get you seated right away."

Two minutes later she returned and led him to the far end of the restaurant where a man in a dark suit was setting a small table for one. The man pulled out a chair and said, "Welcome. Glad you joined us today."

"Thanks." My hubby returned his smile and sat down. Surprised by the amazing service, he chalked it up to the kind of Canadian friendliness and efficiency I always bragged about.

The woman handed him a menu. "You'll probably want one of these specials at the top of the sheet. Your waitress will be right with you."

Later, he told me his taste buds were primed for a burger until the savoury aroma from the platters of turkey and mashed potatoes with gravy coming out of the kitchen made his mouth water. He said he had no choice but to order the Gobbler Special.

The waitress hovered, refilling his coffee cup regularly. Over the din of clattering silverware and loud voices, she went out of her way to make conversation. "Quite a crowd today. It looks like the weather's going to break soon."

While he waited, he was struck by the sight of so many large groups, mostly families, sharing a meal in the late afternoon. During our months of constant commuting, the days of the week were blurring together. He checked his watch to make sure it was Monday and not Sunday.

When his turkey dinner arrived, it was as exceptional as the service. He ate every morsel and had just pushed his plate away when the attentive waitress surprised him with a jumbo slice of pumpkin pie piled high with whipped cream. "This is from your neighbours." She pointed to the next table.

He turned to the group of friendly faces across the aisle. A young woman with a toddler on her lap leaned over. "We just wanted to share some Thanksgiving cheer. You looked lonely over there."

"Oh... yes... thank you." After their kindness, he told me, he wasn't about to confess that he'd forgotten their traditional holiday. Although already full, he managed to stuff down dessert. He bid his new friends farewell and paid the bill at the counter. As he made his way through the crowd still waiting to be seated, he realized how pitiful he must have looked, all alone on Canadian Thanksgiving.

Six weeks later, in late November, my mother was out of the hospital and well enough to travel. My dear husband drove to Vancouver and brought her back the same day. We had so much to give thanks for that year when we celebrated American Thanksgiving south of the border.

~Maureen Rogers
Canadian living in Lake Forest Park, WA, USA

56

The Magic
of the Calgary Stampede

Life is a festival only to the wise.
~Ralph Waldo Emerson

There's something magical about the Calgary Stampede. I stand at the gates, waiting to enter with my daughter, and marvelling at the crowds that swell around me. It's only 8 a.m. on a Wednesday morning but the area is alive with excitement. The sidewalk is littered with strollers and impatient children. I can already smell the sweet sizzle of sausage, pancakes and maple syrup.

My daughter tugs at my hand. It's our turn through the gates. Children are free and I have a coupon I clipped from a case of pop so I can get in for free as well. Gotta love Stampede. Did you know that everyone in the City of Calgary basically shuts down for the ten days of the greatest outdoor show on earth, shucks off their suits and replaces their ties with cowboy hats? Every day, whether it's at a mall or recreation centre, there is a free pancake breakfast that mothers love to drag their children to and entertainment you can't even imagine in the evenings.

Clowns flow through the crowds of children and hand out balloons. My daughter wants a red one. With a wink, a daisy-covered clown bends down and gently ties a string around her wrist. I smile a thank you and try to follow my daughter through the bodies as we approach the sounds ahead of us.

The DoodleBops are playing today. Their song "Words, Words, Words!" is playing over the speakers. The closer we get to the stage the faster my daughter walks. She's wearing the pink cowboy boots that we found at a garage sale and I'm worried she'll trip, but there's no way I can get her to slow down. Her whole body is jumping from anticipation. She's been waiting for this day since the spring when I found out her favourite singing group would be here. Her squeals of excitement that day were enough to wake the neighbours, I swear.

Can I share a secret? I'm a little excited as well. A nervous flutter settles in my stomach. Yes, I know, it's a group of adults who dance and sing to toddlers, but still. I watch these three every single morning. I know their songs inside and out and even find myself talking out loud to them when they ask questions.

What I love the most though? Knowing that if I lived anywhere else in Canada, I might not have this opportunity to make my daughter's young dream come true. Anywhere else we'd be paying an arm and a leg to get in to see their concert. But here, in Calgary, where even the low-income families can partake in the Stampede, I can take her to see them for free. And eat pancakes.

There is a covered wagon located close to the stage where they are flipping the pancakes. The concert won't start for another hour, so we have plenty of time to eat our fill. I glance around me and refuse to wipe the silly grin off my face. If only you could see all the cowboy hats that dot the scene. All in various sizes and colors, but primarily white cowboy hats—a trademark of being a Calgarian cowboy (or girl in my case). I bite my lip as I look down at my daughter's upturned face. She wanted a hat, but things have been a little tight and I couldn't find one for her. So we opted for pigtails and a bandana around her neck. I know she's about to ask me for a hat. I can see the words form on her lips. Today is a magical day for her and the last thing I want to do is take away a little bit of that magic. But, just as I start to remind her she still looks like a cowgirl a hand lands on my shoulder.

It's the mayor of Calgary. And in his hands are two white hats. I glance behind him. There's a crowd of people following him who are also handing out hats, but here, in front of me, is the mayor himself. I'm tongue-tied and embarrassed. Yet he only smiles at me as he holds out the two hats. With a small nod of my head and a shy smile I reach out to take his gift, only to find one of the hats snatched away.

My daughter, not shy at all, has grabbed one of the hats and plunked it on her head. I shake my head and laugh. The mayor bends down to look my daughter in the eye and whisper words I know she'll never forget.

"Now you are a real cowgirl."

Did I mention today was a magical day in Calgary?

~Steena Holmes
Calgary, AB

57

The Secret of the Cedar Chest

Good as it is to inherit a library, it is better to collect one.
~Augustine Birrell

For many years I've kept my guilt regarding the cedar chest a secret. I felt deeply ashamed of the lack of self-control that led to my infamous behaviour. However, this Christmas I've decided enough time has elapsed (the statue of limitations on such crimes must have expired) that I can now confess.

To begin, I must admit to being an incurable bookaholic. I always have been. In fact, one of my earliest memories is of standing behind my mother as she washed the lunch dishes at the kitchen sink, a book in one hand, pulling on her apron strings with the other as I begged her to read, "just one chapter, please, just one chapter."

My mother contributed to my addiction. I cannot recall her ever refusing to leave the sudsy pan, dry her hands, and follow me to the living room. There, we'd curl up together and while away the afternoon, deep in our love for the printed word. A devoted amateur actress, she read with passionate expression. Carried away on the wings of her words, I would listen mesmerized.

The books I remember best from those days were the works of Thornton W. Burgess. My favourite among his bevy of loquacious animals was Reddy Fox. Reddy frequently outfoxed himself through some small flaw in one of his nefarious schemes.

When I finally learned to read on my own, I experienced one of the greatest epiphanies of my life. There was magic to be found on a printed page. It had the power to sweep me away into another time, another place, another spirit. Words flowed over, around and through me, enthralling me to the core. I read everything from the corn flakes box on our breakfast table to the set of University Encyclopaedias published in 1902 that I discovered in my grandmother's attic. (It wasn't until I looked for the word "airplane" and couldn't find it that I realized the venerable age of this fascinating reading matter.)

While other children hounded their parents for toys, I begged for books, books, and more books. The Christmas season presented the paramount opportunity for my supplications. Each autumn, I began to prepare a long list of titles I'd be delighted to find beneath the festive tree. Since we had no bookstore in our town, the Eaton's catalogue was the only place to purchase these desirable items. Consequently one special Sunday afternoon each November my mother and I would sit at the kitchen table with that lovely, plump book while I selected the books I most desired from the limited selection on the two pages that offered reading materials.

My mother, knowing how I devoured the contents of books the moment they arrived in our home, never let me know when she was picking up the parcel at the post office. And definitely, never where she hid the precious package.

Overwhelmed by my reading affliction, however, I'd become sly and unscrupulous. No book could remain unread anywhere within my ability to ferret it out. Thus, one day the year I was ten and desperate for a good read, I began my quest for her hiding place in earnest.

I dug through closets, into their darkest, most remote corners and topmost shelves. I burrowed under sheets and towels in the linen cupboard, and even checked beneath the mattress in the guest room. Nothing.

Stymied, I followed my mother into my parents' bedroom and sat down on the edge of the bed. I watched as she opened the cedar chest beneath the window. My father had handcrafted it for her on their engagement. She kept her most treasured possessions in it; things like her wedding gown, my christening dress, her collection of hand-embroidered linens and, anathemas to a Reddy Fox fan, a couple of fox fur capes. Their presence had always made me shy away from the cedar chest.

I watched as she folded a pillow slip she'd finished decorating with moss roses. When she bent over the cedar chest to store her handiwork, I started to turn away. I had no desire to see the pelts of those poor, unfortunate foxes.

Then something caught my eyes. Peeking out from beneath a lace table cloth, the top corner of a shiny, new BOOK!

My mother hastily lowered the lid and glanced in my direction. Had I seen it? Struggling to appear nonchalant, I began to hum "We Wish You a Merry Christmas" as I swung my legs against the chenille bedspread, and gazed up at the ceiling. She hesitated, then drew a deep breath and headed out of the room.

"Come along, Gail," she called as she started down the stairs. "We have cookies to bake."

My heart dancing with joy, I skipped along after her. Visions of how I'd invade the cedar chest later when I was alone upstairs waltzed through my head.

That evening after I'd been tucked in bed and my parents were safely settled in the living room listening to Charlie McCarthy and Edgar Bergen on the radio, I slipped my bare feet onto the cold linoleum that covered my bedroom floor and tiptoed across the hall. I carried a small flashlight. My father had given it to me the previous Christmas, in case of power outages, he'd said. He'd never intended it to be used in a book burglary in his own home.

Trembling with the thrill of the forbidden, I eased open the cedar chest, slipped my hand beneath the folded linens, (being careful to avoid those fox furs) and felt them... not the usual two but four, count them four, slick new books, their dust jackets as smooth as silk.

I slid out the topmost volume. My breath caught in my throat as I read its title. *The Secret of Shadow Ranch*! The Nancy Drew mystery for which I'd longed for the past two years and for which Eaton's had always sent a substitution!

Resting my back against the cedar chest, I squatted on the floor, opened the Carolyn Keene classic to page one, adjusted my torch and began to read. Although I wasn't then familiar with the term multitasking, I quickly became adept at it. While I read I had to stay alert for the slightest indication that either of my parents was about to come upstairs.

Oh, the bliss of those stolen moments. My heart hammering, I read Nancy's adventures for over an hour. My bare feet felt like blocks of ice on the cold floor. I shivered in my pyjamas but I continued.

Then I heard my father suggesting a cup of tea before bed. Trembling from the enormity of my crime, I eased open the cedar chest, slid the book gently beneath the table cloths and pillow slips and scuttled back into my own room.

Snuggled beneath the covers, the flashlight still warm in my hand, my overwhelming need for a book satisfied, I drifted off to sleep. Visions of Nancy Drew, Bess, and George riding the range at Shadow Ranch replaced the sugarplums that were supposed to dance through children's heads just before Christmas.

In the hard light of the next morning, I admit I had a few qualms. As I sat at the breakfast table and glanced over at my mother, I knew I was destroying her joy in the big surprise she must be hoping to produce on Christmas morning with that long-sought-after Nancy Drew title. But I was incorrigible. That night, as my parents listened to a Christmas concert broadcast from Halifax on the living room radio, I cautiously opened *The Secret of Shadow Ranch* to Chapter Five and read on.

By the time Christmas Eve arrived, I'd devoured all four books and was contemplating re-reading *Shadow Ranch*. No, I told myself sternly. You'll bend a page, you'll crack the spine. Quit while you're ahead.

My extreme enthusiasm as I unwrapped each book on Christmas morning might have been a tip-off to less trusting parents. Their faces flushed with my reflected delight. Cradling my treasures in my arms,

I curled myself up in a corner of the couch and in the flickering tree lights settled down to indulge myself in a full Christmas morning of re-reading.

My criminal activity continued during the next three Christmas seasons. It might have gone on much longer had I not made a major faux pas in my eagerness to defend the work of my then-favourite author, L. M. Montgomery. I'd read all of the Anne books and had been longing for one of the author's more mature stories entitled *The Blue Castle*. Not an easy book to find, it was proving as elusive as *The Secret of Shadow Ranch*.

But joy of joys! A week before Christmas it appeared in the cedar chest. Reading it by the light of my torch, I thrilled to the courage of heroine Valancy Stirling and identified with her need for freedom and self-expression. It was so romantic, the ending absolutely wonderful. When I finished reading two days before Christmas, I hugged it in the darkness beside the cedar chest.

On Christmas morning a bevy of relatives descended on our home. It was my parents' turn to host the Yuletide dinner. One of my maternal aunts wandered into the living room as she waited for the meal to be served and found me in my usual reading corner of the couch, absorbed in *The Blue Castle*.

"Well, Gail, I see you got another book," she sighed in mild exasperation. Not book-addicted, she couldn't understand my fascination.

"Yes, a perfectly lovely book." I put my finger between the pages of the first chapter to mark my place and beamed up at her.

"Another novel, no doubt," she scoffed sitting down opposite me. "I never read anything but the newspaper myself. Those things are nothing but nonsense."

"Oh no they aren't!" I couldn't bear to hear my beloved books defamed. "This one is about a girl who leaves home to nurse a sick friend and falls in love with the town outcast. Later she discovers he's really a millionaire, they get married and live happily ever after."

"Do they now?" I turned to see my mother standing in the living room doorway. My finger slipped from its place at page six.

Her lips curled up into a smile, she winked and turned back into the kitchen.

My mother died three Christmases later, a victim of cancer. Her legacy to my love of literature, however, lives on in my heart and home. Thornton Burgess's *The Adventures of Reddy Fox* and *The Secret of Shadow Ranch* remain beloved parts of my library. *The Blue Castle* occupies a place of honour beside the family Bible.

As for the cedar chest, filled with family photos, it sits in my living room, symbolic of those happy Christmases when a book could make my dreams come true and a mother who understood.

~Gail MacMillan
Bathurst, NB

58

Has the Game Started Yet?

Half the game is mental; the other half is being mental.
~Jim McKenny

"Has the game started yet?" That question was commonly heard echoing through the halls of our suburban Toronto house on Saturday nights shortly after my father and I returned from church meetings. You see, Saturday night during hockey season was Hockey Night in Canada at our house. My poor mother always found herself banished to her small sitting room to watch the old black and white movies on PBS while my dad and I took over the entire family room to watch our beloved Toronto Maple Leafs compete to hopefully make it to the playoffs and then have the chance to win the highly coveted Stanley Cup. Alas, the last time the Maple Leafs won the Cup known to most sports fanatics as "Lord Stanley's Mug" was in 1967... the year before I was born.

The play-by-play was usually called by long-time announcer Bob Cole, along with his color commentator Harry Neale. Now, although Bob Cole was the best hockey announcer in the business, my dad and I were pretty good at announcing the plays ourselves... or I should say, yelling plays at the TV ourselves. My dad would often say, "Pass the puck!" while I could be heard yelling "Come on guys; get out of your zone!" The loudest noise that shook the very walls of the house always came from the victory cries we joined Bob in when the Leafs got a goal and he would announce, "SCORE!"

Even after the first period was over, we remained glued to the

TV set to watch the incredibly popular and ever entertaining first intermission segment called "Coach's Corner" with Don Cherry and Ron McLean. We waited with eager anticipation to see what flamboyant suit Don (a former coach of the Boston Bruins) would come out wearing and what issue he was going to target. In spite of his outspoken manner, Don was a staunch Canadian patriot who was known to call the Russian hockey team "those darn Ruskies." As Don's sidekick, Ron more or less spent most of the segment listening attentively to Don's ranting and raving, occasionally injecting his own opinion (if he was lucky!). Ron would always end the show with a comical line that would even leave Don shaking his head at a loss for words. One of the funniest endings was when Ron said, "Well, there you have it, from the coach who would yell behind the bench... and in front of it too, we end tonight's segment of the Coach's Corner."

Anyone who has attended a hockey game will tell you about the chaos and running around that takes place at intermission time to get something to eat. This was no different during the intermission periods at our house. My father and I would scurry about the kitchen to find something to eat before the next period was set to begin. It was also the only time my mother was invited to leave the solace of her room and come help us find something to eat.... or make something for us if we implored her to. With plates of food in our hands, back to the TV we went.

A nervous anticipation would creep over us as each period progressed to the final minutes of the third period... particularly if the Leafs were up by a goal or two. A sudden rush of relief and exhilaration would descend over the room when the final seconds ticked away and the Leaf players surrounded the goalie for a victory hug when the game was won.

The only time we ever missed watching Hockey Night in Canada was the one time I had the good fortune of "scoring" two tickets to a game from a media representative I worked with during my days as a media buyer for an advertising agency. I took my father, and will never forget the wonderfully anxious feeling that surged through us as we walked up to the "shrine of hockey" known as Maple Leaf

Gardens and looked at the building with our own eyes. It is a common tradition for native Torontonians to actually kiss the side of Maple Leaf Gardens when they see it, and my father and I were no exception to this rule. We paid our homage and kissed the closest brick wall before going in to soak up the electric atmosphere of the arena inside. Once we arrived at our seats, we looked at each other and all we could say was, "Wow! We are actually here!"

We found that watching a game live was not much different from watching it on TV, except that there were no commercials. I could still hear Bob Cole's voice in my head calling the play-by-play and I would say the exact same things watching the game live as I would watching it at home. I also experienced the same relief and exhilaration at the end of the game when the Leafs won the game.

The one amazing thing about watching a hockey game at home is how simple it is to please a hockey fan; all that is usually required is a TV (the bigger the screen the better!), a comfy chair, and a plate of food with a beer or two to wash it all down! And while most sports bars will accommodate every hockey fan's needs if they can't get to watch a game in person; most hockey fans will admit that watching a game in the comfort of their own homes is the way to go!

I'm much older now; and even though I live in the United States, I have not lost my love of the sport forever known as "Canada's national sport." It becomes engrained in the life of every Canadian no matter where their path in life takes them.

When people ask me if I'm a hockey fan, I always answer, "Of course I am... the Canadian government will revoke my passport if I'm not!"

~Mike Rumble
Canadian living in Raleigh, NC, USA

Chapter
8

O Canada

Summer Memories

Ah, summer, what power you have to make us suffer and like it.

~Russell Baker

A Small-Town Kid with a Big-Town Dream

Fishing provides that connection with the whole living world.
It gives you the opportunity of being totally immersed, turning back into
yourself in a good way. A form of meditation, some form of communion with
levels of yourself that are deeper than the ordinary self.
~Ted Hughes

I just wanted to get out of my small hometown when I was younger. And I did. At eighteen I was drafted in the first round by the Colorado Avalanche—my childhood dream team. Denver is great. It's a bigger version of Haliburton County, with picturesque scenery and pick-up trucks, and country music—all the things I like—but it's not where I'm from.

Now, I can't wait to go back to my small town during breaks and over the summer. This is where my roots are and it is where I go to recharge.

Going back home, I get to relax, take time out after the hockey season. Fishing offers that relaxation. And it's the most beneficial thing for me to do in the whole world. With so much pressure in professional hockey, you can stress yourself out. But there's no pressure, no stress in the fishing boat.

Like the other day. After my morning workout, I met one of my buddies at his hunting camp in the northern part of the county. We put a boat on the roof, threw in gear and drove up to a secluded lake with just two houses on it. To get to it, we had to carry the boat up a hill and back down a hill. That was another excellent workout. We put the boat in, paddled out and fished. On lakes like that, it's just you and the lake and the fish. It's awesome.

We fished for bass for a while and made out pretty well—caught sixteen fish! We called it a day there and made our way back, carrying the boat up and down the hill again. By that point, we were drenched in sweat. But it's worth it to get to a lake like that. My buddy and I drove back to his hunting camp and fished a lake there for rainbow trout. I texted another buddy and we went back out for some walleye later that night. I got to fish for three species in three lakes in one day! It doesn't get much better than that.

With days like that, I realize how much I miss fishing when I'm not home in Haliburton. Don't get me wrong, I love playing hockey. Hockey's my life. It's what I always wanted to do and what I am doing. But I get better at hockey and at life by sitting in the boat with a line in the water. It's meditation for me. Sitting there fishing, I can visualize what I'm going to do in the next season. Fishing is so simple. I can sit there, think, put things in their place. Whatever's weighing on my mind, I realize I can do it, I can get through this, I can accomplish that. Everything seems to come more easily.

Haliburton is where I can always be myself too. As a professional hockey player, I always have to be diplomatic and there's a small range of emotion I can show. But with my buddies, I can just be myself. I can be the way I was growing up. That's huge for me. I can get excited about a big fish. My dad says I'm like a six-year-old, I get so excited. And I can show I'm disappointed about the one that got away. With the media, though, I have to put on a face. That is why I want to come home every summer. I get to be Matt again.

I was worried at first about coming home after the hockey season. Haliburton is a hockey-crazy county. But everyone is used to seeing me in town. People let me be me and don't stop me. During the summer months, when the population quadruples with all the cottage-goers, I typically don't go into town anyway. You can't find a parking space in town, and I'm home to get away from the craziness, not dive back into it.

The best part of being home for the summer is the week my family and I spend at Redstone Lake. It's one of 600 in the county and only about a half hour away from our house, but it's my favourite place in the world. It's paradise.

I grew up at that lake. My family never bought a cottage—our time and money went to hockey—but we rented a cottage there for a week every summer. My parents have home videos of me and my sister Jessica up there running around when I was five and she was one. And we still go every summer.

I really believe in going back to my roots. You appreciate the little things that made you who you are. Haliburton is a big factor in that. Growing up, I saw our small community do great things. People really help each other, because in a small town like Haliburton, it's tough. There isn't a large economic base and if it wasn't for the cottage market, the town would be smaller. So fundraisers are huge.

I help whenever I can. At home, I've spoken at different events. And even when I'm not, I can give signed jerseys to fundraisers for raffles. I order a lot of extra jerseys from Reebok and I sign them and donate them to be auctioned off.

One particular effort in Haliburton really stuck with me. A few years ago, a local boy, Dawson Hamilton, was diagnosed with cancer. He was five. His parents were having a tough time making ends meet. They were always in Toronto at the SickKids hospital so it was hard for them to hold jobs. Our community had fundraisers for the family, and I participated in many of them.

I really connected with the family. Dawson had watched me play when I was in the Ontario Hockey League and he came to my first NHL game in Toronto. But in January 2010, he got a lung virus. He couldn't fight it off, and died. He was almost ten. I was in Denver at the time, and flew back for the day to go to his funeral. There was an open casket but no one would let me near it. I found out later that Dawson had asked to be buried in my jersey and everyone thought it would be too hard for me to see that. You don't really realize how much of an impact you have until something like that happens.

I have Dawson's initials on all my hockey sticks. It's a reminder of my hometown, where everyone pitches in to help out their neighbours. It also reminds me of the strength and courage of a little boy from Haliburton County who loved hockey as much as I do.

I want to stay involved in my community. I had a great time coaching the high school hockey team during the Olympic break in 2010. Some of my best memories are of playing high school hockey for the HHSS Red Hawks. And if a kid in the area is working toward something, I like to spread the word. I want to keep those small-town dreams alive because I was a small-town kid with a big-town dream. And I still am.

~Matt Duchene
Haliburton, ON

59

Cottage Life

Then followed that beautiful season... Summer...
Filled was the air with a dreamy and magical light; and the landscape
Lay as if new created in all the freshness of childhood.
~Henry Wadsworth Longfellow

Each year opening up the cottage is an adventure. As we drive onto our property, we're alert for any changes that have occurred during our six months' absence. A new cedar has popped up in the hedge. And just look at the holes a Pileated Woodpecker has made in the dead tree by the gate. There appears to be a fresh crop of squirrels and chipmunks, too. The roof looks good, husband Ron acknowledges pragmatically, while I'm more concerned with seeing if the tulips I planted last October have poked through the earth by the front step.

Then, with the turn of a key, we open a place that has lain fallow all winter. It's as if time has been on pause since we left last fall. Nothing has changed except the atmosphere. Dark and silent and chilly inside, the cottage needs to be awakened from the months of winter dormancy. I hurry to pull up blinds and open windows.

Renewed life and spring flood in as Ron turns on the electricity and the refrigerator begins to purr. Dust and cobwebs stir in the breeze as I peer about for evidence of a mouse or squirrel invasion. It wouldn't be the first time the cottage hosted a rodent family.

Thirty years ago we'd desperately wanted a place in the country (Tabusintac in northeastern New Brunswick, to be exact). But we had three children under the age of five, financially crippling student loans, and little more than the clothes on our backs and a secondhand Volkswagen Beetle as assets. We had exactly one hundred dollars with which to purchase land and building, so our dream of owning a rustic retreat seemed destined to remain in the realm of wishful thinking.

Then Ron discovered a small, abandoned cabin in the woods. Even though its windows had long ago been broken, its door sagged inward on a single hinge, and numerous squirrels, birds, and a raccoon couple were in residence, it appeared structurally sound. It definitely had potential. Ron quickly offered the owner half of our vacation home money for it. Totally amazed that anyone would want it, she readily accepted.

Next Ron convinced a kindly neighbour to pull the little shack out of its isolation and down to the corner of a hayfield we'd managed to purchase with the remainder of our cottage fund. (Later we'd expand to include shorefront in our domain but this was a beginning.) I can't say I was overjoyed when I saw it, but it was the best we could afford and, as Ron had said, it had potential. Or at least four walls and a roof.

While Ron fixed the windows and door, I tried to sweep and scrub away the evidence of its former tenants. Then we moved in, with no electricity and definitely no indoor plumbing. An outhouse we'd salvaged from the local garbage dump became our toilet. All five of us participated in carrying water from a spring one quarter of a mile away.

Keeping up with our demand for water required constant and unflagging teamwork. Three or more times a day we took buckets and pots and headed off in a group. Steve, the smallest, carried a teakettle.

Our neighbours were astonished that we could live under such conditions. The hippie era was drawing to a close and they must have regarded us as its last remnants.

The kids didn't care what anyone thought or how minimally we lived. They loved being able to run free in the hayfields and trees that surrounded our summer home. Each spring, as the school year drew to a close, their anticipation mounted. They got busy planning new activities and adventures and reminiscing about the previous summers' fun. They couldn't wait to get back to the cottage. For them, the joys of country living far outweighed the lack of amenities.

Ron and I were also eager to head back to the country. We loved the freedom from all but family responsibilities that life at the cottage offered. We regarded the lack of a telephone as an asset.

Then "C" day would arrive. We'd pile a summer's supply of clothing, blankets, and books into the Volkswagen and squeeze the kids and our two dogs (a Beagle named Brandy and an eighty-pound Labrador Retriever named Jet) into the back seat. Finally, with a smile in our hearts and a song on our lips, we were off.

The first meal at the cottage traditionally had to be wieners and marshmallows roasted over the old charcoal burning hibachi we'd pull out from under the front steps. And no matter how blackened the food became in the cooking process, it always tasted like haute cuisine.

As darkness fell, we'd slather ourselves with insect repellent and huddle around the hibachi that we turned into a smudge pot by adding handfuls of green grass. Then we'd listen to the frogs' medley in the magic country quiet and watch the stars appear in the soft black velvet that was the night sky.

"Look! There's the Big Dipper!"

"I see the North Star!"

In the warm, gentle darkness, we'd gaze upward and find (or at least believe we'd found) the various constellations.

Days at the cottage were never dull, either. Without television and toys, Joan, Carol, and Steve had to use their imaginations and what they could find outdoors to amuse themselves. They made swings in the trees using discarded tires and rope, rafts for the river from driftwood they found along the shore. These skills would prove valuable in adult life when their jobs required them to come up with fresh ideas.

They were enthralled with the birds and animals that lived in the forest and fields and on the riverbanks, and they developed a deep and lasting respect for all wildlife and its habitat. This fascination inspired Ron and I to teach them to appreciate the environment that supported these creatures and ultimately, ourselves. We explained the evils of littering, the necessity of obeying the golden rule of camping—"Pack out what you pack in and leave only footprints behind"—and how wild flowers and creatures should be enjoyed and left in peace in their natural setting. They listened attentively, then applied our advice in their daily rambles.

They discovered the succulence of blueberries, raspberries, and the tiny wild strawberries that grew in profusion behind the cottage. After we'd assured them that it was okay to pick and eat these tasty treats, they quickly developed their own harvesting philosophies. Joan picked and ate. Carol, destined to become a chartered accountant, picked and saved. Steve watched his sisters for a while, then did what he considered the best of both methods. He ate some and saved others.

Their quest for berries took them farther and farther afield. One day in their wanderings they discovered the ruins of an old hunting lodge. It quickly became the centre of many of their games. Like three small musketeers, with two dogs trailing at their heels, they made and shared summer adventures and projects. Isolated from other children, they formed deep and enduring bonds. They even devised coded nicknames for each other that still fondly surface whenever they're together.

Last year, when someone commented to Carol that the movie *The Blair Witch Project* was frightening because of its forest setting, she was amazed.

"When we were kids at the cottage, the woods were a wonderful, happy place," she said. "We'd take a pillow, a blanket, a Nancy Drew book and go there to read. We always felt perfectly safe and content there. I can't imagine anyone thinking it's a scary place."

Evenings were definitely family times. We'd often explore trails in the nearby woods, hoping to see bird and animal life, then return home pleasantly tired and ready for bed. We also invented a unique after-supper game of hide-and-seek. Ron and I would hold the dogs while the kids darted across the field and into the woods to hide in the trees beyond it. Then we'd release Brandy and Jet to seek them out.

It was never much of a chore for the Beagle, given his innate scenting abilities. Jet usually just lumbered good-naturedly along behind him, confident in his canine buddy's skill. The bottom line was all seven participants enjoyed the game immensely.

One summer Ron purchased a second-hand sixteen-foot outboard motor boat. At first we were ecstatic at the possibilities this new mode of transportation offered. Soon, however, our enthusiasm was tempered as we discovered the old boat had a propensity for breaking down.

Undeterred, we christened the cantankerous vessel the good ship Undependable and adapted to her idiosyncrasies. We learned not to venture too far or too deep and accepted the frequent necessity of towing her home as we waded through the shallows. Once again, it was a family effort with only the dogs remaining aboard to act as Master and First Mate.

These occasions, although at times mildly aggravating, quickly fell into the realm of just another adventure of the Canadian Family MacMillan. They became the stuff familial legends are based upon and taught the kids the importance of maintaining one's sense of humour and sticking together in adversity.

As the years passed, the cottage expanded and got electricity and indoor plumbing.

We celebrated when the first light bulb clicked on, shouted as if we'd hit oil when the first water spouted from the hole in the yard, and happily slept on a plank floor on the first night after two new bedrooms had been added. The cottage was maturing.

But so, of course, were the children. During their teen and college years, the cottage fell largely fallow. With friends and part-time jobs monopolizing their waking hours, they lost interest in country life. Ron and I, not willing to leave them at home unsupervised, didn't get many opportunities to enjoy its rural charms, either.

Sometimes during the brief visits Ron and I would make to check on the old place, I sensed a certain sadness within its walls. Looking out a rear window I saw, in memory, three small, sturdy, sun-browned figures in shorts and T-shirts running barefoot across the field, laughing in pure delight, a Beagle and a Labrador Retriever galloping after them.

The vision brought the sting of tears to my eyes, a lump to my throat. The days were long gone when the old cottage's board walls had echoed with the whoops of children's exuberance and its screen door had slammed multiple times a day on their comings and goings. Now it sat quiet and subdued in the shade of the trees we'd planted with the youngsters so many years ago.

Then, suddenly it seemed, all three offspring were on their own, working, getting married, having kids of their own. Ron and I returned to the cottage, alone except for a new pair of dogs. Forced to accept the emptiness of our nest, we'd decided to turn the cottage into our retirement retreat and began to renovate.

We put in a basement, new plumbing and electrical wiring, added a large deck and a gazebo. Phones, televisions, and even a computer took up residence. The cottage was adapting to the twenty-first century.

Then the kids started returning, fond memories of a happy childhood drawing them back. They brought friends and partners. Our backyard sprouted tents and other camping paraphernalia.

They visited their old haunts and were amazed at how high up in the branches their old tire swings dangled. Trees, like children, grow a lot in fifteen years.

And if I'd once feared the cottage would miss the patter of small feet up its steps and across its old board floors, that problem, too, has been remedied. Last summer Daniel Wilson MacMillan, our first grandchild, arrived at the cottage. His daddy Steve pushed him proudly about in his stroller, showing him where he'd played as a little boy and although Daniel is still too young to grasp the significance of what his father is telling him, I know that someday he will understand.

Later when he splashed about happily as his mom Michele gave him a bath in the kitchen sink, his giggles told me the cottage had come full circle. A new generation of MacMillans has been woven into the fabric that is our family and the little shack from the backwoods will continue to be a basic thread.

~Gail MacMillan
Bathurst, NB

Fish 'N Fries

Good things come to those who bait.
~Author Unknown

I've always loved to fish. Summer in the Land O' Lakes region of Ontario was a paradise for my eleven-year-old self—except when I had to babysit. My little sister wasn't as keen on fishing as I was.

"C'mon, Laura! Please? I'll use my allowance to buy you some French fries and gravy up at the hotel."

Our small town was a hub of activity for those few summer months when the American tourists rented cabins and boats. Some local entrepreneurs survived all year on the money they made during that time. The hotel restaurant's take-out window did a brisk business.

And my sister loved their French fries.

"Well... okay," Laura said, taking the bait.

I planned to carry the poles and tackle box. Before we left I opened the fridge and grabbed a white paperboard box holding three leftover nightcrawlers. I handed it to Laura.

"Why do I have to carry the worms?"

"Because I said so."

She opened the box. A ripe, earthy scent filled the air. "Smells gross—and the worms look dead."

"It's just dirt," I said. "And they aren't dead; they're just cold from being in the fridge."

We walked the mile and a half into town. The morning was slightly overcast, but warm. A couple of cars passed us going in the opposite direction. The drivers beeped their horns "hello" and we waved.

About midmorning we arrived on the edge of town where a grassy picnic area bordered the lakeshore. I put the tackle box and poles down on a green-painted table. Laura set the worms next to them.

"Can I get my fries now?" she asked.

"We just got here," I answered. "Fishing first—then fries."

She stuck her lip out, pouting. I pretended not to see. I really wanted her to fish. And I wanted her to like it.

I took a worm out and cut it into two pieces with my fingernail. Then I slid a juicy hunk onto each of the two hooks. Laura cast her line out. As she sat down to wait, she knocked a stone loose and it tumbled into the water.

"Be careful! You'll scare the fish away!" I said.

"Bossy," she mumbled.

I put the box of worms down under a maple tree. The sun was beginning to shine a little brighter and I didn't want the nightcrawlers to get baked.

A dull roar hummed nearby and I noticed someone mowing the grass on the far end of the picnic area. I recognized Ronnie by his Montreal Expos cap. Ronnie was a gentle and friendly, but simple man. His beaming smile was well known by everyone in town.

"I think I got one!" Laura yelled. She held the pole out to me.

I didn't take it.

"C'mon!" she said.

"You can do it," I said.

"I can't! You always do this part!"

"You do it! This is the fun part—go ahead."

"I—I think the line stopped going out."

"Just be patient," I said. "The fish is probably..."

"It's going out again!"

"Grab the line with your thumb and stop it."

"It's getting tight!"

"Pull the pole back fast and hook it!"

And, somehow, she did it. Biting her lip so hard I thought it might bleed, she yanked the pole back over her head and set the hook.

"Now reel it in!"

About fifty feet out in the lake, a beautiful blue-green bass jumped high out of the water. It twisted and twirled in the air just like a slow motion shot from one of those weekend fishing shows.

"Keep reeling," I yelled.

A couple of people—tourists, since I didn't recognize them—stopped to watch us pull in the fish.

It was big—five or six pounds. Laura's face flushed red. She staggered as she pulled the fish free of the water. The pearly scales flashed in the hazy sunlight. The tourists clapped as I swung it over on to the shore.

The roar of Ronnie's mower grew louder.

Luckily the bass hadn't swallowed the hook and I removed it easily. Laura brought me the stringer and I slipped it through the gill, the fish's spiny teeth scraping my hand. Securing the stringer with a stick between two large rocks, I let the fish back in the lake so he would stay alive longer.

"I did it," Laura said.

"Yep."

"Can you put another worm on?" she asked.

"I can." I smiled.

First I checked my line. Eaten clean. I'd have to put more worm on it, too.

A loon called out across the lake. Suddenly it seemed very quiet. I looked over at the picnic table. Ronnie was standing under the tree with his cap in his hands. His mower wasn't running.

I hurried to him.

His usually smiling face was troubled.

"What's wrong, Ronnie?" I asked.

He pointed under the tree. The remains of my worm container

lay torn and scattered on the fresh mown grass. My worms had been chopped into tiny mangled pieces. Darn it!

Ronnie looked at me, stricken. "I'm sorry," he said.

"It's okay," I said. "It was an accident. Don't worry, Ronnie. You just go on now."

Hanging his head, Ronnie slowly pushed the lawn mower away.

I knelt down and ran my hand through the grass feeling for pieces of worm. I found only two bits that could be used and carefully threaded them onto our hooks. Within a couple of minutes Laura caught a little perch and I pulled in a fair-sized sunfish.

"Well, that's it," I said, stringing the fish. "Let's go get your fries and we'll come back for these before we head home."

"I'm not hungry," she said.

Not hungry for French fries? "Do you feel sick?"

"No. I just don't want fries."

"How about we get some butter tarts from the store?"

Laura shook her head. "Let's just use the money to get more worms at the bait shop."

"You sure?"

"Yep."

I could hardly believe it—Laura wanted to keep fishing.

So we bought a white paper box filled with a dozen fresh, juicy nightcrawlers. We laughed and talked. And we caught fifteen more keepers before we ran out of room on the stringer. It was a perfect day.

"Sorry you didn't get your fries," I said, packing up.

"It's okay," Laura said. "Sorry I never wanted to go fishing. It was kind of fun today, but… you smell pretty fishy, though."

"So do you." I smiled. "Like seaweed."

As we headed up to the highway, Ronnie came hurrying down from the hotel. He had a white paperboard box in his hand. He held it out to me.

"We're all done fishing, Ronnie," I said. "Why don't you keep them?"

He turned to Laura and offered her the box.

She looked at me. I nodded. She took it.

"Thanks, Ronnie," I said. "Thanks a lot."

He turned and walked away.

Laura opened the box and laughed.

"What's so funny?" I asked.

She handed me the open paperboard box. A delicious, salty smell made my mouth water. It was filled with French fries and gravy.

~Leanne Fanning Pankuch
Canadian living in Aurora, IL, USA

61

Adventure on the Halifax Wharf

I try so hard to live in the moment—I don't think ahead very much.
~Sarah McLachlan

We planned a bus tour of historic Halifax as the culmination of a ten-day Maritime holiday. Already we had seen so many things, taken rolls and rolls of film and made memories to last a lifetime. The day before, en route to our historic hotel, we discovered that navigating old Halifax, with its labyrinth of streets whose names occasionally changed without a change in direction, could prove difficult. That fear of getting lost again, coupled with the excitement of the day ahead, motivated us to finish breakfast early and head to the Halifax Wharf to catch our tour bus. After an uneventful drive we arrived with more than an hour to wait.

The sun shone in a cloudless sky, hinting at the warmth of the late summer day to come. My daughter and I wandered along an almost empty wharf while my husband went in search of a cup of coffee. With so few people enjoying this early Sunday morning hour, no one minded how often I stopped to take photos of the many types of boats anchored along the way. Nothing at home on the prairies could compare to the sights and sounds of the wharf.

Tall-masted ships, fun tour boats and older ships belonging to the Maritime Museum bobbed side by side in the relatively calm water. Then we spied a full-size version of Theodore Tugboat, the main character in a children's TV series that my grandchildren loved to watch. I snapped a few photos before we continued our walk.

As we continued exploring, a group of photographers captured my attention. These gentlemen carried expensive cameras, tripods and light meters. Once in a while they passed close enough to allow me to hear snippets of their conversation. My curiosity was piqued when I heard words like "lighting," "angles" and comments on scenes they planned to shoot. I wondered what they planned to film and when. Would we be able to watch a movie shoot? That would be a fantastic finish to a wonderful holiday.

I pushed these daydreams away as we walked back for a couple more photos of Theodore Tugboat. I positioned my daughter as close to the boat as possible. Just before I snapped the picture, one of the men spoke to me.

"Why don't you let me take a picture of you and your daughter? I'm sure you'd like that." As I turned to hand him my camera, he added a few words that caused me to hesitate. "I do have a condition. Well rather a two-part condition. First are you mother and daughter like we assume you are?" he asked, pointing to the other men carrying all the fancy camera equipment. "Secondly would you be willing to be in a video we are shooting?"

My thoughts rushed. How much time until the bus left? I glanced up and down the wharf hoping to see my husband rush toward us. Us in a video shoot? Now? Really? My face must have betrayed the confusion I felt.

He quickly added further explanation. "We're shooting a documentary about the life and times of Canadian and Maritime singer/songwriter Sarah McLachlan. Right now we're doing some background shots using ordinary people instead of actors. This particular shot requires a mother and young adult daughter to walk along the wharf and across the little bridge just beyond the tugboat. This would portray Sarah meeting her birth mother at this spot."

Before I could reply he added, "You do know who Sarah McLachlan is, don't you?"

"Yes I've heard of her," I replied.

Another quick glance at my watch revealed lots of time until the tour left, and since my husband had not returned from coffee, I thought, "How hard could it be to continue our walk hand in hand before crossing that little wooden bridge at the end of the wharf for their video?"

My daughter remained sceptical but I finally convinced her it wouldn't take too long. We should be finished well in time to make it to our tour. Besides, how hard could it be? I gave our consent to be filmed.

Four takes later, having finally slowed my daughter down from a power walk to a leisurely pace, we stopped mid-bridge, right at the mark the crew had placed for us. We gazed around at the buildings on one side, the water and ships on the other while deep in conversation for a brief time. On a prearranged signal from the crew we continued across the rest of the bridge.

"It's a wrap," the camera man said. "We have everything we need for this part of the video. Thanks so much." With those words we were dismissed from service and they continued discussing further scenes.

What an unexpected adventure! What a story to tell about our fun, short-lived acting career on the wharf in Halifax. Our video shoot finished before my husband returned from finding a cup of coffee. In all the excitement of the morning I forgot to ask when the video would air or any other particulars about the photo shoot. I wondered if anyone would even believe my story. I decided right then and there it didn't really matter. I would always have the memory of an unplanned adventure one bright, sunny morning on the Halifax wharf.

~Carol Harrison
Saskatoon, SK

62

Summertime in Saskatchewan

I once drove back through southern Manitoba at night.
I was stunned by the beauty the prairies can offer. I remember the sleepy
farming towns at rest — a reminder of the legacy of honest,
hard working people who built a nation.
~Duane W. Berke

When I was growing up in Saskatchewan, we didn't spend our summers vacationing at Disneyland or on extensive road trips to landmarks. The farthest I was ever able to go was to the rural farm my grandparents owned. As one of more than thirty grandchildren at that time, we ran amok over the pasture and pathways that made up the landscape.

I spent a lot of time with my grandmother, but my grandfather was rarely around. Because of how many of us there were, it was no surprise that my grandfather never called me by my actual name. I realize now he possibly had trouble pronouncing it given that he had a thick German accent left over from a childhood in Austria, but at the time I remember being annoyed that he had no idea who I was.

For Grandpa, summers were for work. He tended the wheat, the animals, and tinkered with old cars. From sun up to sun down, he and my uncles would be out on the combine or tractor. The grandkids operated on an entirely different program, flitting in and out of the old farmhouse, swimming in the farm's water supply when it became too hot, and scampering away to hide when Grandpa would walk across the yard with the slop bucket for the pigs.

In a place like that, overrun with his kids and their kids, it's no surprise that he took to hiding things in his room. We'd watch him walk into the house with bags of groceries, bypassing the kitchen and heading straight into his bedroom. Peeking through the door, we'd see him unpacking boxes of cookies and fruit. He'd hide them in his closet, then shuffle back out the front door and leave for the fields again. And, just like any kids who have had something restricted from them, we raided his closet and gorged ourselves on his cookies. In some ways, I think we saw it as a way to get some attention from him. Stealing his plums was easier than just sitting down to talk.

One morning I bolted for the sunshine and was stopped short by a golf cart sitting by the front door. My dad had brought his cart out to the farm and it sat, white and gleaming, with the keys in the ignition. The entire scenario was too much to resist, especially given that my nine-year-old cousin had shown me just the other day that she could drive a car that had the keys in it. Although we survived that experience, we almost gave my grandmother a heart attack as she raced down the road behind us, flapping a tea towel and yelling.

Peering around to make sure no one saw me, I jumped on the golf cart and tentatively started the ignition. I put my foot on the gas and nearly collided with the front step. Grandpa, obviously hearing the commotion, chose that moment to limp up behind me.

"Shirley, what you doing?" he asked, eyeing me behind the wheel of the golf cart. Given that he had thirteen kids of his own, I'm fairly sure he knew exactly what I had planned on doing. Ignoring the fact that once again, he had called me Shirley and my name was indeed Shelly, I adopted an immediate defence:

"Nothing! Dad said I could move it to the garage for him."

He stood for a moment or two, staring at me, while I pondered whether or not he was going to take the keys or go and get my dad. Instead, he put down his bucket and sat down beside me.

"You drive," he said.

I couldn't help myself from saying, "Really?" I was incredulous.

"Go to the fields." Pointing in the direction of the left field, he sat waiting for me to get going. I turned the key and quickly made my way to the driveway, worried someone was going to stop me. We bumped and jerked our way across the washboard on the dirt road, as I steadied the steering and focused on not hitting the ditch.

My grandparents owned over 100 acres at that time, and I never realized until the homestead was abandoned and everyone had moved on how much land that really was. As summer turned to fall each year, the golden stalks of wheat would dance in the late afternoon sun. I always thought it was beautiful to look at, but I never really had an idea as to the work that went into it. Grandpa pointed at the approach into the field, and I slowly turned the cart into it.

"Keep going," he said when I started to slow down. I continued to drive straight through the wheat field, the golf cart bumping as it forced the wheat to give underneath its frame. I laughed out loud at the sheer fun of it all, and I swerved side to side as I drove. Sneaking a glance at Grandpa, I saw he was smiling too.

"Stop," he said, and I instantly eased up on the gas and cut the engine. We were directly in the middle of the field.

There is a reason why they call Saskatchewan the "Land of the Endless Sky." Once we'd stopped, the sun beat down on us and everywhere I looked there was blue and yellow. The wind was blowing lightly, and there was no noise except for the sound of the breeze rippling through the field. Grandpa hopped out of the cart and walked a few steps. Pulling the heads off a few stalks, he rubbed the wheat between his fingers.

"See?" He took a few kernels and placed them in my palm. I noticed how his hands were weathered and callused from years of hard labour. I looked at the wheat in my hand and squinted back up at him, not saying anything. I wasn't sure what he wanted to hear.

"Not just any wheat," he said. "Good wheat. You keep it." Turning his back to me, he stood in the middle of the field for a long time, staring off into the distance. I turned the kernels over in my hand and then stuffed them in my pocket. I felt a surge of pride. I was happy to be sitting there in his fields, proud that he had worked so hard. Even for a kid, it was easy to grasp how difficult his job was.

A few minutes later we turned around and made our way back to the farm. Pulling in, I saw my dad standing on the steps of the farmhouse, waiting for me. I cut the engine and my grandpa hopped out, saying, "It's okay. I took her out."

My grandpa died the year I got married, and I can't remember a time after that day that I ever connected with him again. I kept the kernels of wheat in my pocket until I got home, transferring them into my jewellery box where they stayed for the next thirty years. When I look at them now, I remember a sunny day in Saskatchewan. And I'm sorry I didn't try harder to get to know him.

~Shelly Wutke
Aldergrove, BC

63

The Solitary Cottage

An inability to stay quiet is one of the most conspicuous failings of mankind.
~Walter Bagehot

"Oops, sorry." Those two simple, solitary, apologetic words once got me kicked out of an outdoors game that I like to play at our cottage. The game is called "The Silent Hike" and it is based on the premise that nature and silence go together. It is played on a series of groomed trails that have been blazed in a forest across the road from the log cottage that my wife Kris and I had built on a lakeside lot two hours north of our Toronto-area home in 1992.

Everyone who plays the game must adhere to one simple rule: You must not talk at any time during the one-hour hike. Not. One. Word.

On one occasion several years ago, on a warm July afternoon, I stood at the edge of the forest and explained the rules to a group of six gamers who included Kris, her brother Bob, his now-deceased wife Ann, and their two preteen sons, Andrew and John.

"You must be quiet as a mouse," I explained. "Even if you see a bear, you must keep your trap shut," I joked. "Utter a sound and you're out of the game. The winner is anyone who can complete the hike in complete and golden silence."

For the first twenty minutes, we tramped through the woods as "noiseless as fear in a wide wilderness," to quote John Keats. I took up a rear position and was thoroughly enjoying the serenity of the hike through the woods. We all became immersed in the tranquility of this walk with nature, where the only audible noise, other than the gurgling sound of the babbling brooks we crossed, was the rustle of snapping twigs under our feet. I was paying close attention to the stillness of the event when at one point, while lost in my thoughts, I came up too close to Ann and accidentally stepped on the heel of her hiking boot. "Oops, sorry," I said, automatically. "That's okay," she whispered, politely.

Well, you'd think we just killed Bambi! Everyone stopped and pointed at us, noiselessly but accusingly, and indicated in no uncertain terms that we were out of the game. Since I had created the rule, I had little choice but to suck up my punishment. We all trooped onward.

Now that I had been banished, I played devil's advocate. When I spotted a tiny snake slithering through the grass, I yelled out: "Hey, John, I'll give you $10 if you can tell me what kind of snake this is." John didn't bite. Neither did the snake. Later, I called out to the tight-lipped adolescents. "Kris and I have two extra tickets to a couple of Toronto Blue Jays games next week. Would you two like to come?" Both boys nodded their heads excitedly and in silent unison. "Which game would you like to see? Wednesday's game against the Yankees or Saturday afternoon against the Red Sox?" The expression in their bulging eyes was painful to watch. "Speak now or forever hold your peace," I teased. "Let me know now or we'll take your mom and dad instead."

Bob thought I was being a tad unfair and he let his feelings be known when he uttered a sympathetic "Awww." Both boys jumped up and down and, still under the gag order, demonstrated a universal sign that their father was toast by drawing their forefinger across their throat.

"Ha," laughed my wife.

And another one bit the dust!

To their everlasting credit, and despite the best efforts of four scheming adults, the two youths completed the journey without so much as a peep. Later that evening, Kris and I hosted an Awards

Barbeque to honour the winners. Everyone got a chuckle when they saw the booty bag of prizes which included aptly named chocolate bars and candy, namely Turtles, Snickers and Smarties. I had tried to find a Noisette bar—delicious caramelized hazelnuts buried in milk chocolate—but they are available only in the U.S.

The Silent Hike is just one of many quiet activities that Kris and I enjoy at the cottage. I can easily spend a speechless summer afternoon chopping wood for the fireplace while she enjoys the sweet serenity of reading a novel on our deck that overlooks the still and deep waters of Lake Manitouwabing.

Whenever I feel like exercising at this soul-satisfying place, which is surrounded by tall pines and maples, I put on my running shoes and run up and down the wooden stairs that lead from the cottage to the lake. When my father Wally died a year after the cottage was built, I had the staircase built in his honour. There are fifty steps, and at Step #25 I placed a gold-plated plaque that reads: "Wally's Stairway to Heaven." If I'm going down for a swim or coming up from a canoe ride, I know I'm halfway there when I stop at Step #25 and whisper a silent prayer. Often, the prayer is one of gratitude for owning such a place of splendid isolation. We feel extremely fortunate, especially when we learned that only seven percent of Canadians own a cottage. Our secluded spot is indeed a treasure. Even a poor little rich girl like the late Diana, Princess of Wales—who seemed to have it all—once lamented: "I've got to have a place where I can find peace of mind."

During snowy winter weekends, at our four-season cottage, we are reminded of the phrase that "serenity is not freedom from the storm, but peace amid the storm."

As much as we love the stillness at our lakeside retreat, we decided to put the cottage up for sale this year. We got a bug. The travel bug! We want to explore more of the world before we get fitted for the "Forever Box." But no matter where we travel and whomever we meet, having owned a cottage will give us lots to talk about.

~Dennis McCloskey
Richmond Hill, ON

64

Our Moment

Dancing with the feet is one thing,
but dancing with the heart is another.
~Author Unknown

July 30th, 2003 is a date that many Torontonians will never forget. In the spring and summer of 2003, Toronto was hit hard by SARS, which was a big blow to the tourist industry. A giant concert to aid the city was organized for Downsview Park. The concert would feature several bands, both Canadian and not, and would be headlined by the Rolling Stones. For a lot of Ontarians, the concert was an event not to be missed, and I was amongst them.

My parents were teenagers of the 1970s and were devoted classic rock fans. They spent their youth going to concerts and they passed their love of music on to me. For my father, there was no greater band than the Rolling Stones.

I happened to be born on a Tuesday in July, thus earning me the nickname of "Ruby Tuesday" from my father. Growing up, my father often promised, "Someday I'll take you to see the Rolling Stones and they'll play your song and we'll dance." Twice we made plans that fell through. Then Toronto Rocks was announced for four days after my twentieth birthday and we both knew this was our moment.

In the weeks leading up to the concert, I couldn't contain my excitement. "Do you really think they'll play 'Ruby Tuesday'?" I asked over and over, knowing that if they didn't, it would take away from my enjoyment of the day. "I know they will," my father would assure me with a smile. He seemed so confident that it seemed impossible to doubt him, even though I knew that there was no way he could know what songs would be on the set list.

The concert was fantastic. The music, the crowd, the general love for our city — it made for a day that I'll never forget. However, as wonderful as the concert was, for me the best part came near the end of the night. The Rolling Stones took the stage and after a few songs, the familiar beats of "Ruby Tuesday" began to play.

"Didn't I always say I'd take you to see the Stones and they'd play your song and we'd dance?" my father asked, taking my hand. I smiled and nodded and we danced there, in the crowd of people, as Mick Jagger sang our song.

"Someday, we'll dance to this when some lucky man takes you away from me," my father promised.

Sadly, that day never came. Six months after that warm July evening, I heard "Ruby Tuesday" again, but this time it was at my father's funeral. He'd been killed in a car accident at the age of forty-eight.

As I sat there, listening to our special song, I remembered that night and how happy we'd been. My father had kept his promise and while we'd never dance at my wedding together, for the rest of my life I'll have the memory of that concert and that one perfect moment with my father.

~Michelle McKague-Radic
Peterborough, ON

65

Adventure into the Unknown

Leave the beaten track behind occasionally and dive into the woods. Every time you do you will be certain to find something you have never seen before.
~Alexander Graham Bell

My husband loved adventure, especially exploring the back roads of BC. One day he suggested we visit Glen and Betty, our friends in Seton Lake. "Sounds good," I said, ready for another adventure.

Driving west past Vancouver one hot July morning, we turned north onto the Sea to Sky Highway. Then, after stopping for a quick lunch at Whistler, we headed north again.

In the town of Pemberton we stopped at a gas station to ask directions. "I suppose it's best to drive through Lillooet to get to Seton Lake?" my husband asked the attendant.

"Oh, no." The man shook his head. "That way it will take a long time through some isolated areas. The mountain road is much quicker."

"Really? But, I've heard this logging road is quite high and used only for service vehicles and trucks. Is it safe?" my husband asked, a bit concerned.

"Oh, sure. I just drove that road a week ago. It's a little steep, but I think you'll be all right," he said as he looked at our older model Chrysler.

"Well," my husband hesitated for a minute. "If you say so, we'll take a chance."

After a couple of miles the pavement ran out, and the car shuffled along on a gravel road dotted with large potholes. Soon, the road, carved out of the side of a mountain, deteriorated into just a single lane of gravelly ruts.

As our car climbed higher and higher, I got my first glimpse of Seton Lake about 500 feet below. "Look how beautiful it is down there!" I exclaimed.

Just then, the car hit something. My husband stopped the car and went to check. "Bad news," he told me. "A rock must have hit the oil pan. The oil is running out."

I was suddenly fearful. Whatever would we do on this isolated mountaintop?

"Maybe I can push the car over the hump. Then we can coast down." My husband looked at the mountain crest just a few yards ahead. "You will have to steer."

When I noticed that the car was so precariously close to the edge of the road, I began to panic. I turned the wheel away from the steep drop, yet I knew it could catapult right over the edge into the lake at any moment. Was this going to be our grave? My mind reeled at that prospect.

As my husband began to push, the car lurched forward. I clung to the steering wheel. "Please, God," I prayed silently, "help me to get it away from the edge." Another lurch and the car shot forward and then stopped just before it hit the rock ahead. "Keep steering to the left!" my husband shouted.

Again, I tried to straighten out the wheels and watched in horror as the car now rolled toward the lake. "Help!" I screamed. Just then my husband appeared at my side and grabbed the steering wheel. "We've made it. We're at the top. I'll drive now," he said, wiping his brow. "That was a close one. I wish the garage attendant had told us how bad this route is."

"Yeah," I agreed, still not sure if the car would suddenly plunge into the mountain lake below. Yet, with my husband steering, the car began to roll slowly down the mountain. In a few minutes we were at the bottom and coasted right into the driveway of Betty's and Glen's house, the first one in the community of Seton.

"We don't have a garage in this village," our friend Glen told us when he heard about our car problem. "However, there is a First Nations man here who sometimes fixes cars out of his driveway. Let's go down and ask."

When the man looked at our car, he shook his head. "There are no spare car parts around here. Sometimes I go to another town to get a part, but most of the time, they don't have any parts, either," he informed us.

We looked at each other in silence. "Well, I could try to patch it," he finally said when he saw our disappointed faces. "I'll take some time. Come back in a couple of days and I'll see what I can do."

Grateful that he was at least going to try to fix our car, we drove back, past the only grocery store, which doubled as a café, and the little library where community gatherings were held, discussing our options.

After a couple of days, we went back to the home of the mechanic. Crawling from underneath our car, he beamed. "I patched the oil pan. Now you can drive the car home."

While we were expressing our gratefulness, my husband pulled out his wallet to pay for the repairs, but the man shook his head. "No! No! If we can help our neighbours, we do it free.

"And we're all neighbours," he said, gathering up his tools. Even though he refused any money, we determined to someday bless others as we had been blessed.

Arriving home in the Fraser Valley safely after a six-hour drive the long way through Lillooet and the Fraser Canyon, we were thankful that God had not only kept us from plunging into Seton Lake, but that he had also led us to a gem of a man who practiced the Golden Rule. This misadventure certainly had turned into an adventure, one that we would always treasure.

~Ingrid Dore
White Rock, BC

66

Sunday Cycling

Nothing compares to the simple pleasure of a bike ride.
~John F. Kennedy

I was born in Ottawa, and have lived there off and on throughout my life. In addition to being the capital of Canada, it's a vibrant, active city. In my early twenties, I spent a lot of time skating along the Rideau Canal, boating along the Ottawa River, or just inline skating across town.

But my favourite outdoor activity was—and still is—cycling. I love the hard work of getting to the top of a big hill—not so much because I like to push myself; no, I love the payoff of speeding down the other side, so much speed that my eyes tear up and I can hardly breathe. If anything, I am childlike in my enjoyment of cycling.

One day, through friends of friends, I was invited to go cycling in the Gatineau Hills, which are just across the river from Ottawa, in Quebec. I had gone cycling there a number of times on my own, but never in a group. And never with these cyclists. And they were cyclists: hardcore gearheads who wore Lycra from head to toe, had those handlebars that you can practically lie down on, and had the newest, flashiest everything. Intimidating to say the least.

I wasn't a beginner: I had clips instead of regular pedals and did wear Lycra shorts (because they came with padding for added comfort!) and my bike was nothing to be ashamed of. Despite this, I was still intimidated—but I accepted the invitation anyway.

We met mid-morning, on a sunny Sunday in late September. We

all gathered downtown in the ByWard Market, a minute's bike ride away from the bridge connecting Ontario to Quebec, Ottawa to Hull. The others knew each other much better and were chatting comfortably, but I felt self-conscious, just waiting for us to get going.

We biked single file out of the Market, past the stands filled with fresh, local produce, the aroma of the bakery on the corner tempting us—or at least me—to linger longer. The others pushed ahead, and I brought up the rear as we passed the Champlain statue overlooking the Ottawa River and the city of Hull.

There is nowhere prettier in autumn than the Ottawa area. The weather is usually mild and sunny, and the colours of the trees are spectacular: the greens are still so vivid, as the reds and yellows burst forth, competing for attention, not just from tree to tree, but you can see colours mingling chaotically on the same leaf.

As we moved from the city into the Gatineau Park and got into a rhythm, I started to relax, enjoying the fresh air and view and starting even to feel a small sense of camaraderie. Whether everyone was still warming up and keeping the pace slow, I wasn't sure, but I was surprised to be keeping up without too much effort.

In fact, everything was going along perfectly until I blew a tire on glass that I had been too busy looking skywards to notice. I felt like too much of an idiot to even call to the others and so I watched them cycle away as I dismounted.

Not being a hardcore cyclist, I had never bought a spare tire to carry around with me. Even if I had, I had never learned how to change a tire. It didn't take me long to realize that the only thing to do was to start walking home.

It wasn't that simple, of course. Because I had the fancy shoes that clip into my pedals, it was hard to walk, and walking would have damaged the shoes anyway. So I took off my shoes and was debating which would be better—walking barefoot or in socks—when I heard a noise behind me.

Mike, one of the keenest of the bunch, had cycled back.

"What's up?"

"I shredded my back tire pretty badly."

"That sucks."

I agreed.

"It's a long walk back."

I didn't need to agree to that one; it was pretty obvious. At that point, I expected him to either lecture me on my obvious lack of spares and tools or to turn around and join the group again. Instead, he dismounted from his bike and took his shoes off.

"I know it isn't much help, but I prefer to keep my socks on when I have to walk. It pretty much ruins them, but it makes me feel like the rocks that I step on won't hurt as much."

Without further explanation, he started walking back the way we came. I arranged my shoes in one hand and grabbed my handlebar with the other, and quickly followed him.

I wasn't sure why he had chosen to join me, so I awkwardly started to talk about the beautiful weather at first and then what I was studying at school, nothing personal, and then another safe subject: cycling.

"I can't tell you how many times I have walked home like this. And I've always wished that someone would walk with me. It gets pretty boring," Mike said, answering the question I hadn't dared to ask.

"Yeah," I said and then paused. "Thanks."

"Cycling is a solo kind of activity; everyone just gets into their own space. But, at the same time, we ride in a pack, so it becomes a team sport too."

I had never thought about it that way. "I just like to ride because it makes me feel like a kid again," I admitted.

"Me too. It's all about the hills, the rush of going down."

"That's what I love too!" I exclaimed. We smiled, and continued our sock-footed walk, stepping on the fiery autumn leaves, feeling the sun's warmth, and pushing our bikes along together as if it was something that we had been doing every Sunday for years.

~Esme Mills
Pender Island, BC

O Canada

Life Lessons

*"All life lessons are not learned at college," she thought.
"Life teaches them everywhere."*

~L.M. Montgomery, Anne of the Island

Every Life Has a Plan

We have all a better guide in ourselves, if we would attend to it, than any other person can be.

~Jane Austen

When I graduated from the University of Toronto in 1982, I had a degree in theory and composition and a dream of both making my own records and writing songs for other artists.

I was advised by everyone I consulted to move to the U.S. I was told the Canadian music industry was too small and underdeveloped to launch an international career.

While touring the southern United States as a backup singer with Rockabilly legend Ronnie Hawkins, I was introduced to some of the top songwriters in Nashville. One of them, Wayland Holyfield, wrote a song with me called "If Only" that was picked up by an emerging redheaded singer named Reba McEntire.

I was so thrilled that another artist, who had a bona fide record deal, wanted to do one of my songs. I packed up my bags and moved to Nashville.

In order to get signed to a major label record deal myself, I was encouraged to copy the style of the artists who were having success that year. I was told that if I broke through with music that was the flavour of the day, one day I would get to do my own.

What did I know? My head told me I was getting advice from the experts. My heart told me I didn't like the music they wanted me to do. Still, for the next seven years, I followed my head, not my heart. I was signed to three separate record deals. Every contract was offered when the record company heard my sensitive singer-songwriter songs, and afterwards they would say, "Okay, we hear you can sing and write but now we want you to change and sound like the pop star of the moment." In 1983, it was Pat Benatar. In 1985, it was Laura Branigan. In 1988—Whitney Houston.

And guess what? Not one of the albums I recorded that the big American record labels in Nashville and then Los Angeles paid for, ever came out. Those albums didn't fool anybody, including me. They sounded like I was trying to be someone else. Meanwhile I was still writing songs that I felt really reflected who I was, songs that were written from my place of bliss. But no one seemed to want those songs. So I told myself that must mean they couldn't possibly be any good.

After my third record got shelved in L.A., it seemed to me that my dreams of becoming a recording artist were over. I was twenty-nine, after all, which is a senior citizen in Hollywood. I decided to focus instead on songwriting, and start a family with my husband Marc Jordan. In 1990, when our daughter Zoe was born, my father was diagnosed with Parkinson's disease. When I became pregnant with our son Ezra in 1993, I wanted to be near my dad and my family, so we moved back to Canada, a place I had never had a professional career and where I was virtually unknown.

Marc and I quickly discovered an industry very different from the American music business. Here, there is a thriving independent music scene, not driven as much by the demands of the marketplace as by artists doing the music they love.

These independent artists didn't have big budget U.S. label deals. Whereas success in the U.S. meant having a number one record, in Canada there was less emphasis on pleasing the marketing departments of major labels. Artists were free to find something interesting to say. They just picked a bunch of their favourite songs, made a CD and hit the road.

"I can do that," I thought. What a concept! No Spandex, no

cleavage, no suggestive lyrics—just good old Canadian-style beautiful melodies and meaningful lyrics. I felt I was finally in an environment where I could release a record.

I wrote the song "I Will Take Care of You" with composer David Pickell to coincide with Zoe's birth and my father's illness. I included it on my independent CD *Cool Rain* in 1996 along with eleven other songs. The big clever marketing concept behind this CD was to pick my favourite twelve songs. It just so happened the kind of songs I had been saving in my back pocket for thirteen years were songs influenced by the singer/songwriters of the '70s—Joni Mitchell, Bonnie Raitt and Linda Ronstadt. That kind of music was in style again. So that is how my debut CD *Cool Rain* was born.

The first time I heard myself on the radio, I was driving along Dupont Street in Toronto. As the familiar opening chords of "Don't Leave Me Alone" with Greg Leisz's mournful lap steel guitar came across my speakers, I was overcome with emotion. I pulled over to the side of the road, listened to the song and had a good cry. It seemed it had been a very long road to get there.

My career took off quickly then, and though I seemed to have achieved overnight success, in reality it had taken me thirteen years. I was thrilled to at last write, record and perform my own songs, in my own way. It finally made sense to me. In the U.S. I had been trying, like other women of the '80s, to fit into the style that the record companies wanted. That wasn't authentic for me. When I finally created material that reflected who I was as a person and where I was in life, however, it all seemed to align. I never thought I would see my first hit as an artist at the age of thirty-six, but that was God's plan for me.

We all make different choices about what we do with our lives and careers, but we can all benefit by being guided from an authentic place, a place that is ours and ours alone. Connecting with your purpose in life is what renowned mythologist Joseph Campbell calls: "following your bliss."

I know now how important it is to follow your bliss. It took me a lot of time and tears to figure that out. I followed my head more than my heart in Nashville and Los Angeles, chasing trends and adapting my music to how other people sounded, rather than following my own bliss. Finding out who you are is not so much something you *discover* but something you *uncover*. I believe we are all born with gifts that make us unique.

If I hadn't let go of the wheel when I did in L.A., I probably would not have had a family *or* a career. We're all faced with choices. I've learned to reach for choices that make sense to my heart. Sometimes, they don't make sense to my pocketbook in the short term, but somehow, decisions made for the right reasons always work out in the long term.

I am grateful for all of the life lessons I learned in the States, and equally grateful for all the twists and turns that brought me home to be near my dad for the last years of his life.

As I wrote in "Let There Be Love," one of the songs of mine that Anne Murray recorded:

Every life has a plan
Though sometimes the map is out of our hands.

~Amy Sky
Toronto, ON

67

Look Beyond the Frame

Man looks at the outward appearance, but the Lord looks at the heart.
~1 Samuel 16:7b

While walking down the hall at work, in a hurry to get home, a new friend gave me a gift. She whispered, "It's just a token of our friendship, something to clutter up your house." I peeked inside the gift bag and saw a black photo frame. "Oh, wow," I said. "I've started a black and white wall and I'm constantly looking for black frames. Thank you so much." I rushed on my way. After I got home I fully opened the bag, took out the frame, and actually noticed what was in the frame.

She had photographed a close-up of a delicate yellow lady slipper amongst lush greenery. There for a fleeting moment, but captured for eternity because she paused to look intently and appreciate its beauty. The photo had been processed with a softening effect bringing the flower forward to where it appeared as if you could almost touch its cool velvety petals. The photo was signed and neatly mounted within the black frame.

My heart sank as I realized how insensitive and thoughtless I had been. I knew I needed to repair some surely damaged feelings. God also brought to my mind an instant and profound analogy—something I needed to learn from this.

I have spent an incredible portion of my life focusing on frames while missing beautiful, delicate treasures in the process. The human body is merely a frame around the person inside. The hearts and souls of people are immeasurably more important than the body. Our frame will die, but our heart and soul live on.

I knew I needed to change my focus from the frames of people to searching intently for the treasures contained within. Young frames, old frames, plain frames and gold frames, all containing delicate eternal hearts and souls. I needed to start appreciating and focusing on my own internal-eternal person, rather than obsessing over preserving and polishing my frame. What would I like to be appreciated for, my beautiful frame or for my loving and caring heart?

I believe my new friend had seen glimpses of my heart and soul, while many others who I worked with knew my frame only. I don't blame them for not taking time to discover me. I blame myself for focusing more attention on my frame than on hearts and souls of those around me. I realized I knew a lot of frames, but few hearts and souls.

There was one soul I needed to attend to immediately. I baked a wild huckleberry pie, wrote the following note and then went to find her. (We had both shared how we loved to pick wild berries in northern British Columbia, and due to medical issues she'd been unable to pick that season.)

Dear Trish,

Thank you for the beautiful delicate picture. I'm so sorry I didn't take the time for a closer look when you gave it to me. Forgive me for thinking the frame was the gift when you obviously put incredible talent and skill into the photo. I will cherish it always. A striking analogy hit me when I realized I'd missed the real treasure.

People are a combination of a picture frame and the art it contains; our bodies are merely a frame for the treasure that lies within. I know a lot of people by their frames only.

Thank you for taking the time to get a few glimpses of

my heart and sharing some of yours with me. I know there is a deep and wonderful treasure within your frame.

God bless you,

Love Susie

P.S. The pie crust may be good, but it's the inside that's special.

~Susie Braun Wilson
Prince George, BC

68

Never Miss a Sunset

The moment one gives close attention to any thing, even a blade of grass it becomes a mysterious, awesome, indescribably magnificent world in itself.
~Henry Miller

Growing up with the golden sands of Sauble Beach at my doorstep, I realize now how rich we really were. Fondly referred to as the "Daytona of Canada," Sauble Beach, Ontario is famous for its eleven kilometres of pure, golden, sugary sand, embracing the warm, clean waters of Lake Huron. When I visited my relatives in the "city," I envied their beautiful houses, their stylish clothes and even the cookies that came out of a bag instead of the oven! As I take a nostalgic look at the past I now know that what we had money could not buy.

We lived on a modest farm on Silver Lake Road, just a mile or so from "the beach." My parents had grown up during the Depression, so frugality was a way of life. On the other hand they were so generous and giving. My dad would grow a huge garden to feed us throughout the winter and there was always enough for the "city" relatives to come and visit and take fresh vegetables home.

We seldom went out for a fancy dinner or to a movie, but one thing that we did from the time the weather turned nice in the spring until the snow came and the lake froze over was to go to the beach. My father always said, "Never miss a sunset." In the early spring we would sit at the beach, watching the icebergs as they moved in and out, and of course watching for that beautiful sunset. As spring turned into summer, we would go to the beach and swim until it was time to watch the sunset. Summer would turn to autumn, when the evenings were chilly and the water would begin to get rough. As we watched the waves, listening to them hit the shore, we would wait for those last sunsets of the season, knowing that soon it would be winter and we would be waiting for spring to once again watch the sunset over the lake.

I grew up, married and moved away from the beauty of the lake and its breathtaking sunset. My parents retired and looked forward to summer when our children would spend summer holidays with them. Our children are now grown with children of their own, but they still talk about the days when Grandma and Grandpa would take them to the beach to swim and how Grandpa always said, "Never miss a sunset."

During his golden years, Dad would spend his time in the spring puttering around, making maple syrup and preparing to plant his garden. He would come back from the sugar bush in time for dinner and to take that short drive to watch the sunset. During the summer, he would work in his garden, or relax under the beautiful twin maple trees in the side yard. Evening would come and he would say to Mom, "We better go for an ice cream cone and eat it while we watch the sunset." Autumn was no exception. He still took that short jaunt to the lake shore most evenings.

Dad had lived there from birth; the only time he had been away from home was during World War II when he was in the army. He always said, "There is no place like home."

It was early spring. Dad called with some urgency in his voice, asking us to come and visit for the weekend. We went and helped him do a few things around the farm. When we finished our work he said, "We better go and watch the sunset." That was the last sunset that I watched with my dad. A week later, we got the call. Just the night before, he and Mom went to the beach and watched their last sunset together. Suddenly he had been called to another home. The news was devastating and our next trip home was for his funeral. Spending the next several days at the farm, grieving and not knowing what to do with myself, I would wake up early, drive to the beach to watch and listen to the waves. I felt as if Dad were with me. Every evening, I would say to my family, "If Dad were here he would say never miss a sunset," and off we would go to watch God's artwork, reminiscing about a wonderful husband, father and grandpa.

The memories of the sunsets of the Lake Huron shores have never left my heart. No matter what season I am travelling in the area, I feel an urge to be at the "beach" for the sunset. The spiritual healing that I have had just sitting on the beach, watching the sunset is more than money could ever buy! Living in our crazy "rat race" world I have learned to "take time to stop and smell the roses" and to "never miss a sunset."

~Nancy Loucks-McSloy
London, ON

69

From Vile to Vegas

*You need only two tools: WD-40 and duct tape. If it doesn't move and it
should, use WD-40. If it moves and shouldn't, use the duct tape.*
~Red Green

My husband and I made our dream purchase one
year ago—a bungalow in the country. It was perfect—close to everything, yet away from it all. A place
bordered by the Niagara Escarpment, the Royal Botanical Gardens
and acres of lush farmland. We can blow kisses to city folk from our
front porch—but we're far enough away to wish upon a star. With a
vegetable garden, water from a well, and one of the prettiest pumpkin
patches you will ever see, our house was truly great—on the outside. But after we moved in, we started to feel like preteens staying at
Grandma's house. There was white shag carpeting, bronzed linoleum
flooring, and ski chalet-style faux-wood panelling. Everywhere. The
house was in need of a change. More like a revolution. And we were
up to the task.

For the first few months, we started with simple aesthetic
improvements like flooring, windows, and painting. Nothing too
major. Then we began to take a closer look at the walls, and the struc-
ture itself, and we were tantalized by the idea of new spaces, bigger
spaces. Like a showpiece bathroom perhaps—something fresh and
contemporary. A hotel-inspired oasis. I could live with the ski chalet
faux-wood panelling, but the bathroom was just too much of a bad
thing. It was settled. Our first major renovation project would be

creating the bathroom of our dreams. And that was where every good design show host would tell you to start.

The bathroom had seen brighter days, that's for sure. The décor was an homage to the avocado and salmon interior design palette of the 1960s. The grout between the mosaic tiles was crumbling. The caulking was yellowed and peeling. And so was the wallpaper—all three hundred and ten pink flowers of it. The gold-framed shower doors surprisingly stood the test of time, as witnessed by the 1976 Simpsons-Sears stamp. And the orange-turned-green copper pipes now resembled Venetian glass (and not in a pretty way). From Here to Eternity would describe the thirteen-litre toilet flush—which easily became twenty-six litres when you had to flush twice. It was the original dual-flush toilet. We were ready to bring our bathroom into the twenty-first century, even if it killed us.

And so our bathroom renovation saga began. We figured after watching umpteen renovation episodes on HGTV, we could take on anything, with a little help from the professionals. On TV, each project started when the show began and was over before the hour was up, but we soon found out that wasn't how things happened in real life.

In real life, a demolition bin the size of your house arrives, eliminating any parking spots you once had. Your neighbours decide it's their disposal bin too. A trail of debris and tools leads from the driveway to the room in question. The first to go are the plaster walls. Then the cellulite ceiling. It peels away to reveal the attic while a lingering chill begins to drip from the trusses. You are invaded by ladybugs and you worry about bats. Even the floor vanishes to an abyss-type purgatory. And your cat suddenly learns she can walk through walls—and fall through floors—into a cobweb-encrusted sump pump hole. Naturally, she has this epiphany at three o'clock in the morning and requires rescuing (with a flashlight and towel) by you, her reluctant hero.

Your head hurts from the cloud of dust you now live in. And your throat is like a raw pepita from the constant swallowing of fumes, which range from floor adhesive to tile mortar to latex paint. There is rainwater leaking from the ceiling vent into an upside down toilet and your contractor decides to stay home and play Xbox while you curse and cry in your gutted sanctuary. A three-week lark becomes a three-month saga.

But the long-awaited day finally arrives. The disposal bin is gone. Your contractor has packed up his tools and you've ushered him out. You can now brush your teeth in the sink, instead of the mouldy laundry tub. And suddenly, it was all worth it.

Renovation horror stories are a major reason why people are reluctant to begin a project such as a bathroom. They can be a real gamble—a complicated, expensive, and often emotional undertaking. Our experience was all of these things, but it was also a rewarding one. My husband describes the whole experience as organic, and I agree. Quarrels and creation. Scribbled sketches. Altered plans. And altered states. For us, the renovation experience was both an intricate relationship and an art form. I can see now why the challenge and excitement of constructing something new can be irresistible.

This winter, friends and family will find us taking it easy. More importantly, they will see us again. No more renovation projects until we fully recover from this one. We have since learned that the many torturous hiccups we endured were actually the norm. In a renovation project, crap happens. Contractors are human. They work hard; they make mistakes, and they rest (yes, playing Xbox counts as rest). More notably, the good ones deliver. And our contractor did deliver the bathroom of our dreams (eventually). Our new space boasts Botticino marble, dazzling chrome, double under-mount sinks, a wicked six-litre siphon jet flush, heated towels, and, dare to dream—cable television.

Our bungalow has flow, form and function. We have Vegas, baby.

~Beckie Jas
Dundas, ON

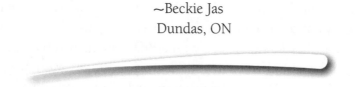

70

Divine Dimes

Angels deliver Fate to our doorstep — and anywhere else it is needed.
~Jessi Lane Adams

Standing at a major crossroads in my life, I carefully chose the items that were of the greatest significance to me as I put the finishing touches on packing my entire life into a single suitcase. I was taking a long-overdue leap of faith. For over a decade I had endured a sea of heartbreaks, disappointment, anger and fear. Only weeks prior I had made the faith-filled decision to leave the unhealthy and unsafe relationship I shared with the father of my children, and the following day I was moving my children 3,000 miles to a better existence.

It had always been my opinion that people who let themselves fall into these situations were vulnerable and weak. I'd never understood how anyone would stay in a relationship that they knew was so incredibly unhealthy. I had always been a strong person, so to find myself in this situation was devastating to my self-confidence. However, one of the many lessons I learned from that chapter in my life was that judging a person for their actions before taking a stroll in their shoes is a serious and insensitive character flaw.

My personal longevity in this relationship came down to a ration of integrity and a pinch of fear. And now as I prepared for our departure, and as they had done every time I had entertained the idea of leaving in the past, doubt and guilt flooded my mind. Was I making the right decision? Would I be able to provide for us? Was separating my children from their father the best-case scenario? Was a flawed father better than no father? Would my children blame me for taking them away from the only life they knew? The fear of the unknown was overwhelming.

I'd lost my mother to cancer when I was nine and though it had been close to forty years since she'd been gone I still missed her very much and thought of her often. I happened to catch a famous psychic on a talk show years back who was discussing signs that our loved ones who have passed on leave for us if we ask them. The most common items that people reported receiving were feathers and shiny pennies. Over the past few years I'd kept up private conversations with my mother, knowing that she was always with me. I would pray for guidance, strength and a sign. It wasn't long after that I started finding dimes. At first I didn't recognize them as signs, but then I would find them in the most unusual places: under my pillow, between the pages of a book, or on a windowsill.

But the most remarkable instance happened that very day. As I'd mentioned, the kids and I left with little more than one suitcase each, so I was going through my belongings and deciding which "memories" would fill up what precious little space I had available. I had already found a few dimes here and there that day so I had a very warm feeling that my mother was there with me and I was heading in the right direction. As I sat cross-legged on the floor halfway into my closet I was about to remove a box I'd gone through that was now empty. It was the very last thing in my closet. I had only a moment ago whispered aloud, "Thank you for the signs... I know now that I'm making the right decision." I lifted up that last box and what I found underneath filled my heart with the most incredible warmth of love I'd ever felt. There, in a clean little pile, were six shiny dimes. I stared at them for a long while, tears of joy streaking my cheeks, and basked in the warmth of the heavenly gift I had been given. After that I never looked back on my decision to leave with anything but self-assured confidence and excitement for a new beginning.

My life since then has been a series of wonderful surprises and fantastic growth. Shortly after I settled into my new surroundings I ran into an old friend who turned out to be the man of my dreams. We blended our families and share a wonderful life with our happy, successful children. I still find dimes in the most unexpected locations and at the most noteworthy times. I keep my divine dimes as a constant reminder of love that never dies, of strength, of integrity and of belief in myself and dreams. They sit beside a picture of my mother in a beautiful ceramic box that was a gift from our children for that very reason.

I found a dime this morning in a jacket that I haven't worn since last year. Some people may say that it's a coincidence that I'd have a dime in my pocket but I know otherwise.

~S. Brunton
Corunna, ON

Flying Solo

The real voyage of discovery consists not in seeking new landscapes,
but in having new eyes.
~Marcel Proust

Day 1—en route to Charlottetown, PEI

"I licked my mommy!" the boy in the seat behind me is yelling excitedly to the flight attendant.

"That's nice," she says as she squeezes down the narrow airplane aisle to mediate between passengers. The father across from me is asking the woman beside him if she will move so his daughter can sit with him, but the woman is refusing. I avoid eye contact with the father and pull my novel up in front of my face so he doesn't ask me.

Two rows in front of me, a baby is screaming. I am a parent. I know the agony of taking children on planes, the frustration when seats don't line up, when kids yell too loudly, when you know you are annoying everyone around you and are powerless to do anything about it. But I can't deny the voice in my head, screaming, "Will you please make that baby stop?"

Perhaps my patience is thin because I am finally alone and want to savour every moment. Leaving behind my family, I'm flying across the country from Vancouver to Charlottetown for a conference. While most people might dread the nine hours in transit, and several of my colleagues chose to travel together, I am revelling in flying solo. The last trip I took alone was five years ago, before I had a child, before

I turned into Mom. Though I wear a wedding ring that states my marital status, no one can tell I'm a mom, and for these nine blissful hours, I'm not telling.

In front of me, there's a monitor with an array of movies and music options. Buttons, buttons, buttons. And all mine to press. I don't have to share my console, don't have to watch children's shows, don't have to keep one earphone off in case I'm needed. I'm not needed.

During the layover in Toronto, I meander shops and sit at a wine bar to eat. I watch moms hauling babes in arms with strollers slung over their shoulders and listen to overtired kids whine and throw tantrums. I just close my eyes. No need to bear witness, offer sympathetic smiles, or share French fries.

Don't get me wrong—I love being with my son, but do I have to feel like "Bad Mom of the Year" when I also enjoy being without him? When I've burned my candle at both ends for so long that I've lost track of what makes me glow, I think it's fair to take some me-time.

An entire week stretches out before me like a fantasy. I'll be in Charlottetown for a conference, but there are delicious days before and after that are all mine—if I can manage to shelve the guilt.

Day 2—Charlottetown, PEI

I'm sitting on the grass in Victoria Park on the edge of downtown Charlottetown, overlooking the Atlantic Ocean. I'm licking a maple walnut ice cream cone and snacking on hot salty French fries and pondering how long I've been here reading my book and soaking in the sunshine. I purposely didn't wear a watch so I could take my time exploring touristy shops and used bookstores. It was an adjustment to be so self-centred, to remember what I used to do with my time. Meandering with no agenda had been my favourite pastime, and I'd forgotten how thrilling it was. Yet every now and then I would look around me, as if I was missing something. Then I remembered, it was me that had been missing for so long.

Day 6 — Basin Head, PEI

I'm walking on the windy beach at Basin Head Harbour with my dear friend, Sarah. After the conference ended, we wasted no time in renting a car and taking off east in search of the "singing sands" recommended by the bellboy at the hotel. As we navigated the coastal highway, all the frustrations of life felt like they slipped away into the ocean. Now, we've taken our shoes off to walk in the cool Atlantic and we try to convince ourselves that we can hear the sands singing. While we arrived at the conference as stressed-out professionals, a sense of freedom has now overtaken us. We ditched our hotel reservations, snuck into potato fields and danced in the red dirt, and just drove and drove, talking and laughing endlessly like we were carefree university students again. As I inhale the salty air, arm in arm with my friend, I feel my spirit replenish.

Day 7 — en route to Vancouver, BC

"I'm three-and-a-half!" the blond pig-tailed girl in the seat behind me yells. I lean over my chair to check out her doll and pet her baby sister's bald head.

Their mom looks up at me with a proactive apology. "She won't be so cute when she's crying, but I promise, once she falls asleep, it'll be quiet."

"Don't worry about it! I'm a mom too. I have a three-year-old," I laugh. This time, I wish I was wearing a badge that said: I AM MAMA! "Let me know if you need any help."

As I watch the film on the monitor in front of me, I take one ear bud out and listen to the coos and whimpers of the baby behind, the bits of conversation between the mom and her daughters. It's all I can do not to leap behind me and cuddle both of them to me. My body is aching for my own little one.

The last seven days were even longer than I imagined. Every evening I would call home, hear from my husband that everything was fine, then get my chance to talk to Lucas. When he found out

I wasn't on my way home, he'd hang up on me. Guilt ate me, but I decided to still devour each moment so that my boy's week without Mommy would be worth it.

Sitting on the plane home now, I scroll through photos of them on my laptop, tears coming to my eyes. While I am grateful for the time I had for renewal, I realize now that I am missing a piece of me. I set back my watch to Vancouver time, so I can calculate how many more hours until we land. I envision running through the arrival gate and picking up my little blond Lucas, swinging him around and kissing him until he squirms out of my grasp, and then falling into my husband's strong embrace and kissing his rough cheeks.

I had to travel across the country to find myself, only to discover that I needed to return home to be whole again.

~Liesl Jurock
Port Coquitlam, BC

To Decorate a Garden

A day is Eternity's seed, and we are its Gardeners.
~Erika Harris

I t had been a long day and was getting to be an even later night. Our family had been at the lake for nearly a month. On our way home, we stopped to visit friends and ended up staying much later than planned. We just wanted to get home. We all wanted to soak in the tub and sleep in our own beds. I was already regretting keeping our little ones up so late, and the plan was to get them into bed as soon as possible.

I hadn't considered that God might have made other plans.

As we were driving through a town we'd lived in two years before, we passed a familiar house. It was the home of an older gentleman my husband befriended at his previous job, several years before. This man lived alone, and over the years we shared many meals and visits. My husband had generally done everything he could to look out for him. Unfortunately, our move two years earlier caused us to lose touch. This gentleman didn't even have a phone.

As we passed by his house, my husband mentioned that we should stop by the following week on our way back up to the lake. I agreed, of course. Then I felt the tug.

"You know, maybe we should stop there tonight. Like, right now." I couldn't believe what I was saying. All I wanted to do was get home.

"No, that's okay. We'll stop next time. We're already pretty late."

We drove on for about a minute. Then, my husband turned to look at me.

"We really are supposed to stop there right now, aren't we?"

I nodded, and we whipped the truck around and drove back to the house. I am always thankful when God speaks loud enough that I can't ignore Him. I couldn't help but wonder, why now? Why was it so important on this night that we stop?

As we all piled out of the truck, we saw the man in his yard, walking toward us. He stopped for a minute and stared, as if confused. Then, his eyes filled with recognition and tears as my husband walked towards him, carrying our girls. There we stood in his yard, him crying as he spoke of how we were family to him, and my daughters picking wildflowers and placing them all around, happy as could be. They didn't seem to mind being up so late, and I was starting to see how important our short visit was to this man.

Then, as if God Himself was answering all my earlier questions, my three-year-old skipped up to me and said, "Mom, we're here just decorating his garden!"

She danced off, and I was the one left standing there in tears. What is it worth to us to touch someone's soul, to "decorate their garden"? Would we give our time? Are we willing to give a gift that meets someone else's needs? Is it something we just talk about, or something our kids see us do on a regular basis?

We had a wonderful visit as we caught up on life, and our excited old friend insisted we couldn't leave without taking home some of his fresh garden vegetables. The pure joy on his face reassured me that we had indeed done the right thing in turning our truck around.

As we passed through his kitchen on our way home, much later that night, my kids drew my attention to something. On his fridge were four pictures, and nothing else. Those four pictures were of my kids and family. Four pictures given to him with Christmas cards each of the years we had sent him some Christmas baking. My eyes welled up with tears for the second time that evening. I had never understood the place we held in his heart.

We knew there had to be more pictures, baking, meals, and visits. It was something we had to do, despite the distance between us.

I can say I hope my kids learned something that night, about how real giving requires real sacrifice, and about obedience to the prompting of the Holy Spirit or your inner voice. But I'm not sure who needed that lesson more, my kids or myself. It's easy to give our leftovers and toss-offs; the challenge is to give up something that is in limited supply and of value to us, such as our time. It may be hard to give away, but who knows, it might look even more beautiful decorating someone else's garden.

~Jaime Schreiner
Tisdale, SK

The Messenger

All God's angels come to us disguised.
~James Russell Lowell

"I want a cart!" Katie said, pulling a buggy free from the rest.

"I don't think that's such a good idea," I replied, realizing that I was fighting a losing battle. "Just be careful not to hit anything or anybody...." My voice trailed off as it so often does in situations like this. Katie had not been an easy baby. She screamed when my husband Mike was not there to hold her, and she slept very little. As a toddler, she threw herself on the ground in fits of anger and frustration so violently that I thought she might hurt herself. Katie only stopped when she slept.

As I watched my five-year-old daughter precociously wheel the shopping cart through the automatic doors and into the closest fruit stand, I recalled all those nights I had tiptoed into Katie's bedroom after everything went quiet. Sitting at the head of her bed, I'd watch her sleep.

"Mommy loves you," I'd whisper into her ear. "Mommy loves everything about you." I was often so tired, it was difficult for me to know for sure if that was entirely true. My greatest wish for Katie was that she would one day settle into that happy-go-lucky child I had always dreamed she could be, but most days it seemed an impossible dream.

"Oh honey, how about we share a cart," I said, as Katie's cart collided with a large overflowing display of citrus.

"Okay, Mommy," she decided. "I'll just ride in yours."

Spreading her coat in the base of the lower carriage Katie eagerly hopped in while I frantically pushed bread, meat, and bruising pears as far to the back of the cart as possible. For the next half hour, I took my time manoeuvring through the grocery aisles. Katie's long legs stuck out to the right, while her head, rested comfortably on her coat, poked out on the left. At least she was comfortable, and for the moment content.

I thought back to what I had read about that cold Toronto morning of Katie's birth. "Beautiful blue-eyed baby girl" is how the nurses on the ward described her, followed closely by "such a pity" as they placed my infant daughter into an incubator. The drug detoxification would not be easy for such a little baby. At the same time, in the next wing over, her birth mother wrapped a large moth-worn coat around her body and quietly stole away.

Those lilac-blue eyes stared into mine as I rounded the aisle. "She certainly looks happy-go-lucky at the moment," I chuckled to myself, "even if it isn't on my terms." But then again, when did Katie ever do anything on my terms?

"I don't even have time to clean the kitchen." My complaints of the previous night rang in my ears and I cringed at my own negativity. More recently than ever I had been wondering if Katie really benefited from the time we spent together. Only Mike and I understood the hard work that had gone into the past five years. Sure, we'd do it all over again if necessary, but I was exhausted, and I prayed it would never be necessary.

"Oh, she is so cute," a woman said, pulling me from my thoughts.

"Yup, a cute handful," I said quickly. Why did I constantly feel the need to apologize for Katie's behaviour?

"I once had a handful too," the woman said. Her eyes filled with grief. This is small town Ontario, and being the owner of a bustling shop, I knew most people by name, and the rest by face. As she spoke, I realized she was nobody I had ever met in my shop or seen around town or for that matter in the grocery store. This woman, though at first seemingly familiar, was indeed a stranger. Still, I've always known when a person needs to talk. Over the years I've learned that it is prudent to listen. Instinctively I placed my hand on Katie's head to quiet her chatter so I could do just that.

"My little girl loved to ride her bike, but I would never let her ride it down the hill," she began. "She was just ten years old. She told me that all of her friends were allowed to ride on their own, but I never felt comfortable letting her out of my sight. She begged me to let her ride down the hill, just once." The woman paused. My throat tightened.

"Fifteen minutes later, she was gone," the woman continued, and then just as abruptly as she had started, stopped speaking altogether.

My body heaved as I caught my breath. Extending my arms I pulled her into a hug. For those few minutes in the grocery aisle all of the other shoppers disappeared, the jingles on the intercom stopped playing, and Katie lay quiet and still in the cart. Sharing her pain as only a mother can was the only thing I could do, and yet I heard the emptiness of my condolences.

In time the woman moved on through the aisle. Plunging Katie and my load of food past the canned goods, I found my way to the big box of stuffed toys. There at the top sat Katie's favourite.

"Do you want to hold the pink unicorn while Mommy checks out?" I asked. Katie didn't need to answer.

It had been a difficult five years. Katie had issues courtesy of a birth mother who abandoned her long before she was even born.

"You've come so far, baby," I whispered watching Katie hug the toy, "but you are safe now. You're happy, and healthy, and you know you're loved."

As I manoeuvred through the checkout, my exhaustion, like a thick fog, lifted. I wondered what more I could possibly want for my daughter.

"More time," the answer came like a whisper on the wind.

As I placed the last of my groceries on the conveyer belt, the same woman stepped up to the checkout.

"She is so cute," she said as if we had never spoken. "You cherish her, just cherish her."

"Thank you," I said. "I will." Looking one last time into her eyes, I longed to ask her name. But when the words wouldn't come I bundled Katie into her coat and hat and left the store with newfound appreciation for my beautiful little girl.

Taking care to get Katie securely belted into her seat, I held her close for a minute and whispered softly in her ear. "Mommy loves you. Mommy will always love you."

Buckling myself into the car, I waited while the heater engaged. Through the rear-view mirror I saw Katie smiling at me. Pushing her music CD into place I let her sing in the back seat while I waited a little longer for the car to heat. Keeping my eyes on the entrance of the store, I waited five minutes, then ten, but the woman never appeared.

Who was she? To me the answer was clear. Glancing into the rear-view mirror, I smiled back at Katie and thanked God for her in my life. Driving out of the parking lot I whispered another thank you to the angels. They had sent me a special envoy, and I would never forget her message.

~Lorelei Hill
Port Elgin, ON

74

The Elves' Christmas Tree

Christmas waves a magic wand over this world,
and behold, everything is softer and more beautiful.
~Norman Vincent Peale

In our family, the last five nights before Christmas Eve were designated as "Chimney Inspection Nights." This meant that during our single digit years, my little brother Will and I had to be in bed very early and asleep so that Santa's elves could come and check that our chimney and the Christmas tree were ready for his visit. If we passed muster the elves would leave candy canes on our bedroom doorknobs. But I think they had an arrangement with my parents, because Santa's helpers always seemed to wait until the night before Christmas Eve to visit. When I was seven, I was glad they did.

That year my public school, in Lorne Park, Ontario, sold Christmas trees as a fundraiser. Families pre-ordered, and a truckload of evergreens arrived just before Christmas break. The eldest child was given the task of picking out his or her family's tree and tagging it for pick-up. I had been carefully instructed by Mum to select a bushy, well-shaped tree with a straight trunk and at least one good side. The responsibility weighed heavily on my shoulders. The trees were Scotch pines and came in a wide variety of shapes and sizes. I examined and rejected many, but finally found and tagged one that met Mum's exacting criteria. At dinner that night I proudly proclaimed the merits of my tree and after eating, Dad and I returned to the school to pick it up. It wasn't there. My tree had disappeared!

Dad went to ask Principal Stevens for help while I kept looking. I hadn't gone far before my heart dropped into my boots. There, lying in the muddy slush was my tag. Someone else must have taken our tree. We didn't have a tree, and with Christmas only two days away, that night was the last night that the elves could visit! What would we do? Would Santa still come? This was serious!

Apologizing profusely, Mr. Stevens led us to a lone pine standing in the corner of the yard. Even Charlie Brown would have been embarrassed to bring it home.

But with Mum waiting, ready to decorate, Dad wasn't about to return home empty-handed. On the way he suggested we not say anything about the mix-up to Mum. We had a tree and that was all that mattered.

At the house we set the tree in the stand Mum had waiting in the corner of the living room and stepped back to admire our handiwork. I heard Mum gasp. Our tree leaned drunkenly to one side, listing like a sinking ship. Its branches stuck out at some very odd angles and there were bare spots everywhere! Dad tried turning the tree this way and that, to improve the profile, but it was no use.

At first Mum was speechless and then she started to question my choice. I was devastated. I had failed her. Dad intervened and hastily explained the problem. Noting my distress, the look on Mum's face softened and hot chocolate was prescribed to ease our pain. Will and I put on our pyjamas and returned to the kitchen where, while sipping our cocoa, Dad and I told Mum the tale of our missing tree. Will and I had regular hot chocolate, but I think Mum and Dad had something a little stronger. It was now past our bedtime and of course a Chimney Inspection Night, so Mum suggested that we postpone decorating the tree until the morning. As Will and I headed off to bed, I took one last look at the tree. I can remember thinking that it looked so bad the Elves might not approve it and Santa might not leave any presents.

In the morning I found no candy cane on my bedroom doorknob. We had failed inspection! I was heartbroken. As I moped down the hallway to the kitchen I passed the living room and looked in to scowl at the cause of my distress.

There, standing straight and tall, with candy canes hanging from many of the branches was the most perfect Christmas tree I had ever seen. Something magical had occurred!

I spotted Mum curled up asleep in the big easy chair and I ran to shake her awake and show her what had happened. Rubbing the sleep from her eyes, she smiled, hugged me hard and agreed with my exclamation that it was the best Christmas tree ever.

When I asked her what might have happened, she suggested that maybe the Elves had heard about the mix-up and decided to help out. That was good enough for me!

Santa did come and Christmas that year was wonderful as usual. I never questioned how the Elves managed to fix our tree that year, but once I was old enough to know, Dad told me the whole story.

Mum had stayed up most of that night fixing my tree. Using hammer, nails and stove wire, she and Dad managed to force it to stand up straight. Next she employed his brace and bit to bore strategically placed holes in the trunk, and then, using branches from the back of the tree Mum filled in the bare spots, holding her transplanted boughs in place with carpenter's glue and green twine. Her finishing touch was pruning the tree to shape with scissors. I guess you could say that Mum created a "real" artificial Christmas tree.

A tradition was started. Ever since that special Christmas, children in the Forrest family have risen to find candy canes hanging on their tree on the morning after Chimney Inspection Night.

This year, three generations of our family will gather to celebrate and reminisce at Christmas and the story of what is now "The Elves' Christmas Tree" will be recounted. It has been embellished a little, but fortunately Mum is still with us to authenticate and describe the details. And when the children's version of the tale is told, they will listen while nibbling on candy canes, and of course marvel at the magic of the Elves' visit.

But I will always hear in my heart, the real story and remember it fondly as a loving and creative mother's way, of preserving the magic of Christmas for her sons.

~John Forrest
Orillia, ON

Chapter 10

O Canada

Winter Wonderland

When it snows, you have two choices: shovel or make snow angels.

~Author Unknown

Winter in Whitehorse

Sixty below, December in Whitehorse
My nose froze shut, my chest complained
Blinding blizzards, black ice, sleet
Howling winds, days dark by five
Ploughs and fir trees, piles of snow

Mountain roads, the drive from Dawson
Static electricity on hotel rugs
Sparks on my hair, sparks on the sheets
My gown freshly ironed on the double bed
A cup of tea in my plug in pot
A hot bowl of soup, a luxurious bath
Oranges and chocolates, a gift from the manager

My Ramirez guitar in the back of the car
The case wrapped up in a borrowed blanket
A long thin crack in its rosewood back
Scotch taped together hoping it holds

Four school shows, young people's smiles
Teachers, questions, wide eyed kids
Evening concert, no empty seats
Music joining us together
Albéniz, Tárrega, Bach and Boyd
Applause, autographs, fond goodbyes

The warmest welcome, the coldest place
"You will come back?"… "Say you'll come back"

Thirty years passed, but I never did.
Maybe one day I'll return
Sixty below, December in Whitehorse.

~Liona Boyd
Toronto, ON

75

Wind Chill Redux

I am told that the Inuit have some sixty words for snow...
for different kinds of snow. That doesn't surprise me; they see a lot of it.
I live considerably south of the tree line, but even I
have seventeen words for snow —
none of them usable in public.
~Arthur Black

"Cold enough for ya?" Frankly, no. It won't be cold enough for me until your lips are frozen shut and you are physically incapable of asking such inane questions.

What is it about winter weather that turns people into blithering idiots? How come normally intelligent beings start spewing forth vacuous meteorological comments?

At first, I assumed that winter temperatures must freeze the lobe of the human brain that governs common sense. How else to explain such time-wasting observations as: "Boy, it's cold outside!" and "How about that snow?" and "Lookit that ice!"

But now I think there must be another reason. After all, not every member of the species insists on stating the obvious over and over again.

The only explanation I can offer is that these folks actually like winter. Why else would they continually underscore its least charming attributes on a daily basis?

Personally, I don't care for winter. And in the case of something I don't like, I find the less said, the better.

I don't enjoy dwelling on the negative things in my life. That's why you won't hear me talking about death, taxes or our longest, loneliest season: winter. It only serves to make me miserable.

So when I hear people standing by the window announcing "Hey, it's snowing!" I have to assume that they are happy about it. Either that or they possess a mean streak beyond the sadistic.

My preferred method for dealing with winter's charms is to say nothing. In my view, winter is a six-month ordeal that is best endured in silence.

There is no need to parse every aspect of this season from hell. I am well aware that winter is cold, snowy and dark. Rather than endlessly remind myself of these obvious facts, I'd prefer to at least temporarily forget them.

But many people, it seems, can't get enough of winter. Despite having experienced it dozens of times before, they insist on asking "Hey, did you see that freezing rain?" or "How about that snowstorm?"

How about that snowstorm, indeed. I just spent ten minutes putting on boots, mitts, a toque, a scarf and three layers of clothing. I spent another twenty minutes shovelling out the driveway and ten more minutes scraping snow and ice off the car. Let's just say I'm not in the mood to joyfully kibbutz about that "amazing snowstorm."

If there's a death in someone's family, how do you react? That's right. You quietly approach the person and succinctly express your sorrow with a quick "I'm sorry." Or you leave the person alone. As far as I know, you don't say "Boy, was that some death!" or "How about that corpse?"

Well, that's the same approach you should take when it comes to winter. If there has been a nasty winter event (e.g.—temperature below minus twenty-five degrees, more than fifteen centimetres of snow or more than five millimetres of ice on the windshield), just let me mourn in peace. Or, if you must, simply say "I'm sorry" and move on.

Don't ask me "Did your car start?" or "Did you get your driveway shovelled?" I made it in to work, didn't I? Your insensitive and silly questions are like road salt on an open wound.

It's only January and it's going to be very cold for a while. And it's going to be snowy, slushy, icy and unpleasant for months after that. I know that. You know that. We all know that.

So do me a favour, please. Don't talk to me about winter. I don't need a gleeful discussion about the wind chill factor or whether or not we broke any records.

Unless, of course, it's happening somewhere else. If Halifax got two feet of snow then I want to hear all about it.

~David Martin
Ottawa, ON

76

Punishment Mittens

Wisdom consists of the anticipation of consequences.
~Norman Cousins

It's like the Bermuda Triangle. There's definitely some kind of vortex between the bus stop, the playground, and the boot room of every elementary school all over this country. But it's not siphoning airplanes and sailboats out of this dimension and into oblivion. It craves something else — something smaller and woollier. It wants mittens.

Like most kids, my five sons do their best to keep this sucking chasm of mitten doom well fed. Between October and April, my shopping list always includes the perennial items of tissues, oranges, and, of course, mittens. It's inevitable, frustrating, and it's starting to get expensive.

Maybe I should have accepted the mitten drain a long time ago. It was certainly part of life when I was a child growing up in this chilly climate. I spent hundreds of frigid mornings frantically digging through my parents' mitten bin until long after I should have already left for school. In desperation, I'd finally surface with mittens that were painfully different in colour or size — or both. At the worst of times, the only mittens I could find were both meant for the same hand. Remember how comfortable that feels?

Still, as a parent I was sure my boys and I could outmanoeuvre the mitten vortex. Fortunately for keen parents everywhere, the dilemma of lost mittens happens to be the quintessential example of a parenting philosophy known as the "Natural and Logical Consequences" method. According to this very sensible approach, parents should not throw themselves between their kids and the direct results of the kids' actions. In the case of the lost mittens, it means a parent should let a careless child experience the full brunt of the effects of losing mittens. The child's hands should be allowed to go unprotected from the elements so the discomfort of cold hands can help the child learn to value his mittens and take better care of them.

But in Canada—particularly the northern boreal forest region where I raise children—the natural and logical consequences of losing mittens and having to go without when it's minus forty degrees might amount to something more than just a logical breakthrough. The consequences could be something much more memorable—like, say, a trip to the emergency room for some frostbite treatment.

With this clever parenting strategy ruled out, I looked for a more concrete solution to the problem of missing mittens. And I found one in an old classic: mittens-on-a-string. But then I learned a bit of cruel elementary school slang for string mounted mitts. Some kids call them "idiot mittens." It's probably evidence of my own social anxiety issues that I stopped short of branding all my kids "idiots" by stringing their mittens through their coat sleeves.

Instead, I let my boys know that the next one of them to lose a mitten would be sentenced to a full month of wearing the hand-knitted, mostly polyester, barn red pair of mitts my grandmother had mailed us all the way from Nova Scotia as part of our last Christmas package. We called them "the punishment mittens." These drafty, single-ply, flea-market mitts were blasts directly from my past. They were indistinguishable from mittens I'd worn when I was in elementary school and somehow I made it through the 1970s with all my fingers intact. But compared to the modern fleece mitts of the twenty-first century, they were abominations—and my kids knew it.

Regardless of the threat, it wasn't long before my oldest son was trudging out to the bus stop with his little white hands clad in the red, twenty-five-cent mittens zapped here from another decade. I felt a little sorry for him. But at least his handmade mittens were a matching set.

A month later, his sentence of wearing the punishment mittens was over and my son had proved he was starting to understand their true value. We celebrated his enlightenment with a trip to the store to buy a brand new pair of sleek but well-insulated gloves in the same shade of navy blue every other boy at school was wearing that winter.

It was an important lesson, not just for my son's benefit but for mine too. It seems keeping my kids in mittens all winter long, whatever the cost or trouble, is really just keeping myself in mittens. No matter what the parenting books say, we all know what happens in the real world when a real mom has a real kid with really cold hands and long-lost mittens.

"Here," the mom will say, tugging somewhat irately at her own gloves. "You can wear mine."

~Jennifer Quist
Lacombe, AB

Wishing for Snow

Getting an inch of snow is like winning 10 cents in the lottery.
~Bill Watterson

Our family owned a small restaurant and motel in Ontario, Canada near the south shore of Georgian Bay. On a clear day, you could climb to the top of the steep hill behind the motel and look out over the bay's beautiful blue water to see the faint outline of Christian Island. For many people, especially those from places like Toronto and London, this was cottage country. For us, it was home.

Winters were usually snow-filled, cold, and often harsh. Many days started with hours of shovelling walkways and plowing snow. If the steps weren't shovelled and the parking area cleared, customers couldn't come in for breakfast and the bus couldn't turn around in the lot where it picked us up for school. I longed for Christmas vacation when we could enjoy winter sports, and not just clear the snow for school and business reasons.

Christmas at our house was never boring. My friend Brian would always come to visit his aunt and uncle who lived in the little house across the highway. He and I were a dangerous combination. I had a knack for doing just the wrong thing at exactly the right time, and Brian was a catalyst in search of gunpowder to ignite. We were teenagers with the brains of developing four-year-olds.

Usually, when Brian arrived for a winter visit, we'd hike miles over the snowy fields with our rifles in hand. You couldn't really call it hunting—it was more like snow-plinking, taking shots at old logs, leaves, scurrying meadow voles and the occasional rabbit. Sometimes, we'd climb high into the rafters of an abandoned barn and drop breathlessly into huge piles of old hay. When the snow was deep enough, we had one passion. We'd chase and challenge each other at high speed along narrow trails on snowmobiles.

This Christmas, however, there was no snow. We had done pretty much everything we normally did in the cold weather. But both of us kept gazing up the hill at the line of three yellow snowmobiles, engines tuned, already fuelled and calling our names. Only the lack of snow held us back.

It was the night of Christmas Eve and we were lounging around when one of Brian's many relations observed that it was snowing. We hurried outside to find that it wasn't someone's Christmas nog delusion. It really was snowing—great big flakes. In an hour, it was sticking to the ground, and in two, we had an inch. That inch seemed good enough to us. We raced up the hill to the machines.

We opted to buddy up and run the larger, more powerful snowmobile. The engine roared to life and down the hill we raced. One very bumpy trip around the field told us that there just wasn't enough snow yet. So we roared across the highway in a bright display of sparks to Brian's aunt and uncle's place where they were serving a Christmas Eve midnight buffet.

It was the return trip that did us in—or almost did. A little after midnight, we went outside and climbed aboard the snowmobile to return to my house. The engine fired up but the single headlamp remained dark because of a loose ground wire. We didn't care. We could see the house lights in the distance. We jumped on, I gunned the engine, and we took off across the front yard hooting and hollering.

We both saw it at the same time; the words were leaving our lips in unison: "Gas meter!"

Our words hung in space for only a millisecond when there was a jolting CRACK followed by a roar. The rear end of the snowmobile left the ground under the influence of 300 pounds of gas pressure and Brian took flight. A second later, I hit the edge of the road and jumped into the air.

I was alone astride the machine when it struck the hard surface of the highway in an enormous and terrifying shower of sparks. The snowmobile came very close to overturning as the skis and tread slammed into the pavement. Behind me the escaping gas roared like a jet engine at takeoff.

I didn't hesitate. I squeezed the throttle wide open and shot across the road and into the opposite ditch where I shut off the key and bailed out. The machine hadn't stopped coasting forward when Brian ran through the ditch and past me at amazing speed. He was in his stocking feet. At the bottom of the ditch he'd encountered mud and run right out of his shoes. The slapping of his socks on the frozen ground faded quickly as Brian kept on running into the darkness ahead.

Brian and I met at the edge of my driveway. We stood open-mouthed as gas screamed into the air from the broken pipe. Condensation in the sub-zero cold immediately turned liquid to sparkling ice crystals which shot up into the air like a geyser. The silvery beauty of the moment was lost on us. Together again, we turned and ran screaming for my father.

The gas company was called to turn off the gas. They, in turn, called the police to stop traffic along the highway lest any spark from a car set off an explosion or ignite the remaining cloud of natural gas. It took two hours to turn it off.

The policeman arrived at our door at 3 a.m. He was not happy to be there. We had interrupted his Christmas Eve celebration and his mood was very dark. After ranting and raving for several minutes he gave us the bad news: thirteen charges would be filed in the morning. "Merry Christmas" was the last thing he said when he left. He didn't sound very sincere and, to tell the truth, we weren't all that merry. My father looked at me, shook his head, and said, "Go to bed, John."

Christmas morning, the policeman returned. This time, he was smiling when he handed us the court papers and only one ticket. It was a $28 fine. This time, his "Merry Christmas" was much more sincere and I was actually feeling a little merry—until I looked at my father. Dad didn't say anything at all. He just looked at me with his head tilted to one side. Then he shook his head.

In spite of the excitement, we all had a good Christmas. The snow fell heavily and, after a few days' suspension of privileges, Brian and I were allowed to resume our favourite winter sport. We were not, however, under any circumstances, allowed to cross the highway. Ever.

~John P. Walker
Canadian living in New Cumberland, PA, USA

Jour de Neige

When snow falls, nature listens.
~Antoinette van Kleeff

Snow days are not just for kids with toboggans. Their rare occurrence is even more exciting when you're an adult. The city pretty much shuts down due to huge volumes of blinding and drifting snow. That's what the radio announcer blares as he reiterates what the emergency services are reporting. Roads are buried, leaving car and bus traffic impossible. Subways and LRT lines are jammed or immobilized. There is no morning commute. "Stay home," the announcer shouts. "All businesses are advised to remain closed and citizens to stay off the roads." A serious matter, yes. And so we heed the warnings.

The scene of one such snow day was my hometown of Montreal. I was about twenty-two at the time, married and working my first full-time job. The snow began late on a Thursday afternoon, just in time for the afternoon commute. Heavy, wet snow came down hard as I entered the building's parking lot, ready to get into my co-worker's car. Three of us travelled together daily, alternating vehicles. Thankfully it was not my turn to drive. After pitching in to clear the snow off we sat in the car for ten minutes as it warmed up and the windows defrosted. Finally we moved on through the parking lot, windshield wipers working furiously. Our driver managed to edge his way into the crawling traffic that would remain with us for the next three and a half hours. Bear in mind that this was normally a twenty-minute drive along a city expressway.

We inched our way homeward along with thousands of others that evening. Every now and then we'd stop the car entirely so one of us could run out and clear the wipers of icy build-up: a common scene that evening. Rare for Montreal drivers, directional signals were used and respected: if you needed to change lanes or exit, no one cut you off. It seemed that the snow brought out the best in people. Inside our car we entertained one another with stories of the worst snowstorms, best toboggan runs and grandest snow forts we'd each built. We sang songs and played "Name That Tune." The three of us made it home safely that night: tired and hungry yet warmly happy. We were comrades, together against the storm.

The next morning, looking out our apartment windows, my husband and I knew that we, and likely most of Montreal, were stranded. The sky was bleakly grey, heavy snow continued to fall amidst high winds, and neither roads nor sidewalks were visible. The morning radio man loudly declared that the city's transportation services were inoperable and that police demanded that citizens stay indoors and off the roadways. Donny and I looked happily at each other, laughed and leapt back into bed for another hour or so of sleep.

By mid-morning, restless with being in the house, we decided to go out and brave the elements. I think that we wanted to "feel" the storm in our faces: the icy wet wind, the heavy snow on our feet. We dressed in our warmest winter gear and ventured forth.

With no moving vehicles in sight, and no sidewalk defined, we stepped into the broad expanse of roadway that bordered one side of our apartment building. We stood together in the stillness of a street that normally bustled with continuous traffic on its four lanes. There was neither sun nor clouds, and the air matched the sky in its greyness. So did the shoulder-height banks of snow; no definition existed between sky and land, just a blending of greys. We saw no one else and no other footprints. Here and there the shape of a car was visible under the snow and we could barely make out the newspaper and mail boxes that we knew stood at the corner. Looking up we saw low-hanging electrical wires burdened with icicles. Traffic lights flashed wildly out of sync. We moved on. Donny and I walked for a couple of hours that morning—it wasn't all that cold. But it was difficult walking and we probably covered little more than a mile. It felt like a no man's land, with not a soul in sight. I remember the eeriness of the day and what we said as we re-entered our safe and warm apartment. We wondered if the moon would feel like this—wintry, grey, icy and simply devoid of atmosphere.

We spent the remainder of our snow day snugly inside our apartment, reading old newspapers, watching news updates on TV, drinking hot chocolate and eating homemade brownies.

Snow days in Canada are a blessing and a curse. For kids it's a day off school but for the rest of us it's making sure everyone gets home safe and sound. Once that mission is accomplished, time may allow for a bit of fun knowing you're entitled, even supposed, to be playing hooky from the necessities of day-to-day life.

~Janet Caplan
Sooke, BC

A Tale of Two Snowfalls

Life is what happens to you while you're busy making other plans.
~John Lennon

A February snowfall in most parts of Canada is not particularly surprising, but in rain-soaked Vancouver, it can paralyze the entire region. The morning of February 14, 1990, it started snowing. My new boyfriend and I had plans to celebrate our first Valentine's Day together at a romantic lakeside restaurant in a suburb just outside the city. We were to meet at his office after work and go on together from there.

By late afternoon it was still snowing. I decided to take a bus rather than chance driving in those conditions. I asked my sweetie to meet me at a fast food restaurant along the route. Suspecting a slow commute, I left an hour for what would normally be a thirty-minute trip. The bus arrived on time and I hopped on. That's when things started to go wrong. Traffic was indeed bad; the bus crept along so slowly that after an hour, I was still close enough to walk back home. I considered doing just that, but this was before the days of ubiquitous cell phones. I had no way to reach my date, who I knew would be waiting patiently for me at the restaurant. I persevered. As long as traffic was moving, I knew I'd reach him eventually. Then the bus stopped completely. The city was gridlocked. Three hours had passed since I boarded, and I was still barely halfway to my destination. It was time to get off the bus.

I stepped out into a whitewashed landscape. There was not a

taxi in sight, and no buses were running back into the city. They were all stalled in the convoy heading out of town. I had to walk home.

When I finally reached my apartment, covered in a crust of snow, my boyfriend had been waiting for me for more than four hours. I looked up the number for the fast food restaurant where he was waiting and called. I crossed my fingers that I'd reach a sympathetic soul. I knew he wouldn't have given up and left. He just wasn't like that. The employee who answered explained that they could not give a message to a customer.

"Please," I begged. "I am sure you will recognize him. He's a young bald guy, and he's been waiting there for hours — without ordering anything." I guessed that he would not have eaten, hoping that any minute I would walk in and we would be able to carry on with our somewhat delayed plans.

"I know exactly who you mean," the employee replied. "I'll tell him."

No more than thirty minutes later there was a knock on my door. It was my sweetie. He had made it to my place in record time. The roads coming back into the city were completely empty; all the traffic was heading out. It took people up to eight hours to get home that night.

We went out for a quiet, late dinner at a neighbourhood bistro. We had no trouble getting a table as most of their reservations had been cancelled.

Fast forward five years to Valentine's Day 1995. My boyfriend was now my husband and I had a new job at Simon Fraser University, set atop Burnaby Mountain. When I took the job, I had been told that I could look forward to occasional bonus days off as the university usually had to close for a few "snow days" each winter.

After our first disastrous Valentine's Day together, we had not tried to celebrate the occasion again. However, after five years without incident, we decided that it was safe to make plans — another dinner in a cosy romantic setting.

When it started to snow that afternoon, my colleagues advised me to leave right away. I assured them that I would just finish up whatever vitally important document I was working on and go. They all went home. By the time I was ready to depart, I was the only person left in my department and the only road off the mountain had been closed. No one was leaving. I could see the line of stalled traffic from my office window. I was stranded, alone, wearing a business suit, stockings and high heeled shoes—hardly appropriate attire for traipsing around in a snowstorm.

I called my dear husband to come and rescue me. This time it took him much longer to reach me. He had to walk all the way up the mountain—the road was closed at the bottom. He arrived with the best Valentine's Day present ever: pants and hiking boots. We made our way down together and have not celebrated a single Valentine's Day since.

Could it be coincidence that there have not been any more Valentine's snowstorms in Vancouver? Hmmm, perhaps we should have made plans for February 14, 2010—the opening day of the Vancouver Winter Olympics.

~Dawn Livera
Burnaby, BC

80

Canadian Winters Are Not for Fashionistas

There's no such thing as bad weather, only unsuitable clothing.
~Alfred Wainwright

At twenty-something, I was ever so fashionable and cute. I donned a meticulously selected outfit, hat, footwear and accessories for every event. The effect of the look was the priority, not its comfort or practicality, which was all too obvious one winter night in Ontario's cottage country.

I jumped in my little red sports car, heading north for New Year's Eve at my family's cottage in Haliburton. Only a sprinkling of snow dusted the ground in Toronto as I began my two-hour journey north. The traffic was clear and the roads dry, until I turned onto the cottage road from the highway, just thirty minutes south of Algonquin Park.

Without snow tires on my sports car, I felt the car veering closer to the deep ditch of the single lane road, without guardrails to protect my fall. I felt my carefully applied make-up dripping down my face as the sweat began to show my fear. I dropped into low gear, pumped the brake and prayed. Like a puppy walking on ice, I made it to the bottom of the road and arrived at the lakefront cottage.

I took a deep breath and assessed the situation. I was fine, and the car was in one piece. One look in the rear-view mirror and I saw my make-up was the only casualty. Some powder and lipstick did the trick. I jumped out of my car, feeling stylish in my short, leather boots with three-inch heels, tight blue jeans, a leather blazer and sleek blond hairdo peeking from under a fashionable hat. I was too cool for a scarf or gloves.

With my first step out of the car, I knew I was in trouble. My boots sunk through a foot of snow and had absolutely no traction to get me up the icy stairs to the deck where I could make my entrance. I held my arms out for balance, took tiny steps, cursed a few times and made it up the stairs and to the front of the deck. Family and friends were skating on the lake and visiting on the front deck. It was hard to tell who was who since their entire bodies were covered in winter wear that was clearly not going to be seen in the pages of *Chatelaine*.

"I'm here," I announced as I struck a pose to show off my coolness. "Hey there," "You made it," and other welcomes rang out. One voice could be heard above others—my older brother—as he took in my "look" and began to laugh, saying, "Good luck with that," and nodding at my attire. With stubbornness that only a baby sister can muster up, I stuck out my chin and said, "I'm tough. Besides, you won't catch me in an outfit like yours!" I grabbed my first beer and headed off to join the others.

In less than ten minutes it became very clear that the boots had to go. The wet snow had seeped through and I was losing feeling in my toes. I went inside the cottage and borrowed a pair of Ski-Doo boots, lined with 3/4-inch felt. They almost reached my knees and had enough tread to scale an iceberg. Off I went—again. Another fifteen minutes passed and my fingers were turning red with white blotches. I went back in the cottage for lined mitts that reached my elbows, and another beer—to keep me warm.

A little more time passed and my ears begin to sting. Off I went again, but this time, I noticed the snickers from onlookers. My sister guided me by my arm back into the cottage. As the baby sister who is more than a decade younger than the other three siblings, space was often provided to make my own mistakes, but this sister decided enough was enough. Out came the balaclava and a full ski suit from neck to ankles. I stepped back out on the deck, greeted with cheers from the group for my warm attire. I heaved a sigh for my lost coolness, leaving it behind while my great hairdo got crushed and my perfect make-up rubbed off on the inside of the balaclava. I rang in the New Year taking active pleasure in the fun—with warm limbs, no surface skin and fully functioning digits.

~Sheri Gammon Dewling
Markham, ON

81

Another One of Those Canadian Mornings

A lot of people like snow. I find it to be an unnecessary freezing of water.
~Carl Reiner

The irritating buzz of the alarm dragged me from my dreams. I stretched my arm from beneath the covers to silence it. My fumbling fingers found the snooze button, pressed and then recoiled in shock at the feel of the frigid plastic. "Oh no, not again!"

Rolling onto my side I hauled the covers higher on my shoulder, pressed up against my wife Carol and kissed her awake. The radio clicked on and the local station's morning man confirmed my fear. We lived in Ontario's snow belt. Overnight a lake effect snowstorm had blanketed the Orillia area with two feet of the white stuff and the temperature had plummeted to well below zero. This would be "another one of those mornings."

Now in our third year of marriage, Carol and I had already overcome many challenges, but learning to cope with winter living in Canada's mid-north had been our toughest test yet. It was late March of 1971 and I was teaching at an elementary school in Orillia. I had accepted the job the previous November and although we were eager to move to the heart of Ontario's cottage country, like most young couples, Carol and I were long on ambition but short on cash.

We managed to scrape together a down payment and over Christmas break we abandoned our comfortable city apartment and took up residence in a rather rustic cottage on the shore of Lake Couchiching. Although it would prove to be idyllic in the summer, our new home was isolated and ill-suited to winter occupancy. A tiny acorn fireplace and temperamental coal oil space heater were our sources of heat. There was no insulation and the windows were single-glazed. We had managed to install an indoor toilet and a bathtub, but frozen pipes and drains were a common and frustrating occurrence.

However, we prided ourselves on our ability to cope. Outfitted in arctic boots and one-piece snowmobile suits we spent that first winter shovelling tons of snow and splitting forests into firewood. We survived being smoked out in the dead of a sub-zero January night, Carol was assured by the doctor that she would recover full use of the finger she chopped while splitting kindling one frigid February morning.

However today's heavy snowfall would present us with a new challenge. We were the only year-round residents on our road and knew we would be lucky if the snow plow reached us by the next morning. Our lane-way, the nearest concession road and even the main roads would likely be choked with drifts of snow. Travel by automobile would be impossible, but it was imperative that we get to work in town.

Carol had just started a new job with the Federal government and was on probation. And even though the radio announced it was a "snow day," with no school buses running, my elementary school in town had no bussed students. I knew a classroom full of children and my principal would be expecting me. So, eager as always for adventure, we decided to improvise and make the twelve-mile run to Orillia on our snow machine.

Donning our one-piece Ski-Doo suits, helmets, goggles and gauntlets, we prepared for the trek. I pull-started our well used single cylinder Ski-Doo snowmobile and took the driver's position. Carol strapped a backpack containing our lunches and my lesson plans on her back and climbed on behind. While breaking trail out of our laneway, I noted we were running heavy and slow, but we successfully fought our way through the drifts up the concession road and finally reached, as anticipated, an unplowed Rama Road. We were the only moving thing in sight as we headed for Orillia, slogging through the white powder at a top speed of about fifteen miles per hour. Our route took us through the Chippewas of Rama First Nation, Indian Reserve.

As we entered the Village, a lone native dog ran out to investigate and began loping along beside us, tail wagging, barking a welcome. However, our canine companion was soon joined by another dog, and another and yet another; the barking turned to baying. Our friendly escort of domesticated dogs became a snarling, slavering hunt pack, now in hot pursuit, intent on bringing down its motorized quarry.

Squeezing the throttle, I hunched forward praying fervently for more speed. Carol, whose left arm was wrapped around my waist in a death grip, was peering back over her shoulder. She alternated between giving progress reports like a race track announcer, "The black one on the inside is gaining!" and beating frantically on the side of my helmet with her free hand, demanding greater speed! Then fear's icy finger touched our hearts. The Ski-Doo's engine coughed and started to sputter. Our speed began to slip away. Visions of Soviet sleigh riders fleeing ravenous wolves flashed before our eyes; we feared a similar fate as the clamouring canines closed for the kill.

Then the Spirit of the North blessed us. The engine backfired loudly, startling the nearest attackers. The carburetor cleared and the snow machine's engine roared back to life. Slowly, ever so slowly; we inched our way out of reach of fang and claw, leaving our panting pursuers in our snowy wake.

We did make it to Orillia that day. We also arranged for less hazardous transportation home. And to ensure use of the car on the morrow, we devoted hours of backbreaking labour to shovelling the lane-way. Later, in front of a crackling fire, we recorded the day's events in our diary, smug in the knowledge that we had survived "another one of those Canadian mornings!"

~John Forrest
Orillia, ON

82

What We'll Do for Hockey

The problem with winter sports is that—
follow me closely here—they generally take place in winter.
~Dave Barry

Growing up in eastern Ontario, I never became accustomed to the bitter cold of midwinter nights. I'd sleep under layers of crocheted afghans and blankets—sometimes even wearing my mittens to bed.

"Wake up!" My father's rough hand shook my shoulder one January night when I was twelve years old.

I groaned, drawing the covers over my head.

"C'mon, we've got to get going," Dad whispered. "The temperature is supposed to drop tonight. I've got to get that water down."

"Too cold..."

"If we don't do it now we won't have ice. No ice—no hockey."

No hockey? No way! "All right, I'm coming."

First, I hurried to the bathroom. There are few things worse than being a girl zipped up in a snowmobile suit out in the Canadian winter with a full bladder. Might as well be an astronaut on the moon.

Leaving my long underwear on, I put on my cords and my heaviest sweater. The wooden stairs were icy under my thin-socked feet. I hurried to the kitchen and grabbed the wool socks and boot liners that I'd left drying near the woodstove. Awake and shivering,

I pulled them on. I shoved on my best toque, tied on my thick scarf, zipped up my snowmobile suit, shoved my feet into my boots, put on tight gloves and then loose mittens and stepped outside into the crisp, cold night.

The snowmobile's trailer was already loaded with everything we needed. After fastening on my helmet, Dad roared the machine into life. The thunderous sound filled the quiet.

"Hang on," he said.

We rode up the hill and around the trees behind the house. The moon cast our shadows on the snow, stretching long and short as the ground dipped and rose. As Dad turned the snowmobile down the trail to our tree-ringed pond, I could see the rectangle he'd cleared for the rink. It looked the right size—about fifteen metres long and less than half that wide. The snow was banked up about half a metre all around. From a distance, it looked like the perfect ice rink already, but I knew it wasn't. Otherwise I wouldn't be outside at 1 a.m. freezing my rear end!

Dad hopped off, removed his helmet, and started setting up the pump. "Get the shovel," he said. "Run it over the whole rink one more time. Then we'll do the broom. We've got to get every last bit of snow off the ice before we flood it."

I took off my own helmet and pulled the shovel out of the trailer. It wasn't an easy job. I tried to imagine that I was driving a Zamboni machine, careful to cover every inch as I turned and headed down the ice over and over again. My fingers started to grow numb beneath my gloves and mittens. Frost formed where my scarf covered my chapped lips and the frigid wind stung my cheeks like hundreds of needles.

Suddenly I fell! The shovel slipped out of my hands and chipped a chunk out of the ice.

"Wake up, sleepyhead!" Dad yelled. "You'll be the one complaining about that hole later. Hurry up! As soon as I get this pump running, we need to start flooding. The thermometer says it's minus twelve degrees Celsius—just about perfect!"

Grabbing the shovel, and trying to ignore the pain in my knees,

I went back to work. I wondered if Wayne Gretzky ever helped his dad make an ice rink in the middle of a frozen January night.

Dad tried to start the pump.

Chug-a-chunk…

Oh no.

Chug-a-chunk…

This was bad.

Chug-a-chunk…

Dad's swearing echoed across the ice. I started humming a church song so I wouldn't have to hear. Like a prayer.

O God, please make that pump work so my dad doesn't bust a blood vessel….

It felt like hours went by as I finished with the shovel and went back over the ice with the broom. Dad tinkered and swore and tinkered and swore and tinkered and swore. I was finished clearing the ice and my fingers were frozen stiff. Trying to keep warm, I pretended that the broom was my hockey stick and practiced flicking the puck into an imaginary net over and over again. I wasn't big and strong, but I was fast and smart — like Gretzky — and Dad said if I kept practicing my shot, who knew what could happen!

But still, the pump wouldn't start.

Chug-a-chunk…

The wind began to pick up. I could feel it whistling through the zipper on my snowmobile suit. I tried to stay positive. At least my feet weren't frozen. Or were they? I wiggled my toes. Were they warm, or just so cold I couldn't feel them?

O God, please make that pump work so my fingers and toes don't fall off….

Dad had stopped swearing. I went over and stood next to him. His face was red with cold and aggravation.

O God, please help my dad, he's trying to make this ice for me, so we can play hockey…. please God…

"I think we might have to give up," he said.

"No! Could we go back to the house and get buckets?" I pleaded.

"There isn't time," he said. "The temperature is falling again."

"Just try it once more, Dad! Please?"

He turned the ignition.

Chug-a-chunk-chug-chug- chug-chug-chug-chug!

"Yes!" I yelled over the bellowing sound of the working pump.

Dad smiled.

He hooked the pump up to a hole he'd chopped in the ice some distance from the pond. It wasn't perfect—the hose leaked a little and it was hard to get the water to spread evenly. After Dad was satisfied with the first layer, we rode back to the house and had some homemade hot chocolate. I took off my boots and warmed up my toes next to the woodstove as I drank.

After an hour—and a quick bathroom break—we bundled up again and went back to spread a second layer.

After another hour, we spread a third.

Finally, exhausted, we came home. I don't remember dragging myself upstairs and getting back under the covers.

Hours later I woke to the bright, bright morning light that can only come from a January sun reflecting off a thick blanket of snow. Every bone in my body seemed old and creaky.

The phone rang in the kitchen. Groaning and shivering, I put on my robe and went downstairs. Mom got there before me. I sat down at the table and put my head down on my hands. I was so tired.

Mom hung up the phone just before Dad came in the back door carrying our hockey sticks and a roll of tape.

"That was your brother," she told him. "He wants to know if you are still having a hockey game today."

Dad nodded. "Yep, the ice is perfect! Hockey today for sure—that is, unless someone's too tired for some ice time?" He looked at me and raised his eyebrows.

"Too tired for hockey? No way!" I said, jumping up. "I'll get my skates!"

~Leanne Fanning Pankuch
Canadian living in Aurora, IL, USA

Saved

The first fall of snow is not only an event, it is a magical event.
You go to bed in one kind of a world and wake up in another quite different,
and if this is not enchantment then where is it to be found?
~J.B. Priestley

I woke that morning with a sense of dread. I couldn't help it — I just couldn't get my project finished in time. I jumped out of bed and rushed the mundane routine of getting dressed, brushing my teeth and the other tasks that I needed to do before the school bus came. I would have to rush through breakfast too if I was going to have time to finish it.

I was in grade six and my project was due. I had procrastinated and now I would have to pay the price. My plan was to hurry and get as much completed before school as possible.

Then it dawned on me. I had completely forgotten about the weather! Mom had said that I might get lucky as the weather reports were calling for a storm. Living on a side road had its perks, one of them being that we had many days when our bus driver simply decided not to drive down our winding side road due to the weather conditions. After waiting outside until your nose was completely frozen, it was a good bet that you would be welcomed inside and not told to wait a little longer!

I ran to the living room where my mom was peacefully sitting in her rocker sipping a cup of coffee. Her smile said it all. I would not be going to school that day!

It was a wonderful day, one that I will always remember. The weather ended up being much worse than anyone had expected. When everyone else was sleeping the weather was raging! That night, there had been freezing rain in huge volumes. The tree limbs were heavy with the burden of the unwanted ice and snow. The road had been completely frozen and transformed into a smooth ice rink.

Instead of classes and assignments that day, my neighbours and I skated up and down our street. How many people can say that they have had their street transformed into their own personal skating rink? The memory of that day is frozen in my heart. What a wonderful day.

Only in Canada! Oh Canada, how lucky we are to call you our own!

~Brenda Redmond
Kingston, ON

O Canada

Inspiring Canadians

Our hopes are high. Our faith in the people is great. Our courage is strong. And our dreams for this beautiful country will never die.

~Pierre Elliott Trudeau

"Emily Carr"

From the CD *The Return* by Liona Boyd

Lyrics courtesy of Liona Boyd ©2011

Mid-Continental Music SOCAN

On the long summer nights when she lay awake
Listening to the sounds that the night owls make
When she walked in golden forests in the fall
She wanted to paint it all

She saw black bears foot prints in the dampened sand
Was awed by the totem poles of her native land
When she heard the loon and the raven's call
She wanted to paint it all

Victorian lady, Emily Carr
Born beneath a lonely star
She lived and loved and traveled far
But she returned to Vancouver Island

Free spirit and dreamer from the start
She moved to Paris to study art
But only nature soothed her restless heart
And she returned to Vancouver Island

Deep forest greens, tangled roots and trees
Swirling grey clouds on a salty breeze
Driftwood carved by stormy seas
On her beloved Vancouver Island

In England he heart broke, she almost died
The wounds of love left deep scars inside
But she packed her bags when her tears had dried
And headed home to Vancouver Island

There the native tribes loved her quiet ways
Named her "Laughing One", those magic, mystic days
And her spirit shone through the books she'd write
In the cedar fire-lit night

Victorian lady, Emily Carr
Born beneath a lonely star
She lived and loved and traveled far
But she returned to Vancouver Island

When her time ran out and confined to bed
Nature's powerful beauty still in her head
With each flower and forest she'd recall
How she'd wanted to paint it all

Victorian lady, Emily Carr
Born beneath a lonely star
She lived and loved and traveled far
But she returned to Vancouver Island

Free spirit and dreamer from the start
She gave the world her vibrant art
And we still feel her restless heart
On her beloved Vancouver Island

Yes we'll always feel her restless heart
On her beloved Vancouver Island

Fare Thee Well

Nothing is so strong as gentleness, nothing so gentle as real strength.
~Saint Francis de Sales

They say a good teacher doesn't have favourite students. A good doctor favours no patient. And of course, a good parent loves all of their children in equal measure. Indeed, this is more than just fine form; it is humanity's ideal.

But with more than two decades of full-time street work beneath my belt, when it comes to Canada's hodgepodge of homeless faces and factions, the honest truth is that in this regard I have always paled in comparison to just educators, fallen short of ethical physicians, and have existed nowhere on par with the very manner in which I adore my own two children. When it comes to the street, I believe the inside scoop is more than simply my suspicion or opinion. The straight goods and quiet truth is that every road-weary outreach worker, wide-eyed do-gooder, and noble saint worth their salt would ultimately confess — we have favourites.

And mine?

Well, my specialty, "on paper," has always been homeless youth. The very agency I spent my young street-service years with was commissioned to "help young people reach their full life potential." But seldom did a day go by on the streets that my heart wasn't stolen while passing by a wobbly, toothless senior whose mind had been weathered far beyond their feeble body. And if hardcore street seniors suffering with mental illness were my secret favourites, few, if any, were as special to me as a tiny kerchiefed ragdoll named Basil.

Ah, Basil. A wonderfully ironic name for one so mysteriously and richly seasoned by a past that no one knew, and that she could barely recall. For the life-giving months I knew her, she was holed up in a vacant vestibule off the artsy Queen Street corridor of Canada's largest metropolis. Her very self, the grandest and most ignored work of art on the stretch. She was magnificently ancient, with a lifetime of secrets stored in her creaky mind, and a gummy smile meant to melt the heart of God. The better part of a century of family and friends were long lost, with sacred stories and tender moments robbed by mental illness, and further trampled by the unforgiving streets. But there was no less love in her frail heart. There never is for the true survivors.

What a rushed passerby sees in the likes of a Basil is never what's really going on. Dirty faces and soiled sleeping bags serve as a sad camouflage. Hearts still yearn, sweet moments still comfort, and tenderness is still priceless. Here, perhaps more than anywhere! And even if they can only be shared with the tiniest of creatures.

Not just "as" tiny as a mouse. But, in fact, for Basil... a mouse.

Basil's best friend was a tiny grey mouse she called Hickory. (Indeed, à la "hickory dickory dock, the mouse ran up the clock".) Often, I would plop down beside her to chat and share a granola bar or piece of fruit and Hickory would be peeking between her bony fingers as she held him between both hands up against the bottom of her chin, so she could whisper to him and cuddle him while nibbling on her snack.

I would always ask if I could hold him, and the answer always came the same way, after a long gaze, a thoughtful pause, and with a heavy sigh.

"No, no, not today I don't think."

Basil would chat away and story-tell to no end, and usually of no sense, often warbling off into little sing-songs patching together lullaby lines and nursery rhymes—all the while making it clear she was not just talking or singing to me. Hickory was more than present, and in better standing. All the same, we would laugh and carry on until my departure, which always ended with a standing bow, and "Goodbye Basil. So long Hickory." To which she would sit up straight, hold Hickory above her head and reply, "Fare thee well, fine sir."

Then one day, after several weeks of visits, when I got to Basil's alcove, I lowered myself beside her slowly. My mind was focused on other matters, and my heart was particularly heavy. I moved slowly and spoke softly. And Basil tracked me with sensitivity beyond that of an able-minded saint, never less a street urchin with dementia. She was warm and quiet. Still lost in the scattered nonsense of her own mind, she shared her stories in a hush and her songs in a whisper.

After several moments of sweet and obscure comfort, she held her weathered hands in front of me. Hickory's little nose twitching between her thumbs.

"You can hold him today," she peeped. "But very gently," she continued. "Very, very gently."

She delicately placed Hickory in my hands, and quickly wrapped her own tiny hands over mine. Then slowly, she drew my hands to her chin, and whispered into them. I couldn't hear what she said, but her warm breath filled my palms as she assured Hickory she was still there. A heaven-on-earth experience found in the most incomprehensible of moments.

I have pondered this relentlessly, only to conclude that while it was her shocking goodness and unthinkable compassion that allowed me to finally hold her tiny, treasured friend, I believe it was something even more hallowed that she had been waiting on before she could trust me with this honour.

She waited until I came to her gently. And until she knew I could be gentle. The harshness of the streets, the fear of the unknown, the judgment of scowling strangers—none of it had stolen the soul of one who knew the priceless value of gentleness. And no matter what she had tragically lost—in mind, relationships, belongings—on the long journey to wee Hickory and the cold streets, even still, she had gloriously retained a vast love and appreciation for gentle moments and gentle gestures.

Many seasons have gone by since those precious visits with Basil and Hickory. But they, and their impact, have stayed with me. I have maintained, throughout my adulthood, that if I have ever truly met angels in this world, they have all been homeless. I remain suspicious of Basil as such, because she knew too well what all angels must surely know and vow to model... that the true hand of God is first, foremost and always, gentle.

Goodbye Basil. So long Hickory. Be very certain, you have fared thee well. So very well.

~Tim Huff
Toronto, ON

The Gift of Life

We acquire the strength we have overcome.
~Ralph Waldo Emerson

When I was born it didn't take long for doctors to realize that something was seriously wrong. Within hours of birth I began to turn blue. My twenty-three-year-old, first-time parents were told that there was something wrong with my heart and if I was going to survive, I would need open-heart surgery and quickly.

Hours later, I was put on a medical helicopter and flown to the IWK Children's Hospital in Halifax, NS (three hours from our home) for emergency open-heart surgery. The surgery was incredibly risky, especially for a newborn. Fortunately, the surgery went well, but doctors were quick to tell my parents that I wasn't out of the woods yet. A year later there was another surgery. Again, doctors were pleased with the outcome but also cautioned that my lifestyle and activity level would always be compromised by my health.

For twenty-three years I battled the symptoms and complications of congenital heart disease. However, despite the hospital visits, medications and other complications from the condition, I was able to lead a mostly normal life. It wasn't until May 2000 that things took a turn for the worse. That is when I began the journey that would change my life forever.

By October 2000, I began to notice that I was increasingly short of breath, and often fatigued and tired, much more than I should have been. Chalking it up to stress and lack of sleep, I ignored the worsening condition for months, until I went home at the end of the year and saw my doctor. The look on the doctor's face told me that I was much sicker than I realized.

Over the course of that school year, I had lost over thirty pounds (at only 4'11" tall, this was significant since I was only 115 pounds to start). At my lowest, I weighed in at seventy-eight pounds!

I was told that I was in severe congestive heart failure and my health was in a precarious state. After undergoing a series of tests, my cardiologist came back with news that no one was prepared for: "You need a heart and lung transplant and you need it now."

In September my dad and I travelled 1,000 kilometres from home to be evaluated at the Toronto General Hospital to see if I was a candidate for a rare and dangerous heart and double-lung transplant. The surgery happens less than a handful of times in Canada each year; in fact in 2001 there hadn't been a single one done in the whole country. There wasn't much hope that I would be accepted on the list because of my precarious health and the fact that I was so small. A donor would be difficult to find. But we had no other options, so we put all of our eggs in the transplant basket and hoped for the best.

Finally, after a full week of testing and a clear warning that the odds were very much against me, I was placed on the organ transplant waiting list. And in October 2001, my father and I left the rest of our family at home and moved to Toronto to start the wait.

The first month was one of the hardest. Every time the phone rang, I jumped, wondering if it was "The Call." But the months passed, and the call did not come. In April, after waiting for four months, I was told that my heart had developed a life-threatening rhythm abnormality. I would need to remain in hospital under twenty-four-hour surveillance until suitable organs could be found.

For six months, I waited in a small hospital room, each day praying that tomorrow would bring the miracle I needed to save my life. Each night I went to bed praying that I would wake up in the morning.

Finally, on September 6th, at 10:15 p.m. we got the call. My mom and I waited for hours for the surgeons to be ready. Finally, at 5 a.m., they came to the door. I looked at my mom and my mom looked at me, both of us searching for the right words to say, knowing that this might be the last time we would speak to each other. I said, "Mom, I'll see you soon." I wasn't going to mention the possibility of a negative outcome.

The surgery lasted seven hours. Despite a few hiccups, the surgery went well. And after a few days in the ICU, and a week in a step-down unit, I was discharged sixteen days post-surgery. Since then I've been blessed to do some things I never thought would be possible. I've been fortunate to be healthy enough to run four marathons and five half-marathons. I've competed twice for Team Canada at the World Transplant Games and become a fifteen-time medalist at the Canadian Transplant Games. Most recently I was also a part of the first ever all-heart transplant relay team to complete an Iron Distance triathlon. But best of all, my illness led me to discover a career.

After my surgery, I began to share my story with service clubs and schools near where I live. It was a way for me to give back to a community that had been so supportive to me and my family while I was sick. I also enjoyed sharing the lessons about life that I had learned during my illness. And soon, I was being asked to speak at companies and associations and people were offering to pay me. I couldn't believe it.

It's now nine years later and I've gone from speaking at service clubs to speaking at big conventions. I never would have guessed that I would become a professional speaker, but looking back at my journey, I realize that I had been in training for the job during my entire illness. My biggest life challenge has turned into the greatest gift I could have asked for. Every obstacle is just an opportunity in disguise.

~Mark R.W. Black
Dieppe, NB

A Stroke of Inspiration

What other people may find in poetry or art museums,
I find in the flight of a good drive.
~Arnold Palmer

I stood on a grassy mound overlooking the twelfth hole on Arizona's Superstition Mountain Golf Club. The early morning sun lay cradled between the mystical twin peaks of its namesake, providing a spectacular backdrop for our photo. My husband John stood with his arm around my shoulders, as a helpful fellow spectator snapped a commemorative photograph. While John retrieved the camera I turned my attention to the fairway, trying to determine the identity of the professional golfer striding toward me. Six months ago I had only hoped to be here, but against the odds I had made it. The memories came flooding back.

The doctor was succinct. "Carol, the mass in your right breast appears malignant. First we'll remove the cancerous tissue and then begin a treatment plan to fight its spread."

My first thought was, will I live? My second was, how soon can we start treatment and my next was, what about my golf? The answers to those questions would contribute to the tough, tender and even humorous life moments which would inspire me in my battle with breast cancer.

Why golf? I am addicted to the game. I took it up late in life and struggled to improve. Canadian Lorie Kane, a player on the Ladies Professional Golf Association (LPGA) Tour, became my role model.

She too was a late bloomer. After finishing runner-up nine times, many sportswriters questioned her ability to win. But she persevered and had now garnered four LPGA Tournament titles.

Her success inspired me to persevere and my game improved.

Now John and I plan our retired lifestyle around golf and when the snow flies we travel south to play. Unfortunately my cancer diagnosis ended my golf season and might also ruin the trip we had planned to Arizona to watch my heroine play. The surgery was successful and the prognosis good. Chemotherapy was four trips to Hell and back but then I caught a break. It was determined that I was an ideal candidate for a new single step procedure. Radioactive seeds would be implanted in my breast, surrounding the site of the cancer. The surgery went so precisely that the doctor proudly advised that my right breast was now featured in his slide presentation. This was not how I had envisioned receiving my fifteen minutes of fame! Best of all, I was given clearance to travel.

At the United States border we presented our passports and reported our destination. Suddenly two guards appeared. We were escorted to an interrogation room and our van was whisked away. A wand was produced and John was scanned, to no apparent reaction. They scanned me and it buzzed like an angry bee.

"She's radioactive."

"Oh no!" I thought. "I can explain," I pleaded.

The guard smiled. "Relax ma'am. You set off our dirty bomb detector. You have a radioactive implant don't you? Do you have your paperwork?"

I presented my card and we were allowed to pass.

In Arizona, our first task was to acquire tickets for the tournament. I wanted to follow Lorie during her practice round on Wednesday and approach her afterward, but John insisted we attend the Pro-Am event on Monday. So there we were waiting and hoping to hook up with her group. The gallery's applause for the approaching golfers brought me back to the present.

It was Lorie's foursome. I hurried down, took up a position at the thirteenth tee, then glanced back to see John lagging near the players' entrance. Lorie was just passing when suddenly she stopped and started talking with him.

Hey, she's *my* heroine! Had I missed my chance? I was disappointed, if not envious. I began focusing on the players already playing the thirteenth, anticipating John's arrival with his tale to tell. Then I felt a hand on my shoulder.

"Hi Carol, I'm Lorie; I understand that I've been an inspiration to you. I'd like to invite you to walk inside the ropes with me."

My mouth went dry and my legs turned to jelly. I almost said, "Who me?" but rallied, and replied, "I'd love to." Lorie lifted the rope and I stepped boldly into the world of professional golf.

To break the ice, Lorie told me about John contacting her months ago to arrange our meeting. Between shots, we chatted about my treatment, her life on and off tour, how we were both struggling to get our golf games back on track and even swapped stories about our home renovation projects. After holing out the seventeenth Lorie dropped a ball on the green, handed me her putter and said, "Have a go!"

These greens were super-fast compared to those I usually played. I took a deep breath and approached the ball as if it were a live grenade. My hands were shaking so badly I was more concerned about missing the ball completely than sinking it. I stroked and John got a great picture, with Lorie in the background, and my ball rolling toward the hole and lipping out! I retrieved the ball and, like a real pro, casually handed it and the putter to her caddy, before joining Lorie on the walk to the next tee.

Now it was my turn. I was carrying a unique pink ribbon cancer pin, mounted on crossed golf clubs. My hand trembled as I held it out. "Lorie, I'd like you to have this. Thank you for inspiring me."

She immediately pinned it on her visor, then put her arm around me and we walked up the path, cresting the hill overlooking the eighteenth fairway. My special walk would soon be over. Little did I know there was more to come.

On Friday, during tournament play, Lorie needed a low number to make the cut. Now a spectator, outside the ropes, I followed her as she had a fantastic front nine, making three birdies. But it was the par she made on the ninth hole that I will never forget. Her approach shot found a sand bunker so deep, when she swung all we could see was the glint of sunlight off her club. I watched in awe as the ball arced overhead and landed within a yard of the hole. The fans went wild. Lorie made the putt, acknowledged the applause and handed her putter to her caddy. Then, as she walked on her way to the next tee, she stopped and presented the ball to me.

Later that year, back at home, I was awaiting the result of my first post treatment check-up, hoping for the best and watching Lorie play on television. She was just one stroke off the lead in a tournament in California. Glued to the screen, I was cheering every shot. When the camera focused for a close-up of Lorie, lining up a crucial putt, I noted my special pink enamel ribbon still pinned on her visor. She took her stance, stroked the putt and made it! And so will I.

~Carol Forrest
Orillia, ON

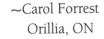

87

Norman the Warrior?

*You are never more like God than when you are
committed to the wellbeing of another, regardless of personal cost.*
~Dr. Larry Crabb

With a severe winter behind us, we were well into the newness of spring. Brave little crocus bulbs began sending their green feelers into the air. Leaves were budding and enthusiastic gardeners had transplants of tomatoes and peppers propped on bright windowsills awaiting the end of the frosts.

You can imagine the disbelief and disappointment I felt when I woke to find the ground covered again in a thick blanket of snow. I was gazing out the window and contemplating the snow when our two pet ducks waddled into view. Norman and Elizabeth, handles our children gave the ducks in honour of my and my wife's middle names, were working hard, very hard, trudging through the chest-high chilly whiteness. They came side by side leaving two duck trails in the virgin snow. However, with fine insight into the ways of efficient snow travel, Elizabeth slowed, and then entered Norman's trail. Now the two made one path, Norman moving into the harsh realities and Elizabeth enjoying the safety of following her man.

Chivalry is not dead, I thought, proudly sharing my name with a warrior like Norman. My chest swelled slightly as I inhaled honourably.

I remained at the bedroom window, watching the only movement in the snow—our ducks. The two waddled about five more steps, at which point Norman stopped. This, needless to say, produced a cessation of Elizabeth's progress as she bumped into the back end of Norman. The two remained motionless—Elizabeth ready to follow, but Norman unwilling to move. "Go Norman, go," I told the closed window. Fed up with her non-moving "leader" Elizabeth pulled out of the position she enjoyed and, leaning hard with effort, once again began plowing snow to come abreast of Norman. Content that he was no longer facing this big, tough, cold world alone, Norman too resumed movement. I exhaled disappointedly. In the fresh snow, the two trails that became one trail were once again two as the two ducks waddled along inefficiently side by side.

This arrangement only lasted temporarily. Norman let his partner gain some distance. "Oh, Norman, don't do it," I said as my breath frosted the window. But at this point he simply slipped behind Liz, leaving her to take the brunt of what life handed the couple. I suppose he hardly realized it was happening, it just felt so good. My shoulders drooped with the thought of my warrior safely travelling behind Elizabeth. Perhaps I could talk the children into changing his name.

I left the window less concerned about the late spring snow and more concerned about the way I handle the "snow" in my life. I think I'm going to return the shovel I bought my wife for Mother's Day.

~Scott Penner
Crowes Mills, NS

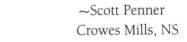

88

Chicken Soup for the Soul.

The Pink Stick Game

Sometimes I think my life would make a great TV movie. It even has the part
where they say, "Stand by. We are experiencing temporary difficulties."
~Robert Brault, www.robertbrault.com

Sitting in Dr. Campbell's office with my husband, waiting for the results of my biopsy, it seemed impossible that this could be the turn my life was taking. You hear stories of younger women getting breast cancer, but they are just stories, right? This is a disease that strikes slightly older women, not thirty-seven-year-old moms with carpools, homework, hockey games and life to attend to. These stories don't really happen to people you know. And they certainly don't happen to you.... this couldn't be my story. But there it was, spoken out loud, never to be taken back, words I will never forget: "Lori I am so sorry to tell you this but you have cancer."

A mastectomy, eighteen weeks of chemotherapy and twenty-five radiation treatments, between carpools, homework and hockey games. I somehow managed to fit it all in. A long and painful chapter in my storybook and not one I like to reread. All but a few pages that is, pages I keep going back to again and again.

It was January 24th, two days before my birthday. I had finally completed my last radiation treatment. It had been a long journey—eight months in total since my initial diagnosis—and I had been looking forward to this day for a very long time. My husband Casey was waiting for me in the lobby at Sunnybrook hospital in Toronto and as we walked hand in hand to the car to begin the drive back to our small town north of the city, we reflected on the past months and discussed what lay ahead for our family. We arrived home in time to have dinner with our three children—Tyler, eleven, Brady, nine, and Eve, six. The kids greeted me with hugs that I think were a little bit tighter and lasted a little bit longer than usual.

We were heading to the rink that night. My son Brady had a playoff hockey game and if his Aurora Tigers Minor Atom AA team won, they would move onto the next round of the playoffs. As a typical Canadian hockey mom, I had always loved going to the rink to watch my kids play. But since my diagnosis, the rink had come to mean even more to me; it was my sanity in those painful months. That's because it was really the only place that I completely forgot about the cancer, and where the ever-present "eyes of pity" could focus elsewhere.

When we arrived at the rink we were greeted with warm hellos. You could tell it was a big game as there was a large crowd of Tiger parents and family members gathering in the lobby outside the dressing room. About ten minutes before game time Brady's coach came out to the lobby and asked the parents to come into the dressing room. He had a few announcements he needed to make before the big game. I was one of the last to file into the tiny room and as I stepped inside I was struck by how quiet it was…. and how pink it was. There in front of me quietly stood seventeen nine-year-old players decked head to toe in pink. Their sticks were taped blade to tip in pink, their hockey socks wrapped up and down with pink, and breast cancer symbols were plastered on their helmets. As Coach Jay began to speak it was difficult to contain the swell of emotion inside me. He had explained to the boys that Brady's mom was going through a tough battle, but that she was winning, and that it was now their turn to battle.

Next my son Brady, a painfully shy child by nature, and his friend Johnny stepped forward in front of their teammates and all the parents, looked at me and explained how I had taught them what it really meant to be a Tiger. They said that I had shown them through my fight that even when it is hard you need to keep fighting.

With tears streaming down my face (as well as the faces of all other parents in the dressing room) my son taped an honourary C to my jacket, explaining to me that tonight I was the captain and they were going to play tonight's game with the same fight and determination I had shown to them all season. And they were going to win this one just for me.

Out on the ice the Pink Tigers warmed up with what seemed to me to be a little extra intensity. Before the puck drop the players skated over to the stands and held their sticks up to me as a final salute to their captain before the big game.

Five minutes into the game Brady took a long pass to go in on a break-away. As the goalie came out to cut off the angle, Brady deked around him to the left and backhanded it in the net. The crowd went wild as the poetry of my son getting the first goal of the game was not lost on anyone. The Georgina Blaze answered back with a nice goal in the second period to tie the game but the Tigers were not to be outdone. Early in the third, Brady battled for the puck in the corner, slid by the defender, rushed out to the front of the net and fired the puck top shelf for his second goal of the game. The roar of the crowd was even louder than the first goal as the Tiger parents screamed, hugged and patted me on the back.

The third period had the Tigers score one more goal to go up 3-1 and as the game approached the final four minutes, it was clear that the coaches were going to do everything they could to get Brady his hat trick. As my tired son headed to the bench for a change, the coach let his wingers off but pointed at the faceoff circle and waved Brady back onto the ice. Another shift and then another and the coaching staff smiled but would not let him off the ice. With one minute left the Georgina coaches pulled their goalie in a last attempt to get back into the game. As Brady skated down the ice towards the puck the crowd was on their feet. Using a last burst of speed and adrenaline he stole the puck in the opposing team's end, headed towards the net, snuck by one defender and then another and buried the shot in the empty net. In classic Canadian hockey tradition, to the cheers of the parents in the stands, I removed the hat that had been covering my bald head, and threw it over the boards and onto the ice.

As I uncorked the non-alcoholic champagne in the dressing room with my son's arms tightly around me, I kept thinking that this story is the stuff movies are made of. They don't really happen to real people you know. And they certainly don't happen to people like you. This couldn't be my story... but it was.

~Lori Futterer
Aurora, ON

The Coach

Leadership is based on a spiritual quality;
the power to inspire, the power to inspire others to follow.
~Vince Lombardi

I was taping a motivational phrase to my son's bedroom mirror when the memories came flooding back...

The final horn sounded in my mind. The bench cleared en masse and the on-ice celebration began. We were winners; but it was the end. As a team, we would never play another game.

Order was being restored when I spotted the tall figure standing alone at the gate of our players' box. I knew he would not join us on the rink. Retrieving the game puck from the melee, I skated toward him and proffered it.

His name was Frank Danby, but to me he was simply The Coach.

The Coach took on the task of forming a new ice hockey team from a group of teenagers that was literally a 1950's version of Disney's *Mighty Ducks*. We were not his first hockey team, but we would be his last. Some of us were local guys who were new to the league and some were cast-offs, cut from teams in neighbouring communities. We had a wide range of size, talent and personalities, some very good players and a lot of other boys who wanted to be. From scorers to checkers we would become The Coach's team, and no one who gave their best was ever cut or benched just to help us win.

Ice time was scarce in those days and older teams drew the worst practice times. Ours was brutal: Saturday mornings at 6:30. We whined. The Coach responded by convincing the arena's manager to let us on earlier and challenged us to skate with him, starting at 5:30! Although he was in his sixties, The Coach was always first on the ice, and even though some of us arrived a little worse for wear, straight from Friday night dates and parties, no one considered skipping one of those two-hour practices.

I can still feel the frigid arena air grabbing at my lungs as we skated our warm-up circuits. The snick, snick of skate blades carving fresh ice was music to our ears. It was a time before helmets, and as we ran our drills the heat rose from our heads, forming vaporous halos in the freezing air above. Gliding, bent at the waist, sticks across our knees, sucking wind, we sprang back into action at each blast of his whistle. We would skate, shoot and check to the point of exhaustion and then beg to be allowed to scrimmage for the pure joy of it. And when it was over, we suffered the delicious agony of tingling toes when the skates came off and warmth began to seep slowly back into our numb feet.

Every Saturday, The Coach was there, teaching and guiding as he put us through our paces. He honed and made the most of what skills we possessed and he set an example for us in his attitude toward sport. For him, winning wasn't everything. What mattered was how you played the game.

I can see him still—a tall, gaunt figure stooped slightly at the shoulders, towering above us behind the players' bench, fedora pushed slightly up on his forehead. His demeanour was calm and his expression was thoughtful and all-knowing. His voice was low and gravelly and he spoke in measured tones, with the odd "humph" for emphasis. He rarely yelled and I can't remember him ever berating a player.

The Coach didn't demand respect; he commanded it! You knew that if you practised and played his way—hard, clean and smart—and gave a hundred percent every time you laced up your skates, the winning would take care of itself. It did, and we became a force to be reckoned with.

Two years in a row we made the finals, but two years in a row injuries forced me to sit in the stands and watch in frustration as teams with perhaps more individual talent, but certainly less character, denied us the goal we sought. Some coaches might have cut me, or others, and found new players, or called it quits, but not The Coach. He knew it was just a matter of a little more time.

The next year came and we never lost again. Two years, undefeated over ninety games, two League Pennants, two County Titles and a City Championship. Nobody beat The Coach's team ever again.

We couldn't have known then the pride he felt, but I understand now. Pride, not just in winning, but in moulding a bunch of boys into a team of young men. The Coach taught us more than hockey skills; he taught us skills for life. And as the years passed, he followed the careers of his boys and spoke often, with pride, of their success in business, education and sport.

I became a coach and my son played hockey. The verse I was taping to his mirror was a mantra shared with us by The Coach; a quote from sportswriter Grantland Rice. It read: "When the one great scorer comes, to mark against your name; it matters not who won or lost, but how you played the game."

As I smoothed the last piece of tape to the mirrored glass, I remembered the end of our last game....

The Coach took the puck from my hand. Tough sixteen-year-old defencemen aren't supposed to cry, so no words were exchanged. He studied it for a moment, turning it slowly in his hand. That battle-scarred black disc represented the achievement of a dream and the end of a four-year journey our team took with him, which would forever mark the lives of a dozen young men. The Coach nodded, slipped the puck into the pocket of his coat, turned and walked slowly down the ramp toward the locker room. Not much of a trophy, but it was enough.

~John Forrest
Orillia, ON

90

Surviving a Stroke
at Age Ten

There is no education like adversity.
~Disraeli

The worst thing that ever happened to me happened on June 25, 2005. Ten days after my tenth birthday. I was your typical ten-year-old. I had best friends who I had known since preschool, lots of hobbies and interests, and I would constantly fight with my younger sister. It was the weekend before the last week of school. The week when you would go on a bunch of fun field trips, clean up the classroom, and basically do no schoolwork.

My family decided to go to our cottage, in Lake of the Woods, Ontario, for the weekend. It was hot and sunny. It was the perfect time to water-ski and to use our paddleboat. My cousins were at the cottage too, and their cottage was right beside ours, so we spent that Saturday together. When it started to get close to dinner, my sister and I decided to go home.

The sun was setting, making a beautiful orange glow over the lake. My sister, my dad and I decided to jump into the lake one last time before bed. When I began to walk up the steps from the dock to our cottage, it all started.

I started to feel a faint headache on the left side of my head but ignored it; I assumed it would go away later. But I was terribly wrong.

As the night progressed my headache got worse. My mom suggested I try to go to sleep early; it would be fine by morning.

I tried to fall asleep, but couldn't. I threw up a couple of times, and the most painful throbbing I had ever experienced continued. It felt like my head was going to explode. I started to explain to my parents that I should go to a doctor, but for some reason I couldn't get the words out. "Are you trying to say you need to go to the hospital?" my dad asked. I could tell he was really worried at this point. At first, my mom thought we should wait until the morning, because by then it was really late, and Kenora, the town close to our cottage, was a forty-minute drive.

But I knew this wasn't just a bad headache. Something was very wrong. I sat on the floor in our living room, pressing my head against the cold wood, but nothing eased the pain.

My parents decided to call my grandma to babysit my sister, and they put me in the minivan. We drove up and down the hills to Kenora. Each bump the car went over, my head ached more. The last thing I remember was looking out the window to the tops of the trees. Then, everything went black. My dad told me months later what had happened after I blacked out.

At the Kenora hospital, the doctors at first couldn't figure out what was wrong with me. They thought I might have West Nile virus. However, after a few CAT scans, it wasn't even close.

At the age of ten, I was having a massive stroke. I was raced to Winnipeg in an ambulance, and underwent surgery on June 26th. The surgery took about eight hours. A week later, I opened my eyes.

I was on a bed in a room I had never been before. The place smelled really bad, and there were big machines and beeping sounds. I looked up to see a bunch of tubes connected to me, one even up my nose. I thought I must be having a bad dream because at the time I didn't remember the headache or even the day it happened. I then saw my parents and my sister walking towards me with extreme relief and sadness in their eyes. I realized it wasn't a dream. I lifted up my left arm and felt something strange on the left side of my head:

stitches. From the top of my head all the way down. Why on earth did I have stitches?

I was taken out of the Intensive Care Unit and put into another room. For the first day all I did was sleep. But when I had to go to the washroom, I realized something horrible must have happened—I couldn't walk. I couldn't control my right leg. I also couldn't control my right arm. And since I am right-handed, I couldn't write or draw. It was horrible! I loved to draw and doodle. But worst of all, I couldn't talk. I could form words in my head, but couldn't say anything except gibberish and baby talk. At least I was alive. My surgeon had not been sure if I would wake up after the surgery.

I spent my summer vacation in the hospital, relearning everything. I had to learn to read, walk, eat, speak, and write. I was frustrated all the time. I had to visit a bunch of doctors for tests and since I couldn't walk, I used a red wheelchair. It's interesting how many stares you get when you are in a wheelchair, even in a hospital.

After months, I was able to overcome all of the challenges. I was able to walk again, I could speak again, and eat again. It took me a longer time to control my right arm; I spent a lot of time drawing pictures that looked like they were drawn by a four-year-old. It took a long time for me to use the keyboard, but by the end of the summer, I could write again. It also took me a while to get back to my old reading level. I remain blind in the bottom right edge of my right eye because of the stroke. Even today, six years later, I trip over tons of things because of that blind spot.

As for school, for the next two years I needed an assistant and mostly had to work in the resource room instead of a normal classroom. I would get tired and need to take breaks or else I would fall asleep. But when I got into the seventh grade, I could work alone, and, surprisingly, made it onto the honour role. At the end of the year I won Highest Mark for General Grade 7 English. A while ago, I couldn't even read a grade two-level book.

The stroke was definitely the worst thing that ever happened to me, but it also taught me the most important lessons: You can't take life for granted. I was a normal, healthy ten-year-old and then

I almost died. Although strokes usually occur in older people, there are different kinds of strokes, including some that kids, even babies, can have. And the most important thing I learned is you can recover and accomplish anything if you set your mind to it.

~Nikki Vincent, age 16
Winnipeg, MB

91

The Man on the Bridge

Act as if what you do makes a difference. It does.
~William James

"It's okay, all is well, drive carefully." This was the message my weary brain formulated back in the fall of 1997 when I first encountered the "man on the bridge." I'd been to meetings in the city of Halifax all day and was tired and anxious to get home to the Annapolis Valley—a little over an hour's drive.

As I approached Mount Uniacke, the weather changed and the road became treacherous—the first storm of the season. Frightened, I gingerly picked my way towards home. Tension rose as tractor trailers swished by and my old sedan moaned and groaned.

Gripping the wheel, I noticed my headlights outlining a lonely figure shrouded in mist on the Highway 101 overpass, just outside Hantsport—my halfway-home mark. As if guiding me through the storm, the mysterious man slowly raised a large hand in a friendly gesture. I sounded my horn in appreciation and continued my journey safely home. Since that November day, I always looked for the man on the bridge. Faithfully, he stood there, almost motionless, his rosy-cheeked face welcoming weary travellers. And whenever our grandchildren were with us, the man gazed kindly as they waved with excitement at seeing his outstretched hand and slight grin. Others mentioned that they too had tooted to the man. People who travelled to work in the city called him their beacon on the bridge.

Then one day on the last leg of a long journey home from New

Brunswick, my husband and I noticed there was no mysterious man standing on the Bog Road Bridge. Where was the large quiet figure? We missed him. No one we talked to knew what had happened to our messenger on the bridge. We didn't even know his name.

Soon a letter appeared in the daily provincial newspaper asking about Nova Scotia's gentle giant, the ambassador who welcomed all to visit his Annapolis Valley. We learned that our overpass friend's name was Freddie. And although he had been ill, Freddie planned to return to his post on the bridge, cautioning all to slow down and enjoy the ride home.

We also learned that complications at birth in 1954 had left Freddie with some challenges. In his early years he had attended a special training school in Truro, NS, but he'd returned to the Valley at the same time an overpass was being built—just down the road from his home. A lover of trucks, Freddie would stand on the overpass bridge facing east, waving to all the truck drivers. They honked their horns in return, pleased to see a stranger's token of friendship. (A long stretch of highway and a steep incline leads to the overpass, which can be seen for at least a kilometre away.)

When the weather is balmy, Freddie, who is a keen hockey fan, can be seen wearing a colourful hockey jersey; he owns jerseys of all thirty National Hockey League teams—many of them gifts. On stormy days he wears a bright safety vest, a gift from his hometown of Hantsport. In good weather or bad, he offers a gift to all who travel Highway 101, helping people to forget their trials and tribulations, if only for a little while.

Through the years his impromptu bit of human bonding has touched many hearts and steadied many nerves. Internationally renowned Wolfville artist, Alex Coleville painted his 1996 work titled, West Brooklyn Road, after being inspired by Freddie. It features a man on a bridge waving to a truck driver.

In no small way, Freddie's sense of neighbourliness has been an inspiration to all of us here in Nova Scotia. Waving, after all, is a gesture of goodwill. And in our fast-paced world, even the grumpiest person feels better after being greeted by a hearty wave.

Freddie has found what we all seek in life: A reason for being. Like a shepherd watching over his flock, he stands tall, guiding us home — on the newly named Nova Scotia bridge: The Freddie Wilson Overpass.

~Phyllis Jardine
Centreville, NS

O Canada

That Famous
Canadian Hospitality

*Canada is one of the planet's most comfortable, and caring, societies.
The United Nations Human Development Index cited the country as
the most desirable place in the world to live.*

~Time magazine

"Thank You for Bringing Me Home"

From the CD *The Return* by Liona Boyd

Lyrics courtesy of Liona Boyd ©2011

Mid-Continental Music SOCAN

Toronto I knew you long ago
Over the years I've watched you grow
I've been away, but now I know
Toronto I've missed you so

Vancouver I lived here once before
Wandered up and down your western shore
And those rainy streets that I'd explore
No one could have loved you more

Maritime provinces I knew you well
Every fishing town and small hotel
Loved your sandy coves and salty smell
And the fog I remember well

Canada oh Canada
Oh how the years have flown
Ad mare usque ad mare
Thank you for bringing me home

Canada oh Canada
Oh how the years have flown
Ad mare usque ad mare
Thank you for bringing me home

It feels great to be here today
Don't care what my critics say
A love affair stole me away
But now I know I'm here to stay

Montreal I knew you long ago
I've missed your joie de vivre and your snow
And a certain man who I let go
Montreal I've missed you so

Let the prairie winds keep blowing strong
Showing me the place where I belong
Knowing in my heart and in my songs
I have been away too long

Canada I left you years ago
But I had to fly, I had to grow
Now that I've returned, one thing I know
I have really missed you so

Canada oh Canada
Oh how the years have flown
Ad mare usque ad mare
Thank you for bringing me home

Canada oh Canada
Oh how the years have flown
Ad mare usque ad mare
Thank you for bringing me
Thank you for bringing me

Thank you for bringing me home

La la la la la la la la…

92

Four Corvettes

Let me close as I did in Gander on September 11, 2002
when I went to that community to thank the people of Gander
and the people of Canada for the overwhelming support and help
that was given to us in the wake of those attacks on September 11, 2001.
~Paul Cellucci, U.S. Ambassador to Canada

Four Corvettes. Four couples. Four weeks. We were going on a road trip with our friends; each of the four couples would be driving a Corvette and we would be away for four weeks. The planning for our adventure took about six months. It takes a lot of planning and coordination to get dates that work for eight people, figure out what everyone wants to see, plan a route, reserve the hotels and pack. Packing for four weeks in a Corvette's tiny luggage space takes lots of creativity. You wind up wearing the same outfits more than a few times. It's a good thing that we were all such good friends! Our strategy was to make everything fit in the car and still leave room for shopping along the way.

Finally it was time to leave. We all lived in California, so our route took us east and north through Montana and then into Canada. We tried to stay off the major highways so that we could see as much of the beautiful, natural scenery as possible. We crossed over the border into Canada after driving through Glacier National Park. The border crossing was a small kiosk on a lovely two-lane country road. There were no buildings or people to be seen—just open road for as far as you could see. There was one person stationed in the kiosk—how lonely for him! We slowed down, preparing to stop but he just tipped his hat to us and waved us on... right into Canada. We didn't even have to stop. Now I must say we were pretty spiffy looking—four Corvettes of various colors, all in a row. I think he was impressed.

We were impressed. Canada is beautiful. Our first few nights were spent in Calgary. And then it was on to the Banff Springs Hotel for some time in the Banff National Forest. What an amazing place. Driving through the Canadian Rockies was so breathtakingly beautiful. On our last night at the hotel we had a fabulous dinner in the main dining room and then sat in the immense lobby talking with our friends. We felt as if we were in a fairy tale. We never wanted it to end.

But end it did. Abruptly. The next morning was September 11, 2001. We awoke to the news of the terrorist attacks on our country. This nightmare just couldn't be happening. But it was. We met our friends in the hotel restaurant for coffee. No one felt like eating anything. There were groups of people gathered around television sets and radios, watching and listening as the horror unfolded. Everyone was in shock. The disbelief on the faces of the people told the whole story. No one knew what to do... or what to say.

We were in a foreign country and all we wanted to do was go home. We wanted to be with our families. We wanted to hug our kids. But we couldn't go home. The borders were closed. No one could cross. Thank goodness for cell phones! At this point we were just midway through our trip. Even though we still had plans to be in Canada for a while longer, it was weird knowing that we couldn't go home if we wanted to. It was a scary, spooky feeling. And we were to be on the road again. We were moving on to Lake Louise.

Our somber group of caravaners hit the road. When we pulled up to Chateau Lake Louise we were again in awe of the beautiful surroundings—both the natural beauty around us and the beauty of the hotel itself. But the thing that impressed us the most was the wonderful Canadian people. Our four Corvettes did attract attention. And our cars had California license plates that made it pretty obvious we were visitors from the United States. Strangers—hotel guests and employees alike—came over to us to offer us their condolences on the tragedy that had happened in our country. Strangers became friends. Without exception, people asked us if there was anything that they could do for us. They assured us that our two countries were united—that the border between us was just an imaginary line. And I'll never forget this. There were two flags flying at the hotel overlooking beautiful Lake Louise—the Canadian flag and the flag of the United States of America. Both were flying side by side—at half-staff. It brought tears to my eyes.

At dinner that night, people in the restaurant were quiet and subdued. No music played. Word had gotten around that the table of eight over in the corner of the room was a table of people from California. People kept coming over to comfort us and to console us. Was there anything that they could do for us? Did we need anything? In times of tragedy, the true goodness and kindness of people comes forth. It certainly did for us at that time.

And the warmth and friendliness of the Canadian people continued as we travelled on down the road. From Lake Louise to Jasper to Whistler to Victoria, the story was the same. The towns were different but the people were the same. They reached out to us to offer a kind word and a hug. We were completely impressed by the physical beauty of Canada and by the warmth, hospitality and generosity of the Canadian people.

When it was time to go home, the borders between our two countries were once again open. We were to board the ferryboat in Victoria and return to U.S. soil in Washington.

This time our border crossing was quite different. Because of the attacks, the security was tight—to say the least. We were required to arrive at the loading area three hours early. Each car that was going onto the ferry was searched completely; each piece of luggage and its contents were checked thoroughly. Mirrors were used to check underneath all cars. Passports were checked and rechecked. Once you and your car had been cleared you couldn't leave the locked yard. Not for any reason. But all Canadian security personnel were polite and professional. They made a difficult situation as easy as possible for us.

Finally we were allowed to drive our cars onto the ferry for the crossing. We arrived at Port Angeles, Washington. We were back in the United States. Disembarking was just as difficult as embarking. You couldn't just drive off the ferry. Cars and luggage were checked again, passports were checked again, people were questioned again. Security personnel even had bomb-sniffing dogs checking around each and every car. Difficult, yes—but we were home!

We will never forget Canada. It is such a beautiful country. And we will never, ever forget the Canadian people. How wonderful they were. They taught us a lesson during the time we were there. We all need to reach out to others with kindness and compassion. It really does help and comfort during tough times and it really does make a difference. Thank you, Canadian people. We really appreciate you. We are making plans to come back soon and explore more of your wonderful country. You'll know it's us. We'll be the four couples driving those four Corvettes of various colors, all in a row. Don't forget to wave when you see us!

~Barbara LoMonaco
Santa Barbara, CA, USA

93

The Friendliest Folks Around

When I'm in Canada, I feel this is what the world should be like.
~Jane Fonda

Excitement bubbled in my chest as my sister Jacque and I walked up the steps of Souris Town Hall, a handsome, three-story building of island sandstone. I nearly pinched myself to make sure I was really in this beautiful seaside town on Prince Edward Island.

"I hope they have pins," Jacque said as we entered what appeared to be a public room. "Tourist season doesn't start for another two weeks."

A woman immediately came to the counter and welcomed us. "Are you in Souris for long?" she asked.

We explained that Jacque had lived there a year, but I was visiting for only a week and Souris was the first stop on our sightseeing adventure.

She and Jacque talked about our plans to go to Basin Head and East Point Lighthouse. Then Jacque asked about pins. The woman got us two each, one with an image of a lighthouse and the coastline along with the name Souris in swirling white letters, and the other with the words "100 years."

"100 years?" I wondered aloud.

"This year is the hundredth birthday of Souris's incorporation.

You might be interested in the play we're having tomorrow night, written for the celebration."

I was very interested. I love local theatre.

"A story of the Irish, Scotch and French Acadians here. All local people in it. It will be held in the Souris Cinema," she explained.

"I saw the Souris Cinema when we came in. Brown building. Big white letters on the side."

The woman's face mirrored my own enthusiasm. "It was closed for the last five years and nearly torn down, but Keir Gallery from Charlottetown bought it and local volunteers have rehabbed it."

A real community effort. This town touched my heart. I thought of something I'd read on the Souris website: "We're the friendliest folks around." Maybe so. "Can we go?" I begged Jacque. "It's a birthday party."

"Where can we get tickets?" she asked.

A second woman joined us from another room. "I heard you talking about tickets. If you can wait five minutes, I think my mother has some," she said and hurried out.

She soon returned with a petite, smiling woman who handed us four tickets discounted to five dollars each. I promptly paid her. "I was home from work making pies and fudge," she said. "If you come to the play, I'll bring you some fudge."

"I love fudge. Especially homemade." I assumed they were having a bake sale to help pay for the theatre's renovation. I'd be glad to buy something for such a worthy cause.

"I'll see you then." She nodded and left.

"She's going to make you fudge." Jacque nudged me with her elbow as we walked to our car. "How cool is that?"

I shook my head. "It's not for me. It's for a fundraiser for the theatre. I'll buy us all some."

"No, she's making it for you. People are like that on PEI."

"No one's going to make fudge for a total stranger," I insisted.

She shook her head like I was hopelessly naïve, but I was sure she was the naïve one.

We visited St. Mary's next, a big church made of island sandstone like the Town Hall. Strains of music reached us as we entered, and to my delight we found a group of high school students at the front of the church warming up their instruments.

"What's going on?" I asked a student when he left his folding chair to get some music from his backpack.

"We're having a concert. Part of the hundred year celebration," he explained. "You're welcome to stay if you have the time."

He and a fellow student talked with us for several minutes about the concert and about the schools involved in it. I thought back to my high school days when I played the oboe. Would I have been as gracious to strangers as these young men inviting us to join in their festivities? Or would I have stuck close to my friends? They seemed to know they had a reputation to uphold as the friendliest folks around.

I watched younger students and adults that must be their parents and grandparents file into the pews. Jacque and I and our husbands listened to the concert, and then we continued our sightseeing. PEI's green fields, red bluffs, woods of birch and oak, and, everywhere, glimpses of white sands and wind-whipped waters enchanted me. Could the tranquil beauty of the province have something to do with how pleasant and gracious the residents were?

When we got to the theatre the next night, it seemed like all 1,500 inhabitants of Souris were there, talking with each other. I learned the play was sold out and people were being turned away, and I felt both guilty and special. "Watch for the lady who's bringing you fudge," Jacque reminded me.

I shook my head and looked around for a concession stand. When I didn't see food anywhere, I decided it must be planned for intermission.

Then I saw the woman who'd brought us the tickets coming toward me carrying a small box hand-painted with a floral design. "I made the fudge today, right after work," she said, handing me the lovely box.

"You made it for me?" I stammered.

"For you. You said you like fudge."

"I love fudge. I…"

She slipped back into the crowd before I could say a proper thank you.

"See?" Jacque said triumphantly.

I couldn't believe it. The woman had made me fudge. No bake sale. Just me, ordinary tourist. I held the box carefully, like a young woman holding a bouquet of red roses.

"I don't even know her name," I murmured. When I saw her take a seat in the auditorium I made my way to her. "I'm Samantha," I said, hoping I didn't sound too bold. "And you're the nicest person I've ever met."

"Audrey Macinnis." She smiled and introduced me to her mother Lily, and her daughter Shelly whom we'd talked with at Town Hall. I wrote down Audrey's e-mail address, and, clutching my precious box, returned to my seat. The lights dimmed as I peeked into it and took a sliver of the best brown sugar fudge I'd ever tasted. Fudge made especially for me. The people of Souris really were the friendliest folks around.

~Samantha Ducloux Waltz
Lake Oswego, OR, USA

It Pays to Ask Questions!

I take tips from Canada on a lot of things.
~Barack Obama

On a sunny summer day, I climbed the steps of the Parliament Building in Victoria, British Columbia, and found the doors locked. It was a weekday, the flags were all flying, tourists were everywhere, and yet the building was shut down tight.

A security guard was standing nearby and I approached him. He was politely listening to a woman complain that the groundskeeper should do something about "that big old scraggly tree" in front of the building. She harshly proclaimed it "an eyesore" and said it was ruining her photographs!

Well, I had done enough homework before my vacation to know that the gorgeous tree standing proud and majestic before the building was a giant Sequoia, the last surviving one of a row that had been planted over a hundred years ago. How dare that woman criticize its existence!

"Excuse me," I interrupted. "But I'd like to ask a question." The annoying woman gave me a somewhat dirty look and stomped off without further comment.

I leaned in close to the security guard. "You owe me," I whispered, and we both laughed.

"What may I do for you?" he asked.

"Why is the Parliament Building closed today?"

"Why, it's BC Day!" he exclaimed. "The first Monday in August! All government agencies are on holiday!"

I thought quickly, but spoke slowly. "BC... British Columbia... Celebrating the day British Columbia became a province?"

"Not quite," he replied. "BC Day is a statutory summer holiday to give Canadians in the province the chance to celebrate their achievements or relax with friends and family. It's a three-day weekend for most folks."

"But—you're working." I smiled.

"Oh, but I like working here." He smiled back. Then he abruptly changed the subject. "What time do you eat breakfast?"

"Breakfast?"

"I'll let you in on a little secret... Since I 'owe you' and all..." He trailed off.

"Please! Continue!" I encouraged him.

"If you come back tomorrow," he began, "it will be business as usual. Enter the doors to the left of the steps, and go to the Security Office on the right." He pointed to the correct doors. "You'll have to surrender your photo ID, and they'll give you a special Visitor's Badge. Then you can use it like a key card to access the restricted hallways."

This was beginning to sound like I'd landed inside some clandestine spy movie plot. "And where, exactly, do I want to go that's restricted?"

"To the Legislative Dining Room!" He beamed. "Food's really good, reasonably priced, and it's not mentioned in any of the tourist brochures!"

I hesitated for just a moment. "And... who should I tell them sent me?"

"Tell them Uncle Petey sent you!"

And the next morning, that's exactly what I did. The man in the Security Office and the woman in the elegantly appointed dining room all got a big kick out of it. The waitress even let me sit in the Speaker's chair while she took my picture.

And the breakfast? Uncle Petey was right; it was excellent!

~Jan Bono
Long Beach, WA, USA

The Jigg's Up

Each little Province is a little nation by itself.
~Charles Tupper

Salmon, lobster, caribou, rabbit, and moose were served up in recipes handed down from generation to generation, every savoury bite a unique blend of French, Aboriginal, Scottish, and Irish ancestry.

We'd read menus all the way up the western coastline of Newfoundland, wrapping our tongues around unfamiliar words and our mouths around unfamiliar tastes: Colcannon. Brewis. Toutons with partridgeberry jam. Some dishes—fried cod tongues, flipper pie, skinned turr—my husband preferred to leave to the imagination. If he didn't recognize it, Norm wouldn't taste it.

Not me. A more adventurous eater, I relished the opportunity to try new taste treats. It was all part of experiencing a culture I found fascinating. So many things were different than our own.

Like vegetable gardens planted in ditches along the highway, rich black soil fragrant and moist, teeming with root vegetables and hearty cabbage heads. Like patient cords of winter firewood stacked and waiting at the forest's edge.

"Don't you worry about someone stealing?" I'd asked a local.

"Oh, dey'd nere tek sumpkin not dere own," he replied.

The language itself was intriguing. Who wouldn't lift a brow at place names like Pick Eyes, Dildo, and Blow Me Down. In some small ports, it was a job to wade through the dialect, deciphering enough words to piece together a patchwork conversation. The flavours of the Channel Islands, Ireland, France, and Iceland seasoned their tongues. Entranced, I kept a journal of "Newfinese" expressions and colourful phrases we heard.

So when the host of our bed and breakfast suggested we "pop over" to the community building that evening for a "scoff," I lifted my pen from the tablet I'd been jotting in.

"A scoff?"

"A Jiggs Dinner. The church is hosting a Thanksgiving. You'll be a bit late, but no matter. I can point the way," Dot offered.

With not even a hint of trepidation, I accepted the invitation, excited to participate in a traditional Newfoundland Thanksgiving.

"What a great opportunity," I whispered to my husband.

"If they serve cod tongues, I'm out of there," Norm hissed.

We were greeted at the entrance where we paid our fee. "Money fer de church," the elderly man explained as he ushered us through the door.

Long tables lined the crowded hall but chattering folks waved us toward two empty seats and encouraged us to fill our plates. I didn't need to be prodded; the most heavenly aroma had greeted us outside and I could hardly wait to dig in. We joined the line at the serving tables where we heaped our plates from bowls and platters.

A Jiggs Dinner, someone explained, was a traditional Sunday and holiday meal, a one-pot meal of salt beef and winter vegetables. Cabbage, potatoes, carrots, onions, rutabaga, beets, and turnips.

"Oh, you mean stew," I said.

"Not stew. It's biled dinner."

"Okay. But what's this?" Norm poked a hesitant fork at the curious pile of yellow on his plate. He nudged a dense slab of dark bread. "And this?"

"Pease pudding is t'one. Tothern's my mudder's figgy duff."

We learned that the split peas as well as the dark molasses bread had been boiled in pudding bags right along with the meat and vegetables, absorbing and flavouring each other.

"Remarkable," we both agreed as we savoured each fragrant bite.

But other aspects of the evening were more familiar—a real taste of home. A politician worked his way through the room, fawning over babies. We listened and grinned when he repeated the same joke at each table. Men swapped stories while women traded recipes. Ladies brought out a spread of calorie-laden desserts—cookies, pies, and cakes. The cooks affected the same balance of modesty and pride I'd witnessed during church potlucks in our home town.

"Maybe I'll get another sliver of this crowberry pie," I said to no one in particular and started to push back my chair.

"Stay where ya're tat. Oi'll bring ya some."

I looked into the sparkling eyes of the grey-haired woman at my left.

Food, language, scenery—so many differences separated us. But something more important kept crossing the cultural boundary. We'd encountered it again and again. I'd learned to recognize it anywhere: Friendliness.

~Carol McAdoo Rehme
Loveland, CO, USA

Eyes Wide Open

Canada is a good country to be from.
It has a gentler, slower pace—it lends perspective.
~Paul Anka

When I first moved to Prince Edward Island, I had to learn to look at people. I know that sounds strange, but living in Boston I was accustomed to making minimal eye contact with strangers. Take for example, someone driving an oncoming vehicle. With over four million people in the greater Boston area, the chances of me knowing someone in a car coming toward me were... well, the odds were not in my favour. So I seldom, if ever, looked at anyone driving an oncoming vehicle. The same held true for the grocery store. I was content to walk in, get what I needed, and leave without conversing with anyone except perhaps the checkout clerk. And why would I? I didn't likely know anyone. I was comfortable in that world. It was familiar. And then I moved to Prince Edward Island....

"Do you not want to know me?" my neighbour of three months asked loudly. We were standing in the aisle of the local country store when George posed his question. I was certain there wasn't a soul in the store who didn't hear him.

What a peculiar question. I was confused. In response to the puzzled look on my face, George explained, "I passed you on the Garfield Road and you didn't even nod."

"I didn't see you," I said. He shook his head in disbelief and walked away.

"I didn't see him," I later told my cousin. She shook her head in disbelief and poured me a second cup of coffee.

"How could you not see him? There's not a lot of traffic on the Garfield Road."

She was right. There was no traffic. But I didn't look. Why would I? And then I remembered where I was... Belfast, Prince Edward Island, population 2,000 souls—many of whom were related to me. It was then that I learned I needed to look at the people around me to become a full member of the community.

~Linda Jean Nicholson
Charlottetown, PE

97

Honorable Hosts

Thank you, Canada. For being such good hosts. For your unfailing courtesy…
For reminding some of us we used to be a more civilized society. Mostly, for
welcoming the world with such ease and making lasting friends with all of us.
~Brian Williams, NBC Nightly News

I was lucky enough to attend the 2010 Winter Olympics in Vancouver. It was a wonderful experience in many ways, and I was particularly struck by the pride Canada displayed on the Saturday night before the closing ceremony. Not necessarily the pride in showing off their city or even in their usual kindness to others, but in their love of hockey.

That pride was never more apparent than it was that evening, hours before they were to face the Americans for the gold medal, as citizens filled the streets — displaying flags, yelling, celebrating, and excited about a rematch against an underdog, less talented USA squad that had defeated them a few days earlier. They had been embarrassed on their home ice in a sport that is their craft. Their expertise. Their pride and joy. It draws absolutely no comparison to anything we support or watch in our own country. Not baseball. Not football. Not reality TV. Nothing. It's their life. And for them, on Canadian soil (er… ice), in the gold medal Olympic game, stacked with talent and expectation, in a rematch against their rival who had already defeated them a few days earlier, there may not have been a bigger game. And the cost of my ticket proved it.

Their excitement the night before boiled over to the Canada

Hockey Place on Sunday afternoon. The crowd was 17,000 strong, packed with red and white, one with a sign declaring: "Hockey is Canada's game." Only a few speckles of Americans wearing blue could be seen, surrounded by hockey-crazed Canadians. When their home team jumped out to a 2-0 lead midway through the second period, it was obvious they were headed towards a gold.

Then, a little magic started happening. A goal five minutes later brought the Americans within one, but desperation clearly set in as the third period wound down. The Americans pressed. Hard. Knowing the clock was ticking and their chance at a second upset of the Canadians was slipping away. With a little over a minute remaining, the United States pulled their goalie, sending in an extra attacker. With twenty-five seconds left, little known Zach Parise tied the game—sending hope through American fans, and doubt through those wearing a Maple Leaf. Canada was devastated while Americans had flashbacks of the 1980 "Miracle on Ice" Olympic gold medal winning team. Canadian fans were nervous, doubtful, and fearful. That is, until Canadian hero Sidney Crosby scored in overtime—the arena, and subsequently an entire country, erupted in celebration. It spilled into the streets—people honking, parading, and yelling, as if their country had been saved. In a sense, it had.

They didn't expect to lose. There was no choice—gold medal or failure. The USA won the silver medal, but had never been given a chance by experts to make it that far. They lost the game, but won a silver. Had Canada lost, the silver might as well have been filled with chocolate. Their country proved that they are the best in the world at a sport they invented. They were proud of it, and they didn't hesitate in showing that pride. For hours. Never rioting, but celebrating. Never taunting, but cheering. Never tasteless, but happy. On top of the world.

I headed south of the border that night—exhausted, tired, and a bit poorer. And when I thought back, it was worth every penny.

The funniest thing is, my fondest memory had nothing to do with the gold medal game, the United States, or even Canada really. In fact, it was Finland. They had beaten Slovakia the night before in the bronze medal game, but they were two countries with few fans in attendance. So afterward a majority of the crowd stayed to watch the medal presentation. Not just staying, but cheering—people from all countries, but mostly Canadians. They were actually cheering for the third place team from another country.

That's the Olympic spirit... and the Canadian spirit too.

~Jim Bove
Redmond, WA, USA

98

Terror and Tea

Kindness is the greatest wisdom.
~Author Unknown

Face your fear, I told myself, you can do this. And I answered myself: Are you out of your ever-loving mind? So I stood like a statue, frozen in time and space, unmindful of the ominous grey drizzle, one hand firmly grasping the railing, my feet still on solid ground, my mind playing its version of solitary ping-pong.

Before me loomed the Capilano Suspension Bridge in North Vancouver, British Columbia, a rough-hewn crossing 450 feet above gardens and waterfalls.

No problem, said little voice number one. It's mid-week, it's late morning, and there's nobody around but you and the security guard. I took a tentative step forward. So far so good. I slowly took a second step, white knuckles showing as I clenched the cables on both sides of the walkway.

It's not too late, said little voice number two. Don't look down! Turn back now!

But I didn't turn back.

Gaining a small bit of confidence with every step, I got to the centre of the bridge without mishap. I cautiously released one hand, and then the other, and groped for the camera hanging around my neck. I wanted proof of my monumental accomplishment.

After snapping several pictures of each end of the bridge as seen from the middle, and a few of the rushing waters below, I re-capped the lens and proceeded at tortoise-like speed. At long last, I collapsed on the bench among the shrubbery at the far end.

Two other middle-aged women emerged from the steep winding trail below. They nodded hello and I inquired about the condition of the pathway.

"The trail's pretty muddy, eh?" the taller woman said cheerfully. "You might want to skip it today." She smiled. "Besides, the only way back is the way you've come." She inclined her head toward the bridge.

I paled. I know I paled, because the shorter woman gave me a look of genuine concern and reached out to touch my arm. "Are you okay, honey?"

"S-sure," I stammered. "I just didn't think about having to cross the bridge a second time."

She smiled. "You got over here by yourself, so you can get back by yourself."

"Either that, or you can use the emergency phone at the bottom of the trail to order pizza delivery," laughed the taller woman as they departed.

Leave it to me, I thought, to be the fall guy for a couple of Canadian comedians.

Fall guy? shrieked voice number two. I told you not to do this! I'm too young to die! I want my mommy! Why did I let you get us into this mess?

Shut up, I told her. You're not helping.

And amazingly, the little naysayer clammed right up.

In the silence that wasn't silence within the roar of rushing water, I eyed the bridge. I thought about the Astoria-Megler "Bridge to Nowhere," the Tacoma Narrows "Galloping Gertie," Ambrose Bierce's "An Occurrence at Owl Creek Bridge."

None of this was helping.

I got to my feet and began the long trek back. A few steps short of midway, my peripheral vision vaguely registered a tour bus pulling into the loading zone.

Approximately four heartbeats later, two dozen Japanese

teenagers, whooping and hollering like teenagers are prone to do, bolted out onto the bridge.

Galloping Gertie had nothing on the moves of this bucking monster. The planks heaved up and slapped down, and the deep rippling motion caused the boards to shriek under the stress. We're all gonna die! screamed you-know-who.

I dropped to my knees, looped my arms around the cabled sides of the walkway and did some bloody-murder screaming myself. My camera, now swinging freely from the strap around my neck, bounced up and smacked my nose a good one. The lens cap careened into the chasm. A shrill whistle blasted again and again. I closed my eyes and both little voices and I began reciting the twenty-third Psalm.

What happened next can only be verified by the fact that I lived to tell the story. I'm pretty sure the security guard played a key role in my rescue. But the next thing I actually remember, after my hands were pried loose from the cable railing, was being handed a cup of hot tea as I sat shivering at a table in the gift shop's snack bar.

"There, there, dear," the nice woman with the tea said, patting my hand. "If you are so afraid of heights, whatever were you doing out on the bridge in the first place?"

Don't tell her, said voice number two. Don't tell her that the only reason you were here was the fact that due to the inclement weather, the Super Skyride to the top of Grouse Mountain had been closed for the day.

I smiled broadly at my new best friend and took a sip of tea. Little voice number two won out. "This is very good, thank you." I took a cookie from the proffered tray. "I've always heard that Canadians are wonderfully hospitable, and now I know it's absolutely true!"

She grinned and nodded, and very politely kept any more questions to herself.

~Jan Bono
Long Beach, WA, USA

99

The Beach
at West Edmonton Mall

Edmonton isn't really the end of the world—
although you can see it from there.
~Ralph Klein

T hey arrived in motor coaches from all over windswept central Canada—young and old, housewives and students, waitresses, drug store clerks, grandmothers and construction workers. All the long northern winter they came to the West Edmonton Mall to go to the beach, to sit under palm trees and sip umbrella drinks while waves broke on the sandy shore and heat baked their chilled bodies and warmed their spirits.

I was in Edmonton, Alberta, on business, but I had finished my business early and had an extra day on my hands. It was obvious to me that I should take advantage of my bonus time to look around and possibly do a little shopping in what was then the largest shopping mall in the world—the West Edmonton Mall. Besides, it was February and mighty cold outside.

The Mall was impressive. Spanning the equivalent of forty-eight city blocks under one roof, it housed more than 800 stores and restaurants, a full-size hockey rink where you could see the Edmonton Oilers practice, an amusement park with a fourteen-story triple-loop roller coaster, the Fantasyland Hotel where you could choose to sleep in the back of a pickup truck or on a raft in a lagoon, and a beach. The beach was surrounded by glass.

On this day I peered through the steamy glass wall of the beach, which appeared to be fashioned after Waikiki Beach in Honolulu. Long and curved, it was covered with soft white sand and real palm trees waving in a gentle breeze. Waves lapped lazily against the shore, unless, as was the case today, there was a surfing contest scheduled. Stepping inside the glass door, I watched in amazement as wave machines under the water produced six-footers and teenagers paddled out on their boards to ride the waves in. Overhead tanning lights replaced the sun, and it was obvious there would never be the disappointment of a rainy day.

As I stood there, a motor coach began to unload and a stream of people wearing heavy coats crowded through the mall entrance nearest the beach, kids running and yelling and women shouting at them to slow down or they would slip and fall. I stepped back to speak with an older woman in a parka who was waiting in line to get in. She was wearing sunglasses and carrying a plastic beach bag and a pillow.

"How do you like this beach?" I asked her. "Have you come here before?"

She nodded, a little cautious about talking to a stranger. "It's a nice place and a bit of sun does me good."

"Is it just as good as a real beach? It looks pretty nice!"

"Well, I know about real beaches, I can tell you! I flew on the airplane to Mexico once. The sand fleas bit me to pieces and I got sick from the food. Never again! I can just get on the coach and be here in a couple of hours. It's a break from the cold."

"Do you stay here at the Mall then?"

"Yes, I'm going to sleep in the back of a pickup truck tonight!" She smiled, excited. "You know, they have those rooms in the hotel. Haven't slept in a pickup truck since, well, since I was a young girl."

Her smile was suddenly embarrassed and her shyness returned. She hurried through the door into the beach. Apparently the pickup truck brought back fond memories.

My curiosity got the best of me and since I was staying an extra night I had to try the hotel. I chose to sleep on the raft in the lagoon, an illusion that was accomplished with mirrors and lavish creativity. Indeed much of the floor and the entire ceiling in my very large room were covered in mirrors. There was a real six-foot waterfall into the rock hot tub next to the mirror lagoon my king-size bed sat on, with ferns and the sounds of tropical birds. No birds, though, just the sounds. When it was time to go to bed, I "waded" in over the mirror lagoon. It was an exotic experience and for the moment I imagined I was on a warm tropical island in the South Pacific.

The next day, after buying more in the shops than I had intended, I decided to go to the beach myself. As I settled under my palm tree, I noticed no one there was quite as white-skinned as I was—the tanning lights were on the job. A lovely young woman in shorts and a bikini top took my drink order and the strains of a slack-key guitar wafted through the warm air. The high notes of children on the waterslides at the far end of the beach tinkled in the distance, and added to, rather than disturbed, my tranquility. I sat back, looked around and said to myself, not bad. Not exactly real, but certainly not bad. I, for one, was enjoying the illusion of the tropics in the heart of Canada.

~Dana Hill
Oakland, CA, USA

100

You Are What You Eat

Because that's what kindness is. It's not doing something for someone else
because they can't, but because you can.
~Andrew Iskander

The year 1984 was a tumultuous one in hockey in Orillia. The Travelways Team, always the talk of the town, gathered in August 1983 for tryouts at the Orillia Community Centre, a huge ice pad built mainly by volunteers and service clubs. The Community Centre had complete seating on all four sides of the ice pad, and the Travelways filled those seats with animated, screaming fans every Thursday night. You really had to see it to believe the undying support given to these hard-playing, fun-loving young hockey players by Orillians, young and old.

Veteran Orillia hockey fans always sat in the same places, cheering, moaning, jumping up when fights on the ice started, and covering their eyes when things got too exciting. The arena was always full of noise. Fans of the "other teams" sat close together in one area of the seating and yelled back at the vociferous Orillia fans as they simultaneously cheered their own team.

It was a year of wins for the Travelways. We were "billets." We (George and Jan) lived right across from the arena in a huge white house with our five children. We were both employed, but billeting hockey players was our hobby. We always joked that we would not have been able to afford to feed the hockey players if we hadn't both been working. The pay given to billets for hockey players didn't even cover their weekly food. Could they eat!

In September, all the Travelways were placed with their billets, and the billets provided food and a bed for their hockey players. We usually took one or two in September. By the time the playoffs rolled around, several billet homes would have opted out, and we would have five or six players staying with us. We loved it. Our children loved it. The house was filled with extra cots and sleeping bags. The couches were full. And that was the position we were in when play-offs started in the winter of 1984.

My sister, her daughter, and several rabbits had joined us. She made wonderful suggestions. It was as if she clearly saw the forest in spite of the trees.

"Why are you wrapping up the food after supper and putting it in the fridge? If you leave it on the counter, it will all be gone by ten, you know." She was right. Any kind of food could never become a leftover with hockey players around. Thus a new, easy routine began.

Hockey players follow rules pretty well, but are also prone to doing things their way. After strict orders not to feed our new Lhasa Apso puppy any pop or candy on Halloween, I watched in horror as the puppy, that the hockey players named "Puck," threw up red pop and other things on the carpet under the table. Just then, Mitch Caouette ran by and made a remark that brought laughter from all directions.

"I'd change that dog's name from 'Puck' to 'Puke' if he were mine."

All good things must come to an end, but in one move, the hockey world in Orillia was literally turned upside down. The city closed the arena. The announcement said that it was unsafe, and all playoff home games would be played at the Gravenhurst arena. We were to play Rayside-Balfour. Some unhappy young men boarded the buses for the playoffs. Now they had bus trips before every game, and soon they were down three games to one. The fifth game would be in Gravenhurst, and it was a series-breaker. If they didn't win it, they were out of the playoffs. Orillians couldn't believe the sudden turn of events. Where was our talented, entertaining hockey team? Our Travelways were the best!! Orillians predicted they would never pull out of the slump. *The Packet* newspaper was full of doom and gloom and the radio station was even worse!

What to do? George and I talked it over. What could we do? We decided that we had a secret weapon which we would use to turn things around. George is an avid hunter, and always shot his share of moose and deer each year. Our children were raised on good old northern wild game. Did you know that moose and deer meat make you extraordinarily strong? All of our children were capable of single-handedly pushing the old LTD (and it was a heavy car) out of ditches before they were ten years old. (Unfortunately, I slid into the ditches often.) That was it! The whole team needed to eat Canadian wild game. Our freezer had been filled in the fall after George's hunting trips, but no one knew that our players had been eating Canadian deer and moose meat all along. Time for a full team treatment.

We invited the whole team to dinner before the fifth game. We had prepared the biggest, most delicious moose stew there ever was for the team to eat. We told them that it was a secret Canadian recipe which would give them extraordinary strength for the game that night. They ate and ate. George and I had used tons of moose meat, garlic, onions, potatoes and veggies, with extra cups of gravy thrown in for good luck. It simmered for hours in the kitchen. Finally, we placed the dumplings on the top and the delicious pot simmered its last half hour. The aroma that filled the house was breathtaking. It was time to eat. The players ate, talked, ate, laughed, ate and slapped each other on the backs. Finally it was time to board the bus. They were in the best of spirits. Now all they had to do was play the kind of hockey they usually played. We did not reveal what made up our secret recipe.

George and I literally held our breath as we followed the bus down the road to Gravenhurst. God bless the guys. They did it. They got on the ice and showed what a great Canadian moose stew can do for you. Goal after goal. They won the game, and went on to beat the other team twice more, moving on to the finals in Weyburn,

Saskatchewan. And they won there, too!! They were the champions. They were unbelievable. George timed his transport truck trips so that he saw every game.

The next year, the championship playoff games were in Orillia. Travelways were tops. They were, without a doubt, the glue that held Orillia together. Hockey forever!

~Jan Hulland
Orillia, ON

That's the Way Canadians Are

We only need to look at what we are really doing in the world and at home and we'll know what it is to be Canadian.

~Adrienne Clarkson

We Americans have varied views of Canada and those who live there. There are several common themes however: kindness, politeness and modesty. I have a Canadian friend who told me this story which bears out the truth of those stereotypes. She would never tell this story (see item three above) but I will on her behalf. It reflects on both how wonderful she is and how wonderful her country is.

It was a cold and rainy night on Vancouver Island when my friend, who I will call Amy, had filled her car with gasoline and was walking out of the little store associated with the gas station back towards her car. A man approached her.

"Do you know where the hospital is?" he asked.

"Sure, it isn't too far."

"I need to find my wife, who has a new job there, and get the key to the house," he said, gesturing to a truck that she could see was laden with furniture and household goods even though it was covered by a tarp. A rental trailer was attached behind the pickup.

Amy gave him directions to the hospital.

"How long will it take to drive there?" he asked.

The man looked incredibly weary and troubled. It struck Amy. "Is everything okay?" she asked.

"Well, yes, I just need to get to my wife."

With a bit more conversation, he reluctantly explained he had run out of money. Amy thought about driving him to the hospital, but decided it would be simpler to just give him some gas money. She handed him $20.

"No, I can't take that, but thank you," he said, embarrassed.

She insisted and after several minutes of back and forth, he took the money, but wanted her address to send repayment. She insisted he just take it, consider it a housewarming gift. He thanked her once again and they parted ways.

Five years later, Amy's oldest son had an asthma attack and she took him to the hospital emergency room. It was a quiet evening with few patients in the waiting room. Amy and the nurse chatted as care was administered to her son.

The nurse talked about living elsewhere in Canada and Amy asked how she liked living on Vancouver Island.

"Yes, we love it," the nurse said. "We moved from back east and fell in love with it here. The people are so kind and friendly."

The nurse went on, "When we came here years ago, my husband had run out of gas near the hospital, with all our worldly possessions in his truck. He had no money for gas, though. He was desperate to get to me and to get our belongings to our house and he didn't really know what to do. Out of nowhere, this kind woman gave him $20."

Amy said nothing. That's the way Canadians are.

~Dan Reust
Englewood, CO, USA

Meet Our Contributors

Asmatullah has been living in Vancouver for the past seven years. At the beginning he found it hard to communicate with people, mainly because he didn't know how to speak the language. Now that he has, somewhat, mastered the beautiful language, he has fallen in love with it. His hobbies are reading books, writing journals and playing soccer.

Nancy Bennett lives on Vancouver Island. She spends her days working on her farm called the Three Sister Farm, where she raises heirloom produce and very small heritage chickens. She has been published in over 400 places including many *Chicken Soup for the Soul* books.

Mark Black is a heart and double-lung transplant recipient turned four-time marathon runner, speaker and best-selling author. Mark is a recognized expert on overcoming adversity and is a speaker for organizations who want to turn the changes and challenges they are dealing with into their competitive advantage. Learn more at www.MarkBlackSpeaks.com or Mark@MarkBlackSpeaks.com.

Bonney Bohan received her B.S. in Home Economics from McGill University, Montreal, and dietetic internship at Vancouver General Hospital. Upon retirement, she established a reading program for hospitalized veterans. Bonney lives in London, ON, with her dog, Tucker. She enjoys volunteering, reading, theatre, music and competitive bridge. E-mail her at pagegirl@sympatico.ca.

Jan Bono's latest book, *Just Joshin', A Year in the Life of a Not-so-ordinary 4th Grade Kid*, is available through Sandridge Publications. She also writes one-act plays, dinner theatre plays, Christmas plays, an every-other-day blog, and edits! Jan's books, plays, and writing services can be found at www.JanBonoBooks.com.

Jim Bove received his bachelor's degree from Radford University and a master's degree from Michigan State University. He is currently the Community Outreach Facilitator for the Redmond Police Department (WA). He has another story published in *Chicken Soup for the Soul: Campus Chronicles*.

Rose McCormick Brandon lives in Caledonia, ON, and on Manitoulin Island with her husband, Doug. She is an award-winning personal experience author who also writes articles on faith and family. She contributes to magazines and book compilations published in Canada and the U.S. E-mail her at rosembrandon@yahoo.ca.

Ms. Brunton lives in Southern Ontario, practices yoga, enjoys music, travelling, cooking and spending time with the people she loves. She aspires to write books that stir the spirit and awaken the imagination. E-mail her at mitzib123@hotmail.com.

Janet Caplan lives on Vancouver Island where she enjoys writing, hiking, walking her dogs and photography. Her writing, mainly about life and dogs, has appeared in *Chicken Soup for the Soul: What I Learned from the Dog*, *Animal Wellness*, *Ocean* magazine, *Dogs in Canada* magazine and other print and online publications.

Harriet Cooper is a freelance writer, editor and ESL instructor living in Toronto. She has published close to 100 personal essays, humour and creative nonfiction pieces in newspapers, anthologies and magazines. She often writes about family, relationships, health, food, cats, writing and day-to-day life. E-mail her at shewrites@live.ca.

Elizabeth Creith is an award-winning freelance writer. Her publishing credits include fiction, nonfiction, memoir and poetry, and a decade as a freelance writer/broadcaster for CBC radio. Elizabeth lives and writes full-time in Northern Ontario, distracted occasionally by her husband, dog, and cat. She blogs about writing, art, and life at http://ecreith.wordpress.com.

Currently focusing on her children, **Leslie Czegeny** enjoys being a stay-at-home mom. Her husband and two daughters keep her busy, but she also finds time to pursue writing, reading, and scrapbooking. She is working towards her Writer's Certificate with the goal of getting her children's books published.

Sheri Gammon Dewling, a former software executive, runs a small consulting business, while raising two small children in Markham, ON. Sheri aspires to turn her life lessons into stories that will inspire others. E-mail her at sheri@justmomsense.com.

Ingrid Dore is a retired teacher/librarian and freelance writer. She is an organic gardener and enjoys walking and visiting with her many friends.

Matt Duchene, a Haliburton, ON native, was a first-round NHL draft pick in 2009 at age eighteen and plays centre for his childhood dream team, the Colorado Avalanche. During the 2010-2011 season, Matt led the team in games, goals, points, and shots—and is the youngest player in Avalanche history to lead the team in scoring. In a game ten days after his twentieth birthday, Matt became the youngest player in team history to score 100 career points. When not playing hockey, Matt likes to fish, play his guitar and spend time with his family and friends. Follow him on Twitter @Matt9Duchene.

Dawn Edwards is a work-at-home mom and author of *Second Hand Roses: The Junktiquing Road*. Her interests include writing, nature, bicycling, and working on her blog, Second Hand Roses. She lives in Sandwich, IL, with her husband Alex and her son Julius. E-mail her at 2ndhandroses@comcast.net.

Carol Forrest is retired and lives with her husband John in Orillia, ON. They winter in Scottsdale, AZ. Golf is her passion and this story describes a personal experience that helped her journey to wellness in her battle with breast cancer. E-mail her at carolforrest@rogers.com.

John Forrest is a retired educator, who writes about the exceptional events and wonderful people that have enriched his life. His anthology, *Angels Stars and Trees: Tales of Christmas Magic*, is in its third printing. He lives in Orillia, ON, with his wife Carol. E-mail him at johnforrest@rogers.com.

Lori Futterer received her Bachelor of Business degree from Wilfrid Laurier University in Waterloo, ON. She is a professor in the School of Business at George Brown College in Toronto. Lori lives in Aurora with her husband Casey and her three children Tyler, Brady and Eve. Lori loves teaching, camping, travelling, and being a hockey mom.

Dalia Gesser toured her children's shows under the name Compact Theatre for over twenty years. Since 2000, she has been sharing her love and experience of the theatre with children through her workshops and classes. She lives north of Kingston in beautiful lake country and can be reached via e-mail at daliag@xplornet.com.

After a twenty-year nursing career and fifteen years in radio, **Pamela Goldstein** turned to her passion—writing. She has three manuscripts, three plays under her belt, and several short stories published in anthology books, including several in the *Chicken Soup for the Soul* series. E-mail Pam at boker_tov2002@yahoo.ca.

Linda Handiak has volunteered abroad as a mason, a goat herder and an English teacher. More information about these adventures can be found in her book, *101 Green Travel Tips*, published by LifeTips. At present, she is a teacher and translator in Quebec.

Carol Harrison received her Bachelor of Education degree from the University of Saskatchewan and holds her Distinguished Toastmaster designation. She is an inspirational speaker and author of the book *Amee's Story* and previous contributor to the *Chicken Soup for the Soul* series. E-mail her at carol@carolscorner.ca or visit www.carolscorner.ca.

Dana Hill is a freelance writer living in Oakland, CA. She is retired from a long airline career and currently works as a bartender at a luxury resort. Dana writes a series of columns for the online newspaper Examiner.com about cooking, and she enjoys traveling and writing about her experiences.

Lorelei Hill graduated from Queen's University, Kingston, ON, with a Bachelor of Education degree. She is a teacher, writer, business partner with her husband Michael, and the mother of two beautiful children, three cats, and one Goldendoodle! Inspired by life's triumphs she writes inspirational fantasy. E-mail her at lorie@coracomputers.com.

Elaine Ingalls Hogg, an award-winning author, inspirational speaker, workshop facilitator, is published in books and magazines in Canada and United States. Elaine enjoys encouraging aspiring writers, travelling with her husband, creating miniature dollhouses and playing the piano. She lives in Sussex, New Brunswick, and may be contacted through her website at: http://elainehogg.com.

A self-proclaimed chocoholic, **Steena Holmes** holds a firm belief that true happiness lies in discovering what your passions are and going after them with every breath. Steena's passions are raising her children, growing old with her husband and writing women's fiction and romance. E-mail her at steenah@telus.net.

Joei Carlton Hossack is the author of ten adventure travel books, specializing in recreational vehicle (RV) travel and spends more than six months each year on the road. She is a memoir and travel writing teacher, entertaining and inspirational speaker and amateur photographer. E-mail her at JoeiCarlton@Hotmail.com or visit www.joeicarlton.com.

Tim Huff is the award-winning author of *Bent Hope: A Street Journal* and *Dancing with Dynamite: Celebrating Against the Odds*, as well as the author/illustrator of the bestselling children's book *The Cardboard Shack Beneath the Bridge: Helping Children Understand Homelessness*.

Tim is a sought-after speaker across Canada, an artist, and a musician. In 2011, after twenty-five years working among homeless and street-involved youth and adults, Tim founded and became Executive Director of The Hope Exchange. www.hopeexchange.ca

Jan Hulland was born in Windsor, ON, and received her B.A. degree from a combination of Ontario university credits and her master's degree from the University of Toronto. She is interested in writing, sports, reading, inventing new programs for children, little theatre and people. E-mail her at jan4u911@hotmail.com.

Phyllis Jardine is a retired nurse living in the Annapolis Valley of Nova Scotia with her husband Bud and black Lab Morgan. Her stories have been aired on CBC radio and have been published in numerous magazines and anthologies such as *Good Times*, *CARP*, *A Maritime Christmas* and *A Cup of Comfort*. E-mail her at phyl.jardine@gmail.com.

Beckie Jas, an environmental media specialist in Southern Ontario, creates education/marketing campaigns for children and adults. Her first children's book: *A Farewell to Featherwagons* will be published in 2011. She has received numerous awards for publication excellence and writes for the Restless Writers at www.restlesswriters.ca. She also writes young-adult fiction.

Carolyn Johnson, a former banker and now freelance writer from Houston, TX, draws on her colourful life experiences in the U.S., Canada, Europe and South Africa for her essays, short stories and poetry. She writes from the heart, the hurt, the heavenly and sometimes the hilarious. E-mail her at cetjohnson@comcast.net.

Singer songwriter **Marc Jordan** began his career in Los Angeles, where he spent fifteen years making and producing records, before returning to his home country to continued success. Marc earned an ASCAP award as well as a Juno Award for Producer of the Year and was the recipient of Male Vocalist of the Year by the Canadian Smooth Jazz Awards three times. As an artist, he has released eleven successful solo albums and has also written hit songs for a number of internationally-known artists such as Josh Groban, Bette Midler, Bonnie Raitt, Chicago, Rod Stewart and Kenny Loggins among others. Marc wrote music for and starred in the 2010 movie musical, *Score: A Hockey Movie*. www.marcjordan.com.

Liesl Jurock, M.Ed. , blogs at Mama's Log (www.mamaslog.com) about modern motherhood. She is an alumnus of The Momoir Project and was featured in *Chicken Soup for the Soul: New Moms*. She works in career education at Simon Fraser University and lives in Port Coquitlam, British Columbia, with her family. E-mail her at lieslmama@gmail.com.

Ruth Knox has loved writing ever since she could first hold a pencil. She believes in the power of the written word to unite people. Born in Alberta, Ruth now lives in Idaho with her new husband, and is working on her first novel. E-mail her at ruthknox@live.com.

George Kourounis is one of the world's most active storm chasers, a renowned adventurer, explorer and television presenter. Based in Toronto, his efforts to document nature's worst weather conditions have taken him all over the globe, into places most normal people are fleeing from. George is a member of the Explorers Club, and was nominated for two Gemini awards for his work hosting the *Angry Planet* TV series. www.stormchaser.ca.

Kathy Linker received her B.A. degree in Psychology from the University of Western Ontario, a graduate degree in Clinical Art Therapy and her Master's of Education degree from the University of Victoria. She has traveled and worked internationally and is writing inspirational stories about her experiences abroad. E-mail her at kathylinker@hotmail.com.

Dawn Livera is an artist, writer, mother and world traveller. She lives with her husband in Vancouver. While they do not celebrate Valentine's Day, they do have a private celebration a few weeks earlier when both their birthdays fall. She can be reached through her blog at aspotofserendip.wordpress.com.

Paul Loewen is a youth pastor in Winnipeg, MB. He loves writing, and is working on several novels.

Barbara LoMonaco has worked for Chicken Soup for the Soul as an editor and webmaster since 1998. She has co-authored two *Chicken Soup for the Soul* book titles and has had stories published in various other titles. Barbara is a graduate of the University of Southern California and has a teaching credential.

Nancy Loucks-McSloy is a community service worker and is currently Executive Director of a Business Improvement Association in London, ON. She is a published writer, working on an inspirational book. Nancy enjoys travel and spending time with her children and grandchildren. E-mail her at nancy.mcsloy@gmail.com.

Cathy MacKenzie enjoys writing poems, short stories and essays and is currently writing a novel. She also paints, pastels being her favourite medium and her four grandchildren her favourite subjects. She lives in Halifax, NS, with her husband Gary, and they spend their winters in Mexico. E-mail her at grannymackenzie@gmail.com.

Gail MacMillan is an award-winning author of dog books. A graduate of Queen's University, Gail has had her work published in Canada, the United States and the UK. She lives with her husband and three wonderful dogs. Contact Gail through her website at www.gailmacmillan.com.

Cindy Martin has a BRE degree, is a writer and speaker and the mother of two special needs children. She enjoys traveling, being with her family and acreage living. Cindy is founder of Step by Step Consulting, designed to help families of special needs children. Learn more at www.lifemeetsreality.com.

David Martin's humour and political satire have appeared in many publications including *The New York Times*, the *Chicago Tribune* and *Smithsonian* magazine. His latest humour collection, *Dare to be*

Average, was published in 2010 by Lulu.com. David lives in Ottawa with his wife Cheryl and their daughter Sarah.

Dennis McCloskey has a Journalism degree from Ryerson University in Toronto. He has been a full-time freelance writer since 1980 and is the author of several books, including the 2008 award-winning biography, *My Favorite American*. He lives in Richmond Hill, ON, with his wife Kris. E-mail him at dmcclos@rogers.com.

Sharon McGregor is a grandmother of five who retires on a regular basis, but just can't seem to make it permanent. She shares her living space with a calico cat, Zoey, who has no doubt about who's boss in the house. E-mail Sharon at sharonmcgr@hotmail.com.

Michelle McKague-Radic lives in Peterborough, ON, with her husband and child. She is finishing up her bachelor's degree in History.

Heidi McLaughlin is an author and international speaker. Her topics include excerpts from her books *Sand to Pearls: Making Bold Choices to Enrich Your Life*, and *Beauty Unleashed: Transforming a Woman's Soul*. Heidi loves to golf, travel and spend time with her family. Contact her through her website at www.heartconnection.ca.

Chantal Meijer lives in Terrace, BC, with her husband Rick of thirty-five years. They have four grown children. Chantal's articles, stories and essays have appeared in regional and national magazines, newspapers, and anthologies, including: *Chicken Soup for the Soul: Christmas Magic* and *Chicken Soup for the Soul: Empty Nesters*.

Christine Mikalson is a wife, mother and grandmother who is enjoying retired life. Besides spending time with family, her passions are writing, Reiki-energy healing, camping and reading. E-mail her at chris_mikalson@yahoo.ca or find her at: http://reiki-labyrinth.blogspot.com.

Bruce Mills is a civil engineer living in Boise, ID. Born in Michigan, he has also lived in Colorado, Utah, Washington, Idaho, and Ireland. Seeing new places is an obvious passion, along with howling out tunes with his guitar, hiking and spending time with family. E-mail Bruce at brucegmills@gmail.com.

Esme Mills loves, among other things, cycling with her children, being Canadian, and vanilla lattes. Feel free to connect with her on Facebook to find out more!

Evangeline Neve was born in Canada, brought up in Europe, and has lived in Nepal since 1996. She loves cooking, writing and photography, has a home for underprivileged girls and teaches disabled children. She is working on a book based on her experiences in Nepal. Contact her via e-mail at lilyneve@yahoo.com.

Linda Jean Nicholson, a native of Massachusetts, is an executive director of a non-profit organization in Prince Edward Island. She is a published author and editor of a monthly seniors magazine. Linda has a passion and thirty years experience researching and teaching family history. E-mail her at lindaj.nicholson@gmail.com.

Molly O'Connor lives near Ottawa. She attended York University in Toronto and Carleton University it Ottawa. Retired from the corporate world, she turned her interests to writing and photography. She has published a collection of short stories, *Fourteen Cups*, and a memoir, *Wandering Backward*.

Inbal Ondhia received her Honours B.Sc. degree from the University of Toronto, and M.Sc.A. degree in Speech-Language Pathology from McGill University. She currently lives in California with her family. Writing and cooking are her creative outlets. She also enjoys reading, yoga, running and travelling. E-mail her at inbal.ondhia@gmail.com.

Author and poet, **Debbie Ouellet** lives in Loretto, ON. Her children's book, *How Robin Saved Spring* (Henry Holt, 2009), received the Horace

Mann Upstanders Honor Book Award. Her teen novels for reluctant readers, *A Hero's Worth* and *Legend of the Ring*, were published by HIP Books (2009 and 2011). Learn more at www.debbieouellet.com.

Born in Kingston, ON, **Leanne Fanning Pankuch** received her Bachelor of Arts degree in English from North Central College, IL. She currently lives in Illinois with her husband, children, and dogs. She is an accomplished vocal musician and writes humorous picture books and middle-grade fiction. E-mail her at leannepankuch@comcast.net.

Judi Peers has published several children's books: *Brontosaurus Brunch*, *Home Base*, *Shark Attack*, *Sayonara Sharks*, *Guardian of the Lamp*, etc. She is also a speaker, literacy advocate, avid gardener, and engaging Bible Study leader. Judi and her husband Dave make their home in Peterborough, ON. E-mail her at judipeers@wordpress.com.

Scott Penner is a pastor at the Truro Alliance Church in Truro, NS, where he and his family live. He enjoys seeing God's truth in the ordinary details of life and spends as much time as possible in the great outdoors. Scott welcomes feedback at spenner@truroalliancechurch.com.

Kelly Pohorelic graduated from the University of British Columbia in 2005 and has since been dividing her time between travelling and working with children on the autism spectrum. She enjoys cooking, writing, and seeing as much of the world as she can. Read more at kelmarie.com.

Daniella Porano is a recent high school graduate and is currently pursuing a Humanities degree. She enjoys hockey, soccer, reading, writing, traveling, and is a proud Canadian. E-mail her at daniella_porano_13@hotmail.com.

Jennifer Quist is a freelance writer producing poetry, fiction, and nonfiction from her home in central Alberta. Her upbringing as a child of a federal government employee took her all over Canada from British Columbia to Nova Scotia, High Level to Halifax—but never anywhere warm.

Sheri Radford lives in Vancouver, BC, with her husband and three cats. She is the author of three very silly picture books for children: *Penelope and the Preposterous Birthday Party*, *Penelope and the Monsters*, and *Penelope and the Humongous Burp*. Visit her at www.sheriradford.com.

Brenda Redmond is blessed to have two beautiful daughters and a wonderful husband who are a constant inspiration to her. She enjoys camping, reading, swimming and traveling. She has loved writing from an early age, and plans to continue to grow as a writer. E-mail her at bredmond3@hotmail.com.

Traveling on "the other side of the border" ranks at the top of **Carol McAdoo Rehme's** bucket list. A veteran author, editor, and ghost-writer, she's always on the prowl for new experiences, new culinary delights, and new friendships. Carol writes from her home office along the Front Range of the Colorado Rockies.

Dan Reust lives and writes in Colorado. This story is about a wonderful woman, Amy, who has taught him many things. He loves her very much. E-mail Dan at danreust@msn.com.

When not travelling with her precocious daughter, **Jody Robbins** can usually be found snowboarding or hiking near Calgary, AB. A former technology sales manager, Jody now explores subjects such as travel and mom-ing it, as a freelance writer. Give her a shout at jodyrstar@hotmail.com.

Laura Robinson is a Canadian actress/inventor/producer and married mother of two. She co-invented the classic game *Balderdash*, and is currently producing a television game show *Celebrity Name Game* for a U.S. network. Laura starred on CBS's *Night Heat*, as well as *Cheers* and *Frasier*. Robinson co-authored/co-created the book and game, *Chicken Soup for the Soul: Count Your Blessings*. Learn more at www.countyourblessingsgame.com.

Maureen Rogers is a transplanted Canadian who still loves to visit her homeland. Her writing projects include fiction, poetry and essays. She has been published online, in newspapers, anthologies and in *Chicken Soup for the Coffee Lover's Soul*, *Chicken Soup for the Soul: My Resolution* and *Chicken Soup for the Soul: My Cat's Life*. E-mail her at morogers@gmail.com.

Jazmyne Rose has been writing since she could hold pen to paper. It has always been her passion and she hopes to unite people all over the world through a love of reading. For more works by Jazmyne check her out on Facebook or MySpace!

Mike Rumble graduated with a degree in Marketing from Humber College. He lives in Raleigh, NC, and enjoys golfing, biking, swimming, and is active in the theatre community in Raleigh. Mike plans to write short stories and continue doing copywriting. E-mail him at merumble1168@gmail.com.

Jaime Schreiner lives in a small town in Saskatchewan with her husband and two young daughters. When she's not spending time with her family and friends, she enjoys freelance writing. E-mail her at jaimeschreiner@yahoo.ca.

Mary Ellen "Angel Scribe" is author of *Expect Miracles* and *A Christmas Filled with Miracles*. She is internationally known for her pet column, "Pet Tips 'n' Tales." Heartwarming, inspirational, educational pet and miracle stories are posted on her website, along with her famous swimming cats' video! Learn more at www.AngelScribe.com or AngelScribe@msn.com.

Annabel Sheila grew up in a picturesque little town in Newfoundland. She writes poetry and stories about nature, the ocean, love, and life, embracing the gentle nudge of her muse with passion. She loves to travel and spend time with her family, especially her adorable grandson.

Gemma M. Tamas came to Canada as a refugee. She is a published author and freelance writer. Her book, *"NO!" Is Not MY NAME!*, was published in 2003 and contains a foreword from Dr. Stanley Coren, author and world-renowned authority on dog behavior. In 2009, she won first prize for her poem in *Northern Stars* magazine. She has three finished manuscripts.

B.J. Taylor gets a thrill out of every hat trick and loves exciting shoot-outs. She is an award-winning author whose work has appeared in *Guideposts*, two dozen *Chicken Soup for the Soul* books, and numerous magazines and newspapers. You can reach B.J. through her website at www.bjtayloronline.com. Check out her dog blog at www.bjtaylorblog.wordpress.com.

Terrie Todd writes from Portage la Prairie, MB, where she is an administrative assistant at City Hall. She and Jon have been married thirty-four years, have three grown children and two grandsons. This is Terrie's sixth story in the *Chicken Soup for the Soul* series. Visit her blog at http://terrietodd.blogspot.com.

Kate Tompkins is a freelance writer/editor who's been living in Quebec with her husband and various pets since two months after the last referendum. When she's not working, she enjoys travelling and attending classic car shows. She can be reached via e-mail at wordcorral@gmail.com.

Melissa Valks is addicted to travel and other cultures. Most of her writings originate from her travel experiences... or better said, her cultural faux pas while abroad. Melissa has had several works published, and has recently written a book about living and teaching in Korea. E-mail her at melissavalks@yahoo.ca.

Nikki Vincent is in the tenth grade. She has always loved to write in her spare time. Nikki also enjoys reading, travelling and spending time at her family's cabin at the lake. She is hoping to become an English teacher.

John Walker has served as a pastor in Toronto, Michigan, and Pennsylvania, though he remains one of God's frozen people. He is the Director of Development for Paxton Ministries, providing mental health housing and support in Harrisburg, PA. John is an incorrigible writer and photographer. E-mail him at john1walker24576@yahoo.com.

Sally Walls has a passion for encouragement and a relational heart. She has been involved in Women's Ministry for twenty years and loves investing in people. She lives in Calgary with her husband and teenage son and enjoys spending her time hiking and skiing in the fresh mountain air.

Samantha Ducloux Waltz is an award-winning freelance writer in Portland, OR. Her personal stories appear in the *Chicken Soup for the Soul* series and numerous other anthologies as well as *Redbook* and *Christian Science Monitor*. She has also written fiction and nonfiction under the name Samellyn Wood. Learn more at www.pathsofthought.com.

Rebekah Wilkinson is a 1995 Fine Art graduate from University of Guelph and currently resides in British Columbia. Rebekah enjoys numerous creative endeavours from painting and drawing to scrapbooking. She is passionate about the arts and enjoys writing about her experiences as an emerging Canadian artist on her blog www.rebekahwilkinson.wordpress.com.

Susie Wilson grew up in a traditional Mennonite home and embraces her Christian heritage. She worked as a teacher and school librarian for twenty years. Susie enjoys hiking, kayaking, snowshoeing and cross-country skiing around her lakefront home in British Columbia. She plans to write children's books and inspirational articles.

Linda A. Wright is a retired librarian living in Florida. She met her spouse in 1970, while they were undergraduates at Boston University. Her pastimes include learning to sing under the tutelage of Roxy, the beagle, and knitting, with the aid of Calliope, the calico cat.

Linda C. Wright left the hustle and bustle of the business world to pursue her passion for writing. She's a member of Romance Writers of America as well as her local chapter, SpacecoasT Authors of Romance. Linda lives on the Space Coast of Florida and loves photography, traveling and reading. E-mail her at lindacwright@ymail.com.

Shelly Wutke holds a B.A. degree in Psychology from the University of British Columbia and is a freelance writer. Her main focus is fiction, but she is also a web copywriter. Shelly is a mom to four children, and resides in Aldergrove, BC. You can view her portfolio at www.iwriteit.ca.

Elizabeth Young grew up in Lancashire, England, but has made Barrie, ON, her home for the last thirty years. Elizabeth has been an avid reader since childhood and written extensively since her teen years. Now that her four children are grown she is able to devote more time to her craft.

Melissa Yuan-Innes is an emergency doctor in Cornwall, ON, currently enjoying a maternity leave with her bouncing baby girl, her talkative son, and her guitar-playing husband. She writes fiction, medical humour, and most recently, a CBC radio drama pilot. She hangs out on Facebook, Twitter (dr_sassy), and http://melissayuaninnes.com.

Lori Zenker watches her kids play hockey in Ontario. She has written a children's book titled, *Promiseland*, and does freelance writing and art. She loves working with her youth group, camping and buying and selling old junk. E-mail her at burmiethegreat@gto.net.

Meet Our Authors

Jack Canfield is the co-creator of the *Chicken Soup for the Soul* series, which *Time* magazine has called "the publishing phenomenon of the decade." Jack is also the co-author of many other bestselling books.

Jack is the CEO of the Canfield Training Group in Santa Barbara, California, and founder of the Foundation for Self-Esteem in Culver City, California. He has conducted intensive personal and professional development seminars on the principles of success for more than a million people in twenty-three countries, has spoken to hundreds of thousands of people at more than 1,000 corporations, universities, professional conferences and conventions, and has been seen by millions more on national television shows.

Jack has received many awards and honours, including three honorary doctorates and a Guinness World Records Certificate for having seven books from the *Chicken Soup for the Soul* series appearing on the New York Times bestseller list on May 24, 1998.

You can reach Jack at www.jackcanfield.com.

Mark Victor Hansen is the co-founder of Chicken Soup for the Soul, along with Jack Canfield. He is a sought-after keynote speaker, bestselling author, and marketing maven. Mark's powerful messages of possibility, opportunity, and action have created powerful change in thousands of organizations and millions of individuals worldwide.

Mark is a prolific writer with many bestselling books in addition to the *Chicken Soup for the Soul* series. Mark has had a profound influence in the field of human potential through his library of audios, videos, and articles in the areas of big thinking, sales achievement, wealth building, publishing success, and personal and professional development. He is also the founder of the MEGA Seminar Series.

Mark has received numerous awards that honour his entrepreneurial spirit, philanthropic heart, and business acumen. He is a lifetime member of the Horatio Alger Association of Distinguished Americans.

You can reach Mark at www.markvictorhansen.com.

Amy Newmark is Chicken Soup for the Soul's publisher and editor-in-chief, after a thirty-year career as a writer, speaker, financial analyst, and business executive in the worlds of finance and telecommunications. Amy is a *magna cum laude* graduate of Harvard College, where she majored in Portuguese, minored in French, and travelled extensively. She and her husband have four grown children.

After a long career writing books on telecommunications, voluminous financial reports, business plans, and corporate press releases, Chicken Soup for the Soul is a breath of fresh air for Amy. She has fallen in love with Chicken Soup for the Soul and its life-changing books, and really enjoys putting these books together for Chicken Soup's wonderful readers. She has co-authored more than three dozen *Chicken Soup for the Soul* books and has edited another three dozen.

You can reach Amy through the webmaster@chickensoupforthesoul.com.

About Amy Sky

Award-winning EMI Records recording artist Amy Sky has always used her songs and recordings to reflect "where" she is in life.

Classically trained with a music theory and composition degree from the University of Toronto, Amy has focused on writing for both herself and others. She has written songs for international recording stars such as Anne Murray, Belinda Carlisle, Heart, Cyndi Lauper, Reba McEntire, Diana Ross, Sheena Easton and Roch Voisine. Since 2005, she has branched into producing for others, including four CDs produced and co-written for Olivia Newton-John, which received rave reviews from *Billboard* magazine. Amy has worked with many stellar guest artists in collaboration with Newton-John, including Patti Labelle, Michael McDonald, Jon Secada, David Foster, Barry Manilow, Sir Cliff Richard, and Jim Brickman.

As both writer and performer, Amy has been nominated for Juno, SOCAN, East Coast and West Coast Music Awards. Themes of family, spirituality, and relationships highlight Amy's interest in and commitment to personal growth. Amy has also sung the national anthem at a number of important functions. She has performed at Toronto's Blue Jays and Maple Leafs game as well as many political events, including special speaking engagements for President Bill Clinton.

Along with her chart success and recording career, Amy has appeared in plays and on TV. In 2001 she performed in an extended run of *The Vagina Monologues* in Toronto. Prior to that, Amy played the lead role of Mrs. Johnstone in the play *Blood Brothers* to critical acclaim at Toronto's Royal Alexandra Theatre alongside renowned tenor Michael Burgess and pop icon David Cassidy. She reprised the role at Artpark, New York in 1998.

A women's health spokesperson, Amy has hosted the Rogers TV parenting series *The Baby Hour*, and has spoken out extensively on her own experience with post-partum depression. In 2006, she was awarded the Centre for Addiction and Mental Health Courage to Come Back award. In 2009, she was honoured with the Mood Disorders Association Hero/Inspiration Award for her commitment to helping remove the stigma from mental health issues.

Amy also commits much of her time to various causes, including championing artist's rights. Twice, she testified successfully in Ottawa before the Canadian Radio-television and Telecommunications Commission, helping to shape and change copyright policy. For her testimony on the groundbreaking establishment of the Neighbouring Rights Royalty, she received the Canadian Recording Industry Association Applause Award.

Amy lives in Toronto with her husband, acclaimed singer songwriter Marc Jordan, and their two children. "Alive & Awake", her latest project, launches in the first part of 2012 with a one-woman show that combines her new book and CD of the same name, and celebrates her personal emphasis on sharing joy and raising awareness of mood hygiene.

You can learn more and contact Amy through her website, www.amysky.com.

About Liona Boyd

Liona Boyd, known as the "First Lady of the Guitar," has introduced millions around the world to the art of classical guitar. Her performing and compositional talents have resulted in five gold and three platinum albums, five Juno Awards, five honorary degrees, and The Order of Canada.

Liona was born in England and came to Canada at the age of eight. She went on to complete a Bachelor of Music degree at the University of Toronto where she graduated with honours and won first prize in the Canadian National Music Competition. After two years of private study in Paris, Liona returned to North America and recorded her first album. She has since had the opportunity to play for many world leaders throughout her career and was also the first Canadian to perform at the Kremlin and the new Bastille Opera House in Paris. She has been a guest on popular TV shows such as *The Tonight Show*, *Today*, *Live from the Pops*, had her own TV specials, concertized with many international symphony orchestras, and represented Canada in music festivals around the world. Breaking with classical tradition she toured with Gordon Lightfoot and Tracy Chapman, and recorded with Chet Atkins, Eric Clapton and David Gilmour.

After a few years absence from the stage Liona has reinvented herself as a singer/songwriter. 2011 brings the release of her twenty-third album, *The Return*, inspired by her return to Canada after twenty years of living in the USA. The CD, with a definite patriotic theme,  was produced in the summer of 2011 when after the death of her father she decided to come back to Toronto. Her websites www.classicalguitar.com and www.lionaboyd.com are where her videos, books and CDs are available, sound samples can be heard and regular newsletters are posted. Follow Liona on Twitter and YouTube.

With Thanks to Our Editorial Advisory Board

We are indebted to our wonderful editorial advisory board—a panel of Canadians who read and graded all the finalists for this book and helped us narrow down the list to just 101. They spent weeks thoughtfully grading and commenting on stories.

Harriet Cooper is a prolific Chicken Soup for the Soul writer who understands what constitutes a great story, and her detailed notes helped guide us through the selection process. Pamela Goldstein is another one of our regulars and her thoughtful comments helped us figure out just how much the stories should be specifically about Canada. David Martin, whose submissions to Chicken Soup for the Soul invariably make us laugh, gave us the male perspective. And Terrie Todd, who has been published in our books numerous times, especially in our Christian titles, gave us her valuable perspective and was our lone representative from outside Ontario.

We were also very lucky to have input from Simon & Schuster's Canadian office, with comments from Rob Philpott and Judy DeFreitas. And finally, Laura Robinson read all of the stories for us too. Laura is one of the co-authors of our very popular *Chicken Soup for the Soul: Count Your Blessings* book and the co-creator of the fun game by the same name. She is also an actress, a singer, and a game designer well known for having invented *Balderdash*. Laura seems to know *everyone*, and it was through her friendships that we were connected with Amy Sky, Liona Boyd, Marc Jordan, Matt Duchene, and George Kourounis for all the bonus material that we included in this volume. Amy and Liona very kindly gave us their material even as they were recording their new albums.

~Amy Newmark

Chicken Soup

www.chickensoup.com

for the Soul